The
CLASSIC GUITARS
OF THE 50s & 60s

THE CLASSIC GUITARS OF THE 50'S & 60'S

PUBLISHED BY
MERCHANT BOOK COMPANY LTD
PO BOX 10
WEST MOLESEY
SURREY KT8 2WZ
UNITED KINGDOM

ISBN 1 904779 06 9

CREATIVE DIRECTOR: NIGEL OSBORNE
DESIGN: SALLY STOCKWELL
PHOTOGRAPHY: MIKI SLINGSBY
ILLUSTRATIONS: MARION APPLETON
EDITOR: TONY BACON

PRINTED AND BOUND IN SINGAPORE BY
STAMFORD PRESS PTE LTD

CONTENTS

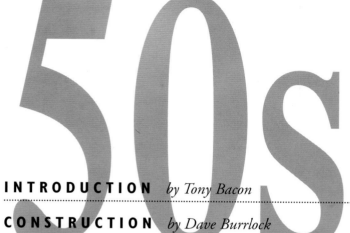

The 1950s created the teenager; the teenager demanded pop music; and pop music's shiniest icon was the electric guitar. This book magnifies the links in that chain, and will plug you in to a decade of astonishing contrasts, blinding invention and great, great music.

The world was changing rapidly in the 1950s. World War II had ground to a bloody halt in 1945. It had shaken some countries to bits, reduced others to bankruptcy, given renewed confidence to a lucky few. Despite the ruins and the indelible marks of suffering, as the 1940s gave way to the 1950s people were determined to enjoy themselves at last, to celebrate their survival and continuing existence. One obvious way was through music.

Sex was popular too. "The abnormally high birth rate since 1940," said a US financial report of 1950, "has continued through 1949 and has resulted in about 33 million births which soon will have an important influence on school facilities, on housing and on food requirements." And, more crucially perhaps, on new trends in leisure and entertainment. "The great social revolution of the last 15 years," wrote Colin MacInnes in 1958, "[may be] the one that's given teenagers economic power… for let's not forget their 'spending money' does not go on traditional necessities, but on the kinds of luxuries that modify the social pattern."

The stage was set for change: many kids who grew up in the war were tougher and more independent than those who had gone before. They were ready for anything – and they wanted more. The new teenagers of the 1950s – only later would they be called 'Baby Boomers' – were greater in numbers than ever before compared to the overall population. Crucially, they had money in their pockets and a new-found freedom in which to spend it, more or less as they chose. A survey of American teenagers' spending habits in 1958 revealed that they represented a buying power of no less than $9 billion. And more often than not, at the top of their wish list was the latest rock'n'roll record.

Businessmen were not slow to appreciate the link between music listening and music making. The Harmony guitar company, for example, teamed up with Decca Records in 1955 for their Dance-O-Rama promotion where, as they described it, "Guitar players will be inspired to buy records and record fans will be encouraged to buy the instrument they like to hear."

Not only did the 1950s host the birth of rock'n'roll, but the new music led inevitably to a concentration on the guitar as one of the prime instruments at the heart of this musical revolution, aimed at and often created by teenagers (or, at least, by teenagers at heart). The United States was the site of this revolutionary melting pot, and the newly created mixtures were whisked rapidly around the world.

And yet these were far from idyllic times. Always close to the headlines in the 1950s was the potential peril inherent in atomic or nuclear power. It seemed only a matter of time before someone would lift the lid of this Pandora's box and finish everyone off for good. The threat of The Bomb was omnipresent – maybe it could

resolve the Korean War, or sort out Suez? After all, it had finished a much bigger war just years earlier. Nuclear fallout shelters sprang up as a rather inappropriate defence. And in the quickly developing climate of the cold war, no-one in the West had much doubt as to who would be hurling the bombs at them.

Reactions to the Communist Threat of the dastardly Russians ranged from the typically unimaginative politician (Harry Truman: "Our lives, our nation, all the things we believe in, are in great danger, and this danger has been created by the rulers of the Soviet Union") to the more subtle innuendo of the movie house, where the sci-fi-Shakespeare of Forbidden Planet starred an unstoppable terror that roamed a doomed world, killing everyone.

As if all this wasn't enough, you just couldn't trust anyone – spies were everywhere. No matter: J Edgar Hoover and the FBI would be the protectors of every true US citizen. Spy fever reached its terrifying climax when American couple Julius and Ethel Rosenberg, found guilty of running a nuclear-espionage ring that passed information to the USSR, were executed by electric chair in 1953 – the first Americans ever sentenced to death for spying, in war or peacetime.

For many people living through the period, the 1950s were a peculiar mix. There were great leaps being made in science and technology, some of which were distant and hard to grasp, like rockets blasting into space, while others such as transistor radios or stereo records were closer to home and easy to appreciate. But underpinning all the innovation was a general unease, a feeling that the world was an unruly place that was spinning out of control. As Jack Kerouac, founder of the so-called Beat Generation, had one of the characters say in On The Road: "I had nothing to offer anybody except my own confusion."

America had the new music, at least for the time being, and so America had the guitars. Meanwhile, Europe had it bad. In Britain, for example, there was one word that came up again and again to describe the mood. Austerity. Post-war austerity. Rationing lasted well into the 1950s, bomb sites were everywhere, greyness and gloom prevailed, and thanks to a cash-strapped government the importing of musical instruments and gramophone records "from the dollar areas" was banned from 1951 to 1959. Rock'n'roll inventiveness necessarily lagged behind the American model, which was streaking ahead with tailfins glinting. Even politician Harold Macmillan's famous line, "You've never had it so good," delivered in 1957 when prospects had brightened, was taken from a US election slogan of five years earlier.

Relatively speaking, the United States had finished the 1940s without the crippling expense and psychological fallout that so many European countries had suffered as a result of World War II. Of course, there were some financial burdens – and the US musical instrument industry, at least, endured a recession from the late 1940s until about 1952. One can tell that there must have been a recession, because the contemporary press was flecked with articles insisting that there was no recession.

In fact the guitar started the 1950s at a disadvantage. A craze for the ukulele had begun at the end of the 1940s in the US, where over three million of the irritating little things were sold up to 1953. Fashion hounds everywhere forced their fingers into cramped chord shapes. The lowly ukulele was even elevated in 1950 to the status of an instrument recognised by the musicians' union in the New York area.

The accordion, too, was on the crest of a popular wave, buoyed up by bandleader and accordionist Lawrence Welk. His proto-MOR 'champagne music' was alone enough to make any self-respecting teenager seek musical alternatives. In jazz and early rock'n'roll it was the saxophone which dominated the instrumental frontline, and only in country, blues and Les Paul's multi-layered chart hits did the guitar start the decade with any kind of musical stronghold.

But by 1954 the guitar's fortunes were changing. A report by the American Music Conference in that year, estimating the number of people playing musical instruments in the US, put the guitar at 1.7 million, ukulele at 1.6 million and accordion at 950,000. The sax was lumped in with 'others' at 975,000.

Two years later, the dramatic rise of rock'n'roll underlined the guitar's versatility and fundamental simplicity, nudging the instrument to a peak of popularity. Charles Rubovits of the Harmony guitar company of Chicago seized on the positive signs when he wrote in a guitar industry report of 1956: "More people have the growing desire to do things themselves rather than be spectators; more people have more leisure time; more people are more easily exposed to music through television, creating a desire for self-expression; and more people have and will have more money to buy the things they want. Desire for fame and fortune is another motivating influence working in our behalf. Although we know the heights are reached by only a few, those attempting to gain this goal are many, proving this sales factor to be a reality."

Sidney Katz, president of the other big Chicago-based guitar manufacturer, Kay, told a trade gathering a few years later to overlook their own musical prejudices and chase the teenagers' dollars. "No matter how you feel about rock'n'roll and Elvis Presley," he said, "for business they have been great, and guitar sales have been rising steadily as a result. People are getting tired of sitting in front of a television set; they want to get together and entertain themselves – and there's no better instrument than a guitar for building a convivial atmosphere," Katz concluded. No doubt he had stressed exactly what his audience of businessmen wanted to hear: that big guitar sales would bring the American family closer together, singing wholesome songs together around the hearth. None of that rock'n'roll rubbish, that's for sure.

Reactions among parents and the establishment of the 1950s to Elvis and his brand of guitar-based jungle music ranged from the outraged to the morally indignant. "Rock'n'roll is the most brutal, ugly, vicious form of expression," Frank Sinatra told the New York Post in 1957, describing it colourfully as "the martial music

of every delinquent on the face of the earth." A vicar in England told the Daily Mirror that the effect of rock'n'roll on youngsters was "to turn them into devil worshippers; to stimulate self-expression through sex; to provoke lawlessness, impair nervous stability and destroy the sanctity of marriage." With that kind of manifesto, most teenagers merely wanted to know where to sign up.

Musical snobbery was rife, too. Steve Race, a British big-band pianist – and Light Music Advisor to the ATV television company – wrote in Melody Maker in 1956: "After Presley, just about anything can happen. Intonation, tone, intelligibility, musicianship, taste, subtlety – even the decent limits of guitar amplification – no longer matter. I fear for the future of a music industry which allows itself to cater for one demented age-group, to the exclusion of the masses who still want to hear a tuneful song, tunefully sung." It's a pity that Race didn't copyright that last bit, because it's been used ever since by every generation who can't help but criticise their kids' worthless music.

Jazzmen of the 1950s, too, were horrified by the inept noise and artless rhythms of the new music. Leading jazz guitarist Barney Kessel, used to his modestly amplified hollow-body electric guitar, but as a sessionman necessarily responsive to new sonic requirements, told a reporter in 1956: "I had to buy a special 'ultra toppy' guitar to get that horrible electric guitar sound that the cowboys and the rock'n'rollers want." And that same year a writer to the letters page in the jazz musician's chief magazine, Down Beat, was clearly affronted. "The epitome of this musical suicide is reached by persons of the ilk of Elvis Presley, who seems to have a talent for sneering, jumping up and down, crossing his legs, standing on his head, playing down to his audience – in fact, a talent for everything but music. What makes it worse is the fact that this guy is making out so well while more talented and deserving artists pick up the crumbs."

During the pages that follow, we'll analyse the decade's guitars and place them in the context of the music of the time. The guitars themselves, photographed to reveal every detail, provide the chronological order of the book, while around and about them a team of the world's top guitar writers bring their expertise to bear on the key elements in the story of the guitar-laden 1950s.

We see Chet Atkins at work on his pop-country hybrid and Les Paul constructing his New Sound, widening the popularity and appeal of the electric guitar; marvel at Tal Farlow reshaping the boundaries of jazz guitar playing; we hear the low-down twang of Duane Eddy's hit records; watch Scotty Moore at work with Elvis Presley, and Frank Beecher behind Bill Haley; investigate everything from the black R&B of Chuck Berry to the white pop of Buddy Holly; and examine Stratocasters and Explorers, Duo-Trons and Byrdlands, Emperors and Clubs and Switchmasters. Classic Guitars Of The Fifties for the first time explains how the electric guitar grew up and established itself during ten mesmerising years. This book tells it like it was. ■ TONY BACON

1950

EPIPHONE was established in New York in the early 1900s by Epaminondas Stathopoulo, and their first electric guitars appeared in the 1930s. This 1950 ad (right) features TV session man Al Caiola with a Zephyr Deluxe Regent model.

△ **EPIPHONE ZEPHYR EMPEROR REGENT**
Also known as Zephyr Emperor Varitone
Produced 1950-1958; this example 1954

A startling mix of old and new, this traditionally styled hollow-body electric boasted three pickups, a panel of six tone-modifying switches, and a laminated maple top.

CONSTRUCTION

Almost all of the constructional concepts for the solidbody and semi-solid electric guitar were established in the 1950s, and more advances were made in those ten short years than in the two decades that followed.

Although numerous electric guitars existed before the 1950s, these were primarily hollow-body types (similar to the Epiphone shown here) or 'Hawaiian' lap steels. By combining the playing position of an electric 'Spanish' hollow-body guitar with the solidity of a lap steel Leo Fender created what was as far as most musicians were concerned the world's first solidbody electric guitar, the Fender Broadcaster. First produced in 1950, and renamed the Telecaster by August of the following year, this is the instrument that laid the foundation and created the benchmark for factory-produced solidbody electric guitars.

Apart from the obvious solid body, it is Fender's bolt-on neck which has become the key constructional feature that still allows instruments to be built in a cost-effective manner today. Initially the feature was instigated as a safeguard against component failure: a bolt-on neck was far easier to replace than the traditional glued-in or 'set' type favoured by older guitar companies such as Gibson. Quite simply, Fender's bolt-on neck made electric guitar manufacturing easier and more economic.

Both Fender and Gibson were factory-production manufacturers. Leo Fender didn't hand-build his

1951

This was Gibson's top-of-the-line hollow-body electric guitar and, at nearly 3½in deep and 18in wide, their biggest. It was based on the existing Super 400C acoustic model, but with a slightly thicker top and stronger internal bracing to help prevent feedback. The P90 pickups of early models such as the example shown here were soon replaced by Alnico types and, later in the 1950s, by humbuckers.

PLAYERS *could raise or lower the Varitone tailpiece (above) to subtly alter tone by using an Allen key in the small hole on the unit.*

BODIES of most 1950s Gibson hollow-body electrics had this 'rounded' cutaway (above); it became 'pointed' during 1960.

DISTINCTIVE touches on the Super 400CES fingerboard include the split-block inlays (above) and 'pointed' end (left).

THE SUPER 400's characteristic pickguard of 'marbleised' tortoiseshell (above) was created by a special plastic overlay.

double offset cutaway horns, three pickups, an advanced vibrato and that contoured body. Its design took Fender's crucial component-based production method a stage further – the Stratocaster's scratchplate/pickup assembly was one separate part, just like the neck, and the body.

Viewed from a 1990s perspective the Telecaster, Les Paul and Stratocaster remain the key instruments of the 1950s, but the decade threw up many more constructional ideas that are important to the modern electric guitar. Rickenbacker are credited with the first production through-neck guitar, their 1956 Combo 400. By making the neck and central body section from one piece (or a laminate of longitudinal stripes) the vibration of the strings, and therefore the instrument's resulting sustain, is uninterrupted: there is no neck-to-body joint. However, some makers believe that the through-neck's central section limits low-end tonal response. Nonetheless the through-neck design has been featured by numerous companies, notably Gibson with their early 1960s Firebird design, and present-day Rickenbacker production. This expensive method is today popular with bass makers.

While the lion's share of attention has historically been focused on the Les Paul, Tele and Strat, Gibson's ES-335 was perhaps one of the most versatile instruments of the era, and has remained popular since its launch in 1958. In many ways the instrument exemplified Gibson's heritage more strongly than the company's Les Paul models. Gibson had established landmark hollow-body electrics with the launch in 1951 of the L-5CES and Super 400CES (as shown on these pages), and four years later the company experimented by marketing their first hollow 'Thinline' electric acoustics, the Byrdland and the ES-350T. In outline these models looked like typical Gibson archtop jazz guitars, but their bodies were much thinner, making for a less cumbersome instrument and one which to an extent reduced feedback when amplified.

In fact Gibson wanted a guitar with the tone and playability of a solidbody but the appearance and feel of a 'real' archtop guitar, and it was the ES-335 that supplied this combination. The new model boasted a fresh double-cutaway body shape constructed in traditional form with separate top, back and sides made from laminated maple,

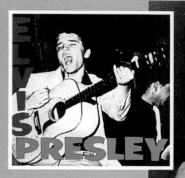

MOST PROMINENT of all players of the Super 400CES in the 1950s was Scotty Moore (main picture, right) who used one during most of his work backing Elvis Presley in the studio and on stage. Moore signed the main photo and sent it to amplifier maker Ray Butts in 1956 to show Butts his EchoSonic amp in action.

BLOCK fingerboard markers and a 'torch' headstock inlay decorate the L-5CES (below).

△ GIBSON L-5SEC
Early examples of the L-5CES were labelled L-5SEC
Produced 1951-current; this example October 1951

Just before Gibson issued an electric version of their Super 400C guitar, the company combined elements of the acoustic L-5C and electric ES-5 models to create the L-5CES ('cutaway electric Spanish'). Like the Super 400CES, the L-5CES had a traditional carved spruce top, carved maple back, and maple sides.

A SPLIT-DIAMOND inlay on the headstock (right) instantly identifies a Gibson cutaway electric as a Super 400CES.

but with an added solid centre block (much like Les Paul's original 'Log' design) stabilising the top and back and giving the pickups, bridge and tailpiece a firm mounting. The design also meant that the neck joined the body at the 19th fret, so players had superb access to the upper frets.

Rickenbacker approached the 'semi-solid' guitar from a different angle. In the mid-1950s they began hollowing out their solidbody guitars, routing the body from the back to leave a solid centre section, and with an additional back piece sealing the completed body. Rickenbacker did this to reduce body weight, and while at first they employed their semi-solid construction method on certain Combo models the company employed it most effectively on the Capri line. Launched in 1958, these models evolved into the soon-to-be-classic Rickenbackers such as the 330 and 360.

Gibson's post-war move to using laminated maple in guitar production had a direct effect on the long-term success of their ES-335. Using pressed, laminated maple (effectively maple ply) for a guitar's front and back reduced production costs but, even on earlier guitars such as the ES-350, contributed to a more fundamental tone with less of

△ D'ANGELICO EXCEL
Produced 1936-1964; this example 1952

Many players added pickups to acoustic guitars, commonly the DeArmond 'floating' units made by Rowe (see ad, right) which float free of the guitar's top and thus avoid interfering with the tonal integrity of the hollow body. With a guitar such as John D'Angelico's archtops, the idea was to amplify the guitar's inherent tone. But with the L-5CES and 400CES shown on these pages, Gibson built modified electric versions of acoustic guitars and began to seek a new and unique voice for the electric guitar.

DJ ALAN FREED begins his R&B radio programme out of Cleveland, Ohio. Between now and 1954 he starts to call it a 'Moondog Rock 'n' Roll Party', and later claims he invented the term 'rock'n'roll'.

I LOVE LUCY, definitive 1950s TV sitcom, starts a ten year run with Lucille Ball as Lucy Ricardo and Desi Arnaz as Ricky the hard-pressed hubby.

WINSTON CHURCHILL (Conservative) replaces Clement Attlee (Labour) as Prime Minister in the UK, where post-war austerity fades a little as the Festival Of Britain is opened by King George VI in London.

J.D. SALINGER's 'Catcher In The Rye' is published. It is the story of Holden Caulfield, who sums up forever how oh-so-lonely it is to be an adolescent.

ARMISTICE negotiations, which become prolonged, open in Korea in July. Elsewhere, King Abdullah of Jordan is assassinated, and Libya becomes an independent state.

LES PAUL & Mary Ford achieve their first number one hit with 'How High The Moon', exemplifying Paul's multiple-layered recording techniques. The jazz magazine Down Beat seems surprised when Les Paul tops their readers' poll for Best Guitarist; runners-up votes are split between more traditional jazzers Billy Bauer, Tal Farlow and Chuck Wayne. In fact Paul will win the Down Beat poll for the next two years running.

LITTLE RICHARD's band, captured for 'The Girl Can't Help It' movie in 1956 and probably with Nathaniel Douglas on Telecaster, shows how Fender's guitars began to grow in popularity during the 1950s, reaching far beyond the company's initial market locally in California. Fender's solidbody guitars became a national sensation that other makers couldn't fail to notice.

A BLACK pickguard and fretted maple neck means an early Telecaster: a white guard was used from 1954 and a rosewood board from 1959.

LEO FENDER's full initials (standing for Clarence Leo) appear on his patent for the combined pickup and bridge unit, mounted into a simple metal plate, that is at the heart of the sound of the Telecaster. The strings pass through the body and are anchored at the back by six ferrules, giving solidity and sustain to the resulting sound, while the slanting pickup also enhances the guitar's natural treble tone.

FENDER began to advertise the newly named twin-pickup Telecaster along with the single-pickup Esquire during the early 1950s, and among the guitars' virtues listed in this 1952 ad (right) was 'no feedback'. This claim was directed at musicians who were used to the howls of feedback that would be heard from most hollow-body electric guitars when their amplifiers were turned up loud.

THE ORIGINAL **Fender** ELECTRIC STANDARD GUITAR

1. Fine fast action.
2. True intonation.
3. Wide range tone effects.
4. Steel re-enforced adjustable neck.
5. Strings adjustable for length and height from fret board.
6. Pickups adjustable for tone response.
7. No feedback.
8. Last fret position accessable.
9. Modern design.
10. Single and double pickup models available.

All models
beautiful top

Distributed B

RADIO & TELEVISION EQ

207 OAK STREET   SANTA ANA, CALIF.

Oct. 30, 1951   C. L. FENDER   2,573,254
COMBINATION BRIDGE AND PICKUP ASSEMBLY
FOR STRING INSTRUMENTS
Filed Jan. 13, 1950

HANK THOMPSON and his BRAZOS VALLEY BOYS
Nation's No. 1 Western Recording Artist Recording exclusively on Capitol Records

Nation's No. 1 Western Swing Band.

PERSONAL MANAGEMENT—
JIM HALSEY
15½ S. WALKER, OKLAHOMA CITY, OKLA.
PHONES—REGENT 6-8081, REGENT 6-0002

WESTERN SWING was a lively dance music that grew up in Texas dancehalls during the 1930s and 1940s, making notable and early use of electric guitars. Hank Thompson's Brazos Valley Boys created a commercial fusion of Western swing and honky tonk, hitting number one in 1952 with 'The Wild Side Of Life'. This 1953 line-up (left) includes Thompson with a personalised Gibson/Bigsby, next to him the band's musical director Billy Gray on Gibson ES-5, and Bill Carson with a Fender Telecaster. Carson had obtained his Tele direct from Fender, partly paying for it by acting as a musical guinea pig for new products. Some of his misgivings over the Telecaster led to Fender's development of a new solidbody model, the Stratocaster, in 1954.

▽ FENDER TELECASTER
Produced 1951-current; this example 1953

The longest-running solidbody electric guitar model ever, the Telecaster is loved by a diverse range of players from all areas of music for its inherent simplicity and clean, cutting sound.

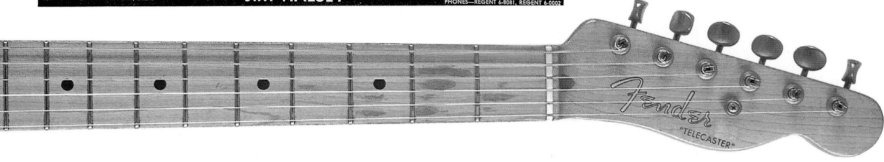

the acoustic-like harmonics contributed, for example, by a more traditional carved spruce top. Guitars with these laminated materials were preferred by many players for amplified work, and in the case of the ES-335 the laminated woods in combination with the guitar's semi-solid construction limited its acoustic properties anyway. When players in later generations used the ES-335 with high volume stage amplification its construction combated unwanted feedback, allowing controlled 'musical' feedback along with the 335's ever-present and distinctive woody tone. Like the Stratocaster, Telecaster and the humbucker-equipped Les Paul, the ES-335 proved to be a survivor of any changes in musical style and fashion.

This versatility is surely the key to the longevity both of guitar designs and construction

methods. Over time, the mark of a successful guitar is that it becomes successful in applications that were not envisaged by its designers. Guitars such as those made by Gretsch and Rickenbacker that tend towards the idiosyncratic have never achieved this iconic status, yet remain viable choices thanks to their individual sonic thumbprints. Fender's Jazzmaster of 1958 was intended to improve upon the Stratocaster, but it didn't. Despite the Jazzmaster's thicker sounds from wider single-coil pickups, a new vibrato design and a new body shape with an offset waist, plus some nifty electronics, it nonetheless lacked a Stratocaster's simplicity – which can often be at the root of a guitar's versatility.

One of Gibson's final flings in the 1950s was the development of their 'Modernistic' designs: the Explorer and

the Flying V. At the time, these guitars were seen and perhaps even intended as little more than a joke. But they proved within the space of a decade following their launch that the solidbody electric guitar could in fact adapt to any shape, could still sound good, and might even represent a fashion statement – perfect instruments, as it turned out, to propel the more overt musical styles such as glam and heavy metal that were to emerge during the 1970s and 1980s.

Cynics in the 1990s sneer at contemporary guitar design, saying it's all been done before. And in fact there is little doubt that virtually all the solidbody and semi-solid guitar design classics were originated in the 1950s. But at the time few of the companies or individuals involved could have had any idea of the monster they'd created: the modern electric guitar. ■ DAVE BURRLUCK

MOST MAKERS had by the late 1940s followed Gibson's lead with a cutaway body (left).

△ VEGA E-300 DUO-TRON
Produced 1949-1956; this example 1951

Vega began in Boston around 1900 as a brass and banjo maker, by the 1930s adding guitars to the line. Electrics like the E-300 used traditional techniques, with "electric parts that in no way affect the body tone" thanks to a pickup fixed to the fingerboard and controls floating on the tailpiece. "So all the tonal advantages are in this instrument with or without amplifier," Vega explained.

STAN KENTON (above) was an ambitious jazzman, prone to calling his band's 'Orchestras' and popular with audiences if not critics. He is seen here during 1952 with his guitarist Ralph Blaze who plays a blonde Vega E-300 Duo-Tron.

THE GIBSON STORY *by André Duchossoir*

At the start of the 1950s Gibson were a successful US guitar-making company, some 45 years old, steeped in tradition... and faced with a dilemma. Should they continue to produce only the acoustic and 'electrified' acoustic guitars that had brought them such success, or should they also meddle with the new solidbody electric guitars that a small competitor was beginning to sell in increasing numbers? The answer came in the shape of their solidbody Les Paul model.

SOLIDBODY electric guitars immediately found favour during the 1950s with the new generation of urban bluesmen (such as Freddie King, seen below with Les Paul gold-top) and honky tonk-style country & Western bands. Both were attracted by the penetrating tone, bright treble response and unusual sustaining power of the new instruments.

THE GIBSON STORY

Gibson's earliest attempts in the field of electric stringed instruments date from the mid 1920s, but it was not until 1935 that the company's first production model, a metal-bodied Hawaiian lap steel, was commercialised. In 1936 Gibson's hollow-body ES-150 'Spanish' electric was issued and became arguably the best-known electric guitar of the pre-war era thanks to its association with the pioneering electric jazz guitarist, Charlie Christian.

On the threshold of the 1950s Gibson produced some of the most popular electric guitars, but these various ES models, including the ES-295 shown here, were still largely rooted in pre-war concepts and patterned after traditional archtop acoustic designs. The most visible evolution since World War II had been the multiplication of pickups, culminating with a three-pickup layout on the ES-5 which premiered in 1949, but the hollow-body electric guitar — what might be termed the 'electrified' guitar — reached its apogee in 1951 with the inception of Gibson's Super

▽ GIBSON ES-295
Produced 1952-1958, re-issued 1990; this example June 1953

Until 1952 Gibson's guitars had come in traditional sunburst or natural finish. The gleaming gold of the hollow-body 295 was a shocking, eye-catching novelty that matched the visual impact of Gibson's new Les Paul solidbody model.

400CES and L-5CES. These superlative models, still considered by many as the finest jazz guitars, were essentially versions of the company's renowned acoustic counterparts, fitted with stronger bracing and twin pickups. But by the time these guitars were launched, a new challenge was already underway.

The success of the Fender Telecaster prompted Gibson to tread new paths where sounds and visual style mattered more than heritage and craftsmanship. Reluctantly but realistically, the company jumped on the bandwagon that Leo Fender had set rolling and came up with their own electric solidbody in 1952. To make up for a late start Gibson smartly enlisted the services of Les Paul, an accomplished guitarist and electronic wizard, to lend his name to the new guitar. Meanwhile, Gibson chief Ted McCarty and his associates developed a solidbody model that manifested everything the brand stood for, including a carved maple top that Fender could not duplicate.

The Les Paul model, painted with a gleaming gold top at Paul's request, was an instant success — in 1952/53 nearly 4000 were sold, more than 30 per cent of the combined production of all the archtop electrics made at that time at Gibson's Kalamazoo, Michigan, factory. After 1953 the sales of electrified archtops dropped, while Gibson forged ahead with a complete range of

WHITE single-coil P-90 pickups (left) on the original ES-295 were replaced by humbuckers in 1957.

THE ES-295 was launched some months after the gold-top Les Paul in 1952, and was effectively a gold finished ES-175 (see page 20/21) with a new tailpiece, white pickups and an attractively decorated white pickguard. But players of hollow-body guitars proved too conservative to be tempted by this shiny bauble, and the 295 did not last very long in the Gibson line.

Gibson SALUTES LES PAUL

Congratulations, Les Paul, on winning the Down Beat Guitar Poll. We're proud of the interest in guitars fostered by your artistry, and we're proud, too, of the wonderful Gibsons now under construction for you and Mary. We are confident these fine instruments will inspire you to new feats of wizardry in your musical accomplishments.

GIBSON, INC., Kalamazoo, Michigan

LES PAUL & Mary Ford became huge stars in the early 1950s with hits like 'How High The Moon' that featured Paul's distinctive multi-layered recording techniques. He experimented with instruments too, and in the 1940s made his 'Log', an early semi-solidbody electric (seen with Paul and Ford on Ed Sullivan's TV show in 1951, left). Gibson eagerly signed the famous guitarist to endorse their new solidbody electric guitar in 1952, a relationship previewed in the company's ad, shown far left, where the Epiphone logo on the headstock of the 'Log' is carefully hidden.

solidbody models bearing the Les Paul name: the top-of-the-line Custom, plus budget Junior, TV and Special.

As befits a high-end model, the black Les Paul Custom was endowed with Gibson's latest advances, such as the fully-adjustable Tune-o-matic bridge and a powerful Alnico pickup with adjustable magnets. The latter was a first effort towards improving Gibson's ubiquitous P-90 single-coil pickup of early 1940s origin. But a real evolution would only materialise with the advent of the humbucking pickup, devised in 1955. The humbucker marked a watershed in guitar electronics and ultimately became an industry standard, the success of which relied on more than its ability to 'buck the hum,' or cut noise. In 1957, both the regular Les Paul and the Custom were upgraded with the new pickup unit, used henceforth as the staple device on the company's senior models.

A request by famed country guitarists Billy Byrd and Hank Garland served as a catalyst for Gibson to design

Melody Maker
INCORPORATING 'RHYTHM'

DANCE MUSIC IS HUSHED AS NATION MOURNS

God Save the Queen

KING GEORGE VI dies at Sandringham, England, while Princess Elizabeth is away on a Commonwealth tour. The new Queen takes up residence at Buckingham Palace three months later.

THE LES PAUL model (below) began to come off the Gibson production lines in 1952. It soon became clear that the guitar's trapeze tailpiece was inappropriate, and it was replaced during 1953 with a new unit (see overleaf).

WITH 'CRY', Johnnie Ray is the first white singer in the US to hit both pop and R&B charts, heralding the erosion of music's racial barriers.

ALL-GOLD versions of the Les Paul gold-top were made by Gibson during the 1950s.

△ GIBSON LES PAUL 'ALL-GOLD'
Special order 1952-1955; this example 1952.

While most Les Paul 'gold-top' models were just that, some were issued 'all-gold', with a gold body top, back and sides.

THE FIRST detonation of a hydrogen bomb – many times more powerful than an atom bomb – takes place at Eniwetok Atoll in the Pacific Ocean by the US. The first accident at a nuclear reactor occurs at Chalk River, Canada, without apparent casualties.

15th OLYMPIC GAMES are held at Helsinki, Finland.

MR POTATO HEAD becomes the first children's toy to be advertised on television.

GIBSON president Ted McCarty (left) holds a special all-gold hollow-body made in 1951 at Les Paul's request for a hospitalised guitarist. It prompted Gibson's all-gold ES-295 production model.

LES PAUL promotes his new namesake model (right) in the gold-top's first ad, from 1952.

Gibson
Les Paul model

It's a Sensation!

Designed by Les Paul—produced by Gibson—and enthusiastically approved by top guitarists everywhere.

The Les Paul Model is a unique and exciting innovation in the fretted instrument field; you have to see and hear it to appreciate the wonderful features and unusual tone of this newest Gibson guitar. Write Dept. 10 for more information about it.

Gibson, Inc., Kalamazoo, Mich.

THE WORLD'S first fare-paying jet airliner passenger is Mr A Henshaw of Mablethorpe, England, who travels on a BOAC Comet on its first commercial flight from London to Johannesburg in May with 35 other passengers.

TED McCARTY (right) was president of Gibson from 1950 to 1966, overseeing what many regard as the guitar company's golden period. A new one-storey extension added in 1950 to the Kalamazoo factory (far right) marked Gibson's confidence as the decade began. The before and after shots (January 1950 above; July below) also show the original 1917 building.

its new thin-body electrics. Premiered in 1955, the Byrdland (named after its originators) and its sibling, the ES-350T, became the leading members of a family of electrics that would offer an alternative to the radical new solidbody designs without offending tradition-conscious archtop players. The two Thinline models looked like regular hollow-bodies, but were much more shallow, making them more manageable and less prone to feedback. Both the Byrdland and the ES-350T were also fitted with an extra-narrow short-scale neck to facilitate extended fingering and dazzling solo runs. Gibson had struck the right chord and the Byrdland was adopted by BB King among others, while a blonde 350T became the trademark of Chuck Berry. But blues and rock were not yet fashionable enough to warrant a photo of these two artists in Gibson's brochures.

Indeed, many dealers' reports had it that Gibson were perceived as too conservative and its products not as flashy or innovative as those of some other manufacturers. Irritated by these comments, Gibson boss Ted McCarty decided to bite the bullet when in late 1956 figures showed that sales of solidbody models had ceased to grow.

McCarty's response was a radical line of electrics appropriately dubbed the 'Modernistic Guitars'.

First sighted as prototypes in 1957 but available by 1958, the Flying V and the Explorer featured unusually angular, aggressive-looking shapes that instantly set them apart from anything else. In the late 1950s, though, their futuristic design was ahead of its time, and what now seems a bold initiative was a flop back then. A mere 81 Flying Vs and 19 Explorers were shipped in 1958, often to dealers who used them as a prop in their window displays. A third design called the Moderne never made it to the production line, and today its untraced prototypes are considered as the true Holy Grail of electric guitars. If anything, the Modernistic Guitars succeeded in shaking Gibson's stodgy image and in showing that a solidbody could take any shape at all – provided, of course, that customers were prepared to go along with the idea.

In 1958 Gibson suffered another blow, albeit less catastrophic, with its attempt to revive the slumping sales of the Les Paul model. To broaden the guitar's market appeal, its gold finish was replaced by a more traditional cherry sunburst, and it was soon renamed the Les Paul

Standard. Practically unnoticed in the late 1950s, this change of guise would eventually create the most sought-after solidbody guitar, acclaimed for its sound as much as its looks. Like the Modernistic Guitars, yesterday's failure would turn into tomorrow's treasure.

Despite the original fate of these influential designs, not everything turned sour in 1958 for Gibson, and the company scored at least two major hits. The double-cutaway body shape introduced to revamp the Les Paul Junior, TV and Special did exactly what it was intended to do: their combined sales doubled within a year.

The other success of 1958 was the ES-335T, which enabled Gibson to break new ground while maintaining its heritage that was rooted in f-hole guitars. Following from the design of the Thinline electrics, Ted McCarty came up with the idea of incorporating a solid maple block inside a guitar's body to blend the resonance of a hollow-body with the sustain of a solidbody. A slimmed-down body depth

GIBSON's peak output of the original gold-top (this example, right, has new tuners) occurred in 1953 when a little over 2200 units were made, beaten only by the LG-1 flat-top and the electric ES-125. Gibson's highest-yet production figure would come in 1959 when 4364 Les Paul Juniors were shipped.

THE SWITCH above the neck selects between pickups. The upper position (marked 'Rhythm') gives front pickup; the lower position ('Treble') selects the rear pickup; and the central position, as shown here, provides both pickups.

1st Annual Combo Issue

DOWN BEAT

July 15, 1953

Richard Rodgers Sounds Off
(See Page 3)

★ ★ ★

Sauter, Finegan, & Goldfish
(See Page 2)

★ ★ ★

'Star Night' Cast Complete
(See Page 1)

★ ★ ★

On The Cover
Les Paul, Mary Ford

DURING the first half of the 1950s Les Paul was the most famous guitarist in America. Despite moving from his jazz roots to achieve a string of pop hits with singer Mary Ford, Paul could still make the cover of the top jazz magazine Down Beat (left). Paul invariably modified the guitars that Gibson sent him: note the unusual knobs and the crude vibrato of this gold-top.

and a graceful double-cutaway shape that gave unparalleled access to the 22-fret neck contributed to the superior functionality of the new model. Along with the stereo ES-345T and the ES-355T, a new genre of electrics was born: the semi-acoustic (or semi-solid) guitar.

The 1950s saw the coming of age of the electric guitar. In a matter of years, electrics looked and sounded like nothing else before, while similarly dramatic changes affected the music. This formative period witnessed the transition from 'electrified' to electric guitar, and by the end of the 1950s solidbody and Thinline electrics had surpassed full-body archtops in popularity. In this highly challenging and competitive context, Gibson introduced many historically significant designs which are still firm favourites today. ■ ANDRE DUCHOSSOIR

CLOCK RADIOS are introduced, waking folks with such news as Republican 'Ike' Eisenhower's inauguration as 34th US president, the end of the Korean war, the conquest of Mount Everest, and Queen Elizabeth II's coronation.

CRAZY MAN CRAZY by Bill Haley & his Comets is arguably the first hit rock'n'roll record, reaching number 12 in May.

LUNG CANCER is reported as attributable to cigarette smoking; meanwhile L&M still advertise their cigarettes as "just what the doctor ordered".

COLOUR TV is demonstrated for the first time when NBC broadcast a test transmission using three trial systems beamed from the Empire State Building in New York.

JUKEBOX favourites include Willie Mae Thornton's 'Hound Dog', an early take on country rock with a rip-roaring guitar solo by Pete Lewis of Johnny Otis' band. The Leiber & Stoller song will later provide a big hit for Elvis Presley.

JAMES BOND debuts in Ian Fleming's first novel, Casino Royale... but not in Simone De Beauvoir's seminal feminist work, The Second Sex.

DEAD: Django Reinhardt, Dylan Thomas, Joseph Stalin. Born: Tom Petty, Mike Oldfield, Robert Cray.

△ GIBSON LES PAUL 'GOLD-TOP'

Produced 1952-58, 1968-72, re-issued 1985; this example 1957.

More changes were made to the gold-top during the later 1950s: in 1955 Gibson's new adjustable Tune-o-matic bridge was fitted, improving intonation, while two years later the company's new noise-cancelling humbucking pickups were added. Left-handed guitars were made to special order and in small numbers; this rare left-handed gold-top is owned today by Paul McCartney.

△ GIBSON LES PAUL 'GOLD-TOP'

Produced 1952-58, 1968-72, re-issued 1985; this example 1954.

The 'trapeze' tailpiece fitted to the original gold-top (see page 17) was quickly replaced with this bar-type in 1953, when Gibson also increased the angle at which the neck met the body. These changes overcame criticisms of the original's limited sustain and inaccurate intonation, and made hand-damping effects possible.

LOGOS were silk-screened on to the holly wood veneer of the headstock face (above). While 'Les Paul Model' was the name used by Gibson for the gold Les Paul, aficionados refer to the guitar as the 'gold-top'.

1953 IN CONTEXT

JAZZ GUITARS *by Charles Alexander*

When Charlie Christian joined the Benny Goodman band in 1939 the electric guitar was almost unknown in jazz, and yet just over a decade later, as the 1950s dawned, jazz guitarists were rarely to be heard without the assistance of an amplifier. Jazz guitar music revealed its public faces and its musicians' musicians, from Barney Kessel to Johnny Smith, as players wrestled with old-school swing, still hip bop and the latest strains of cool and modern jazz.

Barney Kessel

Tenderly
Just Squeeze Me
Bernardo
Vicky's Dream
Salute to Charlie Christian
What is There to Say
Lullaby of Birdland
I Let a Song Go Out of My Heart

vogue
RECORDS
L.D.E. 085

THE BEST-KNOWN jazz guitarist of the 1950s was Barney Kessel (above). Kessel's first influence was the early electric jazz guitarist Charlie Christian, and in a 1953 interview Kessel repeated Christian's advice to him: *"If you can make some interesting harmony after you know how to swing, that's fine. But to begin with, swing alone is enough to get you by."*

JAZZ GUITAR

Charlie Christian's swinging, horn-like lines and the sound of his hollow-body Gibson with its bar pickup had inspired a generation of guitarists to amplify. By 1950, eight years after Christian's premature death at the age of 25, the electric guitar was commonplace in jazz.

Prior to Charlie Christian the jazz guitar had been primarily a rhythm section instrument and guitar players were rarely permitted to play solos. Now the guitar, like the piano, could function both in the rhythm section and the front line. At the same time there was an economic motive for guitarists to amplify and to sharpen their soloing skills, as the decline of the large swing orchestras was putting the traditional acoustic rhythm guitarist out of work.

The emergence of the electric guitar as a jazz instrument in the 1940s had coincided with the bebop revolution, spearheaded by saxophonist Charlie Parker and trumpeter Dizzy Gillespie. This new form of jazz, with its fast tempos and rhythmic and harmonic complexity, demanded far greater technical skills than the earlier swing style. Charlie Christian's jazz lines and phrasing were rooted in swing, rather than bebop, and bear the influence of the great swing-era saxophonist Lester Young. Most of the major jazz guitarists of the 1950s acknowledged Charlie

GIBSON's hollow-body electrics generally came finished either in sunburst (as here) or natural.

THE ES-175D was at first fitted with a pair of Gibson's P90 pickups (as on the example above), but during 1957 the company's new noise-cancelling humbucking pickups began to appear on Gibson guitars, including the 175D.

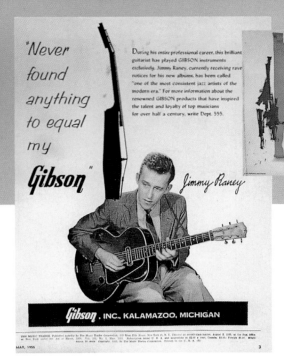

JIM HALL's wonderfully understated playing on a Gibson ES-175D was at large in the 1950s on his own solo albums (centre left). Herb Ellis (left) was also a Gibson ES-175 man, opting for a single-pickup version.

JIMMY RANEY, master of the 1950s 'cool' school of jazz playing, is often seen (as above and inset) with a Gibson ES-150 guitar, the company's original electric-acoustic hollow-body design that dates back to the mid-1930s.

Christian as their primary inspiration, and elements of this pioneer's style are in evidence in the hard-swinging, bluesy styles of Barney Kessel and Herb Ellis.

Barney Kessel was born in 1923. He grew up in Muskogee, Oklahoma, and from an early age was fascinated by the blues and jazz he heard around him. He bought his first guitar at age 12 and within two years was playing with a local jazz group – the only white musician in the band. Many touring bands passed through the area

and Kessel would jam with the musicians after hours. Hearing word of this remarkable young guitarist, Charlie Christian came to Muskogee to hear the 16-year-old Kessel play. This visit from his idol encouraged Kessel in his chosen career and within a year he had left for Los Angeles.

By the time he recorded his first album as a leader in 1953 when he was 30, Kessel was already a seasoned performer. He'd worked with the big bands of Chico Marx, Artie Shaw, Charlie Barnet and Benny Goodman, recorded with Charlie Parker and Billie Holiday and toured the US and Europe with the Oscar Peterson Trio. A mainstay of LA's busy radio and television recording scene, Kessel was also in demand as an accompanist for leading jazz vocalists such as Sarah Vaughan, Ella Fitzgerald and Anita O'Day. His guitar introduction and backup on Julie London's 1955 recording of 'Cry Me A River' is legendary.

In short, Barney was the best-known and most popular jazz guitarist in the US during the 1950s, topping the jazz guitar polls year after year in magazines such as Down Beat and Esquire. This led to a series of superb Poll Winners albums for the Contemporary label with bassist Ray Brown and drummer Shelly Manne, which established the guitar trio format and also demonstrated the range of expression of which the electric guitar is capable in jazz: from delicate

chord melody ballads to driving, blues-laced single-line solos. From the late 1960s until the early 1990s, when he suffered a stroke and could no longer play, Kessel pursued an active touring career with his trio and, from 1974 together with Herb Ellis and Charlie Byrd, as a member of the Great Guitars.

Herb Ellis was born in Texas in 1921, and his career began to follow a similar pattern to Kessel's – indeed their paths have at times intertwined. Ellis's big break came when he followed Kessel into the Oscar Peterson Trio in 1953. Ellis fitted in perfectly and stayed for five years. One of the best four-in-the-bar rhythm guitarists anywhere, Ellis drew pulsing chordal work from his Gibson ES-175, compensating for the lack of drums. He could negotiate Peterson's complex arrangements and solos quite convincingly, while never losing his earthy, bluesy quality at even the fastest of tempos.

The Trio toured incessantly and recorded extensively with many of the top jazz artists of the time, giving Ellis a high profile which opened the door to a two-year stint with vocalist Ella Fitzgerald and 17 years in the Los Angeles studios, where he would play on movie scores and on weekly television shows, while also performing on countless record dates.

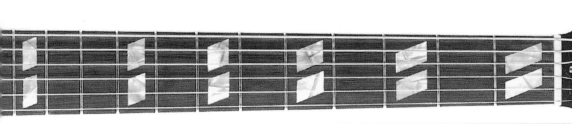

THESE ANGLED fingerboard markers are usually referred to as 'split parallelogram' types.

THE SO-CALLED 'crown' headstock inlay (above) was used by Gibson on nearly every one of the ES line of electric-acoustic instruments.

△ GIBSON ES-175D
Produced 1953-current; this example 1953

Gibson first issued the hollow-body ES-175 as a single-pickup guitar in 1949, but within four years introduced the optional ES-175D model which was fitted with two pickups and the necessary extra controls (the 'D' in the model name stands for double pickups). The 175 has become prominent over the decades primarily as a jazz guitar, and it has long been Gibson's best-selling electric-acoustic guitar. The sharp cutaway of the model was unique on a Gibson instrument for some years, and the ES-175 popularised a pressed, laminated maple/basswood body which contributes to its distinctively bright sound.

KENNY BURRELL (with ES-175, left) grew up in Detroit in a musical family and, taking up the guitar at age 12, was inspired by jazz guitarists Charlie Christian and Oscar Moore, but also by bluesmen such as Lightning Hopkins, Muddy Waters and T-Bone Walker. These influences are reflected in Burrell's sophisticated blend of hard-swinging bebop lines, soulful bluesy statements and rich chordal passages. After a six-month stint with Oscar Peterson, he settled in New York in 1956 and made his first solo album the following year. Soon he was one of the busiest jazz guitarists on the New York scene, recording with a wide range of artists including Duke Ellington and John Coltrane, and making several classic albums as a leader, such as Midnight Blue, and Guitar Forms.

JOHNNY SMITH (right) rose to fame through a 1952 recording with Stan Getz of 'Moonlight In Vermont', complete with Smith's clear, reverb-tinged sound, his fleet-fingered but relaxed three-octave runs, and above all his lush, close-voiced, chord melody style. In 1956 Guild produced the Johnny Smith Award archtop acoustic (with add-on pickup, right). This was based on the guitarist's favoured D'Angelico guitar, but Smith disliked the result and did not take up the Guild. Gibson produced a Johnny Smith model in 1961. Smith retired from performing in the mid 1970s to concentrate on his music store business.

Guild
JOHNNY SMITH AWARD MODEL *Guitar*
(In Limited Production Only)

GUILD's Stuart model, like many archtop Guilds, came in two finishes which were distinguished by different model numbers. The Stuart, for example, was known as the X-500 in sunburst, while the natural version (like this example) was the X-550.

GRETSCH (below) used plain, pearl and sparkle plastic finishes on drums, so why not on guitars as well?

THE HARP-STYLE tailpiece (above) was a distinctive feature of many Guild guitars, made for the US company by Müller in Germany.

△ GUILD STUART X-550
Produced 1953-current; this example 1958

Guild were started in New York in 1952 by Alfred Dronge and George Mann along with a team of mainly ex-Epiphone workers who had decided not to move to Philadelphia with their old company. Guild, who in 1956 also moved out of New York City (to Hoboken, New Jersey), were best known through the 1950s for high quality archtop guitars, of which the Stuart X-550 electric model was top of the line, while in the 1960s Guild's flat-top acoustics were also well regarded. The company changed hands several times, and in 1995 were bought by Fender.

BASSES, GUITARS **Kay** CELLOS, MANDOLINS

BY AN IRONCLAD FACTORY GUARANTEE

...ng, KAY, 1640 Walnut St., Chicago 12

THE KAY Musical Instrument Company was established in Chicago in the early 1930s, growing from Stromberg-Voisinet which was run by Henry Kay Kuhrmeyer and whose most popular guitar line was called Kay-Kraft. By 1935 the Kay company was based in Walnut Street, Chicago.

△ KAY THIN TWIN K161
Produced 1953-1958; this example 1954

The K161's more friendly name came from its 'Thin' body and 'Twin' pickups, and Kay were proud of what they called its "new type body construction": hollow maple, but with a central block of wood running from neck to tailpiece on which to mount the two single-coil pickups.

V-SHAPED *markers (below) recall Guild craftsmen's earlier work with Epiphone.*

AS NEW as new can be!

Here's an entirely new kind of Spanish electric guitar, the Kay "Thin Twin." Two high fidelity pick-ups, each with separate tone and volume controls, permit you to accentuate bass, treble or both. Just flip the 3-way selector switch for the effect you want! New type body construction for sustained tones. Lightweight. For free folder, write Kay, 1640 Walnut St., Chicago 12, Illinois.

KAY
THIN TWIN
"ELECTRIC"

3-WAY SELECTOR SWITCH
TWIN TONE CONTROLS
TWIN VOLUME CONTROLS

KAY's 1930s founder Henry Kay Kuhrmeyer sold his company in 1955 to a group of investors including former Harmony manager Sidney M Katz, and by the end of the 1950s Kay had become one of the largest guitar producers in the US. Most Kay instruments were aimed at beginners and were of average quality, designed to sell at competitive prices. The Thin Twin (a 1953 ad is shown, left) was a good example of how Kay would echo existing market trends – it was a thin, lightweight, solidbody-style instrument – with lower-priced alternatives.

Later in the 1950s Jim Hall, a graduate of the Cleveland Institute of Music, attracted much attention when in 1958 he joined the innovative Chico Hamilton Quintet. Since that time Hall has been one of the most distinctive voices in jazz guitar. At the end of the 1950s saxophonist Jimmy Giuffre invited Hall to join his drum-less trio. This group, renowned for its 'Train And The River' theme, was featured in the movie Jazz On A Summer's Day, filmed at the 1959 Newport Jazz Festival.

A masterful improviser with an unerring sense of melodic development, Hall possesses an instinct for understatement that distinguishes him from the majority of guitar players. With Hall every note counts, and space and colour play an important role. His sound is clear and mellow (on earlier recordings from a Gibson ES-175 but

more recently from a D'Aquisto), but he doesn't shy away from dissonance or earthy, bluesy phrases. These qualities, together with Hall's sympathetic and harmonically informed accompaniments, have led him into fruitful musical partnerships with vocalist Ella Fitzgerald, with saxophonists Sonny Rollins and Paul Desmond, with trumpeters Chet Baker and Art Farmer and with bassists Red Mitchell and Ron Carter, and his early 1960s duo recordings with pianist Bill Evans are widely regarded as high points in the careers of both these musicians.

The Hollywood studios offered many 1950s musicians an attractive financial alternative to the precarious living to be made on the jazz scene. Howard Roberts (1929-1992) was already a fluent, driving jazz guitarist when he moved to Los Angeles from Phoenix, Arizona, but was soon

making a living "as an industrial guitarist", to use his own phrase, and his versatile guitar work crops up in countless TV and movie soundtracks from The Flintstones to The Sandpiper and on albums accompanying artists from Elvis Presley to Peggy Lee. By night Howard was performing on the LA jazz scene with leading artists such as Dexter Gordon, Bud Shank, Al Haig and Chico Hamilton, and in 1955 he won Down Beat magazine's New Star award.

Curious about every type of music from traditional blues to contemporary rock and classical music, Roberts made a thorough and valuable study of harmony, counterpoint and composition. A series of albums on Verve and Capitol underlines his versatility and his willingness to experiment with orchestral settings and rock contexts. Roberts wrote several practical handbooks for guitarists including Howard

△ GRETSCH SILVER JET
Produced 1954-1963, re-issued 1989; this example 1955

In 1953 Gretsch launched their first 'solidbody' electric, the Duo-Jet – actually a semi-solid concoction with a pressed top – and the following year applied a sparkle plastic finish courtesy of their drum department for a chintzy partner, the Silver Jet.

THE GRETSCH *logo with a large T (above) used during the 1950s and after is described by collectors as the 'T roof' logo.*

COLOURFUL *finishes became a distinctive element of Gretsch's guitars in the 1950s with models such as the green Country Club and the sparkling Silver Jet (far left). Gretsch exploited this in publicity; a catalogue from 1955 (left) shows a trio of bright semi-solid models, the red Jet Fire Bird, black Duo-Jet and orange Round Up.*

1954

TAL FARLOW's lightning bebop lines caused a stir in the 1950s, not least in the Red Norvo Trio; seen (far left) on the cover of Down Beat, Farlow is in front of bassist Charlie Mingus and alongside Norvo, the group's vibraphone-playing leader. Farlow also had a fine solo career, his LPs including Swinging Guitar (1956, left), the cover of which featured his Gibson ES-350.

Roberts Chord Melody, Howard Roberts Guitar Book, Howard Roberts Super Chops and the 3-volume Praxis Guitar Compendium. In later years, Roberts co-founded with Pat Hicks the Guitar Institute of Technology in Los Angeles and wrote its original syllabus.

For players such as Tal Farlow and Jimmy Raney, it was the bebop lines of saxophonist Charlie Parker and pianists Bud Powell and Al Haig that figured most prominently in their musical development. Farlow, who grew up in Greensboro, North Carolina, relied on the radio to hear the popular music of the day and became fascinated by the virtuoso jazz pianist Art Tatum. Farlow particularly admired the way that Tatum would vary the harmonies of a song, and began to explore similar ideas on the guitar. Moving to New York in 1944 he witnessed the bebop revolution at first hand and absorbed the playing of Charlie Parker, Dizzy Gillespie, Bud Powell and Miles Davis into his own work.

By the time Farlow joined the Red Norvo Trio in 1949 he was already a fine player but, rising to the musical challenge presented by vibraphonist Norvo, Farlow worked hard on his technique and developed the ability to play long, flowing bebop lines at ultra-fast tempos. He also became a master at playing complete solos using artificial harmonics. Farlow's four years with Norvo introduced him

to a wide audience and confirmed his standing as an innovative jazz guitarist. A succession of excellent albums throughout the 1950s showed a player of exceptional technique and creative powers who could re-harmonise a song with the most sophisticated chord melody arrangement and then follow it with chorus after chorus of inventive, swinging improvisation.

In 1950 Farlow developed a short-scale guitar by reducing the length of the neck in order to enable bigger left-hand stretches. This allowed more unusual chord voicings, but also reduced string tension. A decade later he would collaborate with Gibson on the design of their Tal Farlow model, with its distinctive scrolled cutaway.

Unlike many of his contemporaries, Tal was never attracted by the lure of commercial studio work and, in spite of a period away from the spotlight during the 1960s, he has made his musical career solely in jazz. Still active in the mid-1990s, he remains possibly the most influential of those jazz guitarists whose careers flowered in the 1950s. Many later players, among them John McLaughlin and Pat Martino, have quoted Tal Farlow as a primary inspiration.

While Tal Farlow was applying the hard-bop idiom to the guitar in the late 1940s and the 1950s, Jimmy Raney was

SIMPLICITY ruled in the design of the Les Paul Junior (below) as Gibson competed with lower-priced guitars.

GIBSON's Les Paul Junior had a solid mahogany body and a rosewood fingerboard.

A CUSTOMER in 1956 could buy all six Gibson electrics in this Kansas City shop window

(right), including the Les Paul Junior, for $1610. Today they'd fetch around $20,000.

GUILD never attracted the same calibre of players to endorse their guitars in the 1950s as did Gibson, despite a brief but unsuccessful collaboration with Johnny Smith (see p22). It's hard to imagine that ads like the 1959 example for the X-350 shown (left) did much to widen the appeal of Guild's guitars.

△ GUILD STRATFORD X-350
Produced 1954-1965; this example 1954

This Guild model emphasised the earlier connections of the company's workers with Epiphone, being very similar in pickup and control layout to the Zephyr Emperor Regent model (see p8).

RIGHT-WING Republican senator Joseph McCarthy is discredited by the US Senate. A wave of anti-communist hysteria, blacklists and McCarthy's investigations committee were unleashed after his unsubstantiated claim in 1950 that the State Department was infiltrated by communists.

GIBSON guitars were by far the most prominent among the instruments used by the leading jazz guitar players of the 1950s. Of the guitarists in the prestigious Down Beat poll for 1956, for example, Gibson could count six of the top ten as being 'their' players: Barney Kessel, Tal Farlow, Les Paul, Herb Ellis (above), Jimmy Raney and Jim Hall.

approaching it from a different angle. From Louisville, Kentucky, Raney began his professional career in New York in 1944 at the age of 17 when he joined the Jerry Wald Orchestra. The bebop movement was transforming jazz music then, adding fresh harmonic and rhythmic ideas and introducing a rich repertoire of compositions. Studying at first hand the playing of its leading exponents among them saxophonist Charlie Parker and pianists Bud Powell and Al Haig, Raney worked out a way to apply their complex lines to the guitar.

Raney's gently swinging style combined clarity with harmonic subtlety. Long, flowing, improvised lines, sparkling with surprises, would weave their way through the outer reaches of the harmonies – always melodic but never obvious. Raney's reputation as an innovative guitar

stylist was established through the recordings he made with saxophonist Stan Getz in 1952 and was confirmed by his subsequent albums with Red Norvo, Bob Brookmeyer, Zoot Sims, Jim Hall and others. Particularly outstanding are the 12 tracks he recorded in Paris in 1954 with a French rhythm section while on tour there with the Red Norvo Trio.

In the 1970s, after several years off the jazz scene back in his home town of Louisville, Jimmy teamed up with his son Doug, also a fine guitarist. Touring worldwide, he opened up a fresh and creative phase in his career. Increasing deafness and deteriorating health forced him to stop touring in the late 1980s, however, and Jimmy Raney, the master of the 'cool school' of jazz guitar, died in May 1995. ■ CHARLES ALEXANDER

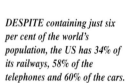

DESPITE containing just six per cent of the world's population, the US has 34% of its railways, 58% of the telephones and 60% of the cars.

TRANSISTOR RADIOS are introduced, made by Regency.

∇ GIBSON LES PAUL JUNIOR
Produced 1954-1961; this example 1956

Once Gibson established that their $225 Les Paul gold-top model would sell, they came out with a cheaper solidbody, the plain, slab-body, single-pickup, sunburst Junior, at just $99.50.

KLUSON of Chicago made most of Gibson's tuners during the 1950s, including these cheap three-on-a-plate types.

DOO-WOP heaven as The Spaniels make 'Goodnight Sweetheart Goodnight' and The Penguins record 'Earth Angel'. Meanwhile, Elvis Presley makes his first recordings.

IN THE UK, food rationing officially ends, celebrated by a bonfire of ration books in London. In the US, the term 'fast food' comes into use.

CUSTOMS of the first few years feature a P90 pickup at the bridge and a more powerful Alnico type at the neck (below).

△ GIBSON LES PAUL CUSTOM
Produced 1954-1961, 1968-current; this example 1956

As well as the lower-priced Junior, Gibson expanded their Les Paul line upwards in 1954 with the classy $325 all-black Custom, complete with multiple binding and gold-plated hardware.

WEST GERMANY win the soccer World Cup, beating favourites Hungary 5-1. Roger Gilbert Bannister, a 25-year-old British medical student, runs the first sub-four-minute mile.

LEO FENDER (right) set up the Fender Electric Instrument Co in 1946, after his K&F operation with musician Doc Kauffman was dissolved. At first there was just a handful of workers involved in the new Fender company, but this grew quickly and by 1959 Fender would employ over 100 people at the Fullerton factories.

THE FENDER STORY *by Walter Carter*

Pop music of the 1950s bolted away from the smooth and cerebral Sinatra, the refined crooner, and toward the raucous and raw Elvis, with his most basic, unrefined expressions of emotion. So too guitar makers began the decade pushing the electric archtop tradition to its highest level of refinement, only to be undermined and toppled by a plain, uncrafted creation that reduced the electric guitar to its most basic form. That creation was the Fender guitar.

THE FENDER STORY

The silhouette of a Fender Stratocaster would become by the end of the decade an icon for rock'n'roll music, but at the beginning of 1950 the Fender Electric Instrument Co was a little company in Fullerton, California, that didn't even make a standard electric guitar. Just as no one could have predicted rock'n'roll, no one – not even Leo Fender himself – could have predicted the coming revolution that Fender's solidbody electric guitars would lead.

Clarence Leo Fender was a most unlikely revolutionary: a low-key, somewhat reclusive man; an accountant by training, a radio repairman by vocation. He never even learned to tune a guitar, much less play one. He and his early partner Doc Kauffman had made a crude, virtually unplayable solidbody electric in 1943 to test a pickup design, but the products of the business he started immediately after World War II were small guitar amps and the simplest sort of electric guitar, the Hawaiian 'lap steel'. Leo's business started so small that, according to Fender lore, he baked the finishes on early instruments in Kauffman's kitchen oven. Fender steels were plain – the antithesis of the flashy Gibsons and Nationals of the time.

In the late 1940s Leo decided to apply these simple, proletarian designs to a standard or 'Spanish-neck' electric guitar. Given the look of his Hawaiians, it's likely that his decision to make his guitar with a solid rather than hollow

body was based as much on practical considerations – he was not in a financial position to tool up and produce conventional hollow-body archtop instruments, nor to challenge the major manufacturers on their own turf – as it was on some grand vision of the solidbody electric guitar as the vehicle of the future for popular music.

Fender's solidbody electric guitar, dubbed the Esquire, was introduced at a 1950 trade show. Like Leo's early lap

FENDER's advertising during the 1950s was far superior to that of the average guitar manufacturer, not only in press ads (like the cool cat of 1957, below) but also in the company's catalogues and general promotional material.

steels, it had a homemade aura, with a single pickup (Gibson's latest had three), a flat-topped 'slab' body that any woodshop student could cut out on a bandsaw, a maple neck that didn't even have a separate fingerboard or a truss rod, and a sickly maple-coloured paint job that let the grain of the ash wood show through (although one or more of the originals may have been black-painted pine). The guitar industry laughed at Fender's 'plank' or 'toilet-seat' guitar and continued to put pickups on hollow-body archtop guitars.

Sales of the Esquire and the subsequent two-pickup model, the Telecaster (née Broadcaster), were slow: about 1000 to 1500 a year, according to Don Randall, Leo's partner in Fender Sales, which had been formed to market Fender instruments. "The backbone of the business was the lap-top steel guitars, the double-necks and the triple-necks," Randall says. "After the Stratocaster came out and after the Precision Bass came out, of course rock'n'roll was beginning and kids were teaching each other to play instead of going to [teaching] studios, and then the thing became more or less geometric in its take-off."

Bill Carson, a country artist who was playing guitar in the early 1950s for Hank Thompson, was an early evangelist for Fender. "I started hanging out there and being somewhat partially reimbursed for expenses by Leo

THE STRAT came for most of the 1950s with a fretted maple neck, like this example (below). In other words, the frets were fitted into the face of the one-piece maple neck, without a separate fingerboard. From around 1959, however, the Strat began to appear with a separate rosewood fingerboard.

△ FENDER STRATOCASTER
Produced 1954-current; this example 1956

Fender's Stratocaster first appeared in 1954, when its sleek lines and contoured body proved a shocking and futuristic departure from conventional guitar design. A vibrato-equipped version like this sold then for $249.50, or $20 less without vibrato ('hardtail' as it's now nicknamed). The Strat's distinctive looks, crisp sounds and easy playability would soon make it a world-beater.

26

DON RANDALL ran the all-important Fender Sales operation, which had been formed in 1953 when Fender's existing sales arrangement with Radio & Television Equipment Co was re-organised. Randall is seen (below) in a new Piper Apache aircraft purchased by Fender Sales in 1957 and which Randall would pilot on cross-country sales trips.

KEY PERSONNEL (left) at the Fender company during the 1950s included George Fullerton (left) who had started in 1948, Freddie Tavares (centre) who came on board in 1953 and was strongly involved in the development of new instruments such as the Strat and later Jazzmaster, and Forrest White (right) who joined a year later to run the Fender factory.

to do prototypes, take them out and play them myself and also leave them in clubs now and then," he said. Jimmy Bryant, the hot-picking country guitarist who recorded legendary duets with steel guitarist Speedy West, was an early convert, and Fender gained a foothold in country music that would in time lead to domination.

The Telecaster was not without problems, some of which related to the guitar's simple three-section bridge. As Carson said in 1995, "You couldn't tune it then; you can't tune it now." Carson also disliked the sharp edge of the Telecaster's unembellished slab body, which dug into his ribs. He and another southern California country guitarist, Rex Gallion, are credited with suggesting contours in the back and top so that the guitar would, in Carson's words, "fit you like a shirt". "They didn't really want to build the guitar that I wanted them to build, which ended up being

THE STRAT's headstock (below right) was probably influenced by the design of an earlier Paul Bigsby guitar, which in turn seems to be based on European headstocks of the early 19th century.

△ FENDER STRATOCASTER
Produced 1954-current; this example 1954

This famous guitar, owned by David Gilmour of Pink Floyd, bears serial number 0001 – but it is not the first Stratocaster made. Fender components are often dated, and this Strat's neck is dated May 1954, the vibrato cavity June, a month or two after production began. More likely this was a special-order guitar – it has a non-standard coloured finish and gold-plated hardware – that was made even more special with a one-off serial number.

EARLY STRATS *can come with gold-coloured anodised aluminium scratchplates (like the example above). While these provided good electrical shielding, their electrolytic anodised 'skin' tended to wear through, leaving unsightly patches, and they were quickly replaced with plastic units.*

SYNCHRONIZED

Tremolo Action...

in the new "Comfort Contoured"
Stratocaster

ANOTHER "FIRST" FOR *Fender!*

First again in the field of amplified music . . . . . . lling new "Stratocaster" by Fender! . . in design — unequalled in per- . . a flick of the wrist means live, . . — perfect pitch.

. . thrill in store for you when . . evolutionary new instrument. . . pick-ups, a special tone . . a new surface mounted plug . . all mean faster action, better, clearer music . . . whether you play it "straight" or while using the revolutionary Tremolo Action lever.

The Stratocaster features advanced design in body too! Here is an instrument actually "comfort contoured" for you! Its engineered to fit the artists body . . . designed to be "part of the player."

See the new, revolutionary Fender Stratocaster at your dealer soon . . . play it . . . and be the first to experience this new amplified music thrill!

The "Stratocaster" is available with or without "Tremolo" Action.

Write for our latest brochure and name of nearest dealer.

Fender
SALES, INC.   308 EAST FIFTH STREET   SANTA ANA, CALIFORNIA

PROMOTION *for Fender's new Stratocaster guitar began to appear in the first half of 1954, such as this trade press ad (right) from May. Here the accent is on the new guitar's "revolutionary Tremolo* Action lever", *in fact the world's first self-contained vibrato unit: an integrated adjustable bridge, tailpiece and vibrato system which provided the Strat player with pitchbend and shimmering chord effects.*

The "CHIRPING" CRICKETS

MCA CORAL
RAINBOW SERIES

BUDDY HOLLY (second from right) fronted the first truly self-contained pop group, The Crickets, who wrote most of their own material, played virtually all the instruments on their records, and performed live as a group. Holly's gleaming Stratocaster was almost as notable a visual trademark as his horn-rimmed specs, and the guitar's appearance on an early sleeve design (left) had many a fledgling guitarist poring over its unfamiliar outline, the Strat seeming especially futuristic when compared to the staid and old-fashioned look of the Gibson hollow-body electric pictured alongside. Holly more than any other player in the 1950s established the Strat as a sleek, desirable, modern guitar.

▽ FENDER STRATOCASTER
Produced 1954-current; this example 1959

Having started the decade without a Spanish electric, Fender had eight models by the time this guitar was made in 1959: the Esquire, Telecaster, Strat, Duo-Sonic, Musicmaster, Jazzmaster, and bound-body Custom Esquire and Custom Telecaster.

STRATS in colours other than the standard sunburst were sold on a limited, ad-hoc basis until 1956, when Fender first listed 'player's choice' colours as an option. In the following year these Du Pont paint finishes, as used on many General Motors cars, were called 'custom colors' by Fender, a name that has stuck ever since.

THIS 'FIESTA RED' (above) was one of Fender's earliest custom colours. Original coloured Strats from the 1950s are rare.

the Stratocaster, because they didn't want to tool up for it," Carson says. "The company was pretty poor at that time."

In sales, Don Randall was also pushing for a new guitar to compete with the gold-top Les Paul that Gibson had introduced in 1952. "The Telecaster was a plain slab guitar," he explains. "We had to have a prettier guitar. The Stratocaster evolved from that."

Fender's new guitar of 1954 fulfilled all requests. A six-piece saddle allowed individual string adjustment. A 'tremolo' (vibrato) system returned the strings to true pitch. The body shape was a fluid, modernistic double-cutaway with contoured back and top. There were three pickups, probably not due to any players' demands for more tonal

possibilities, but simply because the Fender team felt that three pickups surely had to be better than two.

Randall was the staff model-namer: "I named the Broadkaster, because at that time radio was the big thing," he says. "We were just coming into the television field. When Fred Gretsch called me and said they owned the name Broadkaster [used on Gretsch drums], then television was the next thing – Telecaster. Stratocaster – the next highest thing would be the stratosphere."

Carson, the guinea pig for Leo's experiments, recalls the prototype Stratocaster. "The bridge was backwards, where you had to stick a screwdriver under the string to adjust it. I broke one [string] the first night I had it in a club. The

screws adjusted from the neck side, and it's almost impossible to get a screwdriver under there. I had an easier time when we got that bridgeplate reversed.

"The guitar was very crude," he adds, "with no finish on it, no plated parts on it, but it played in tune all the way down the neck, and every session player in that part of the country, of which there were not very many at the time, would borrow that guitar. I had a hard time getting it back from them."

Unlike the slow-starting Telecaster, the Strat came blazing out of the blocks. "Solidbody guitars were beginning to move pretty well at that time," Randall says, "and when we came out with this one it was quite an innovation, with the

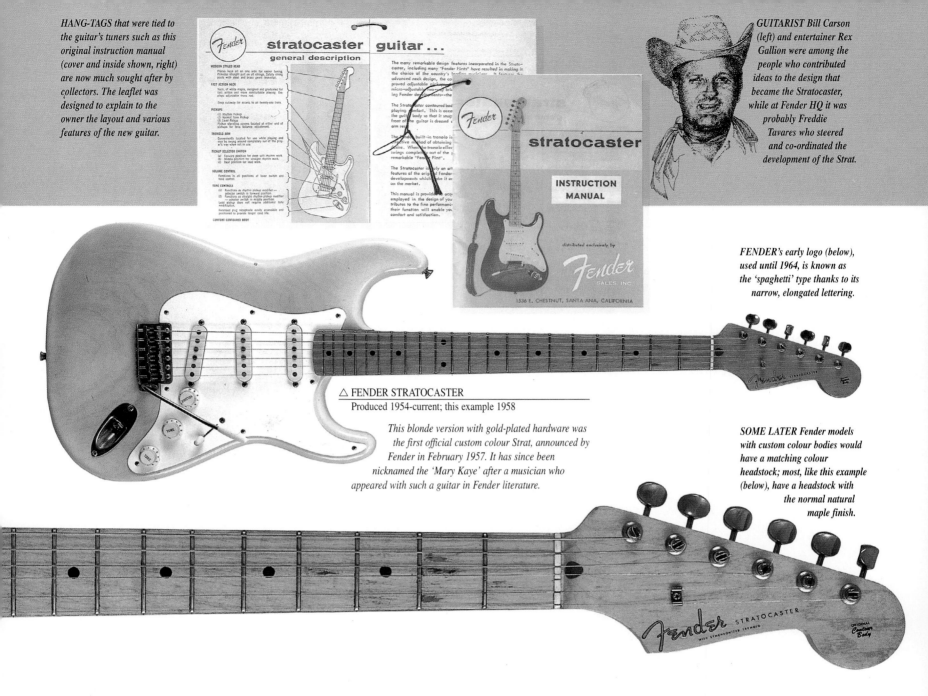

GUITARIST Bill Carson (left) and entertainer Rex Gallion were among the people who contributed ideas to the design that became the Stratocaster, while at Fender HQ it was probably Freddie Tavares who steered and co-ordinated the development of the Strat.

△ FENDER STRATOCASTER
Produced 1954-current; this example 1958

This blonde version with gold-plated hardware was the first official custom colour Strat, announced by Fender in February 1957. It has since been nicknamed the 'Mary Kaye' after a musician who appeared with such a guitar in Fender literature.

FENDER's early logo (below), used until 1964, is known as the 'spaghetti' type thanks to its narrow, elongated lettering.

SOME LATER Fender models with custom colour bodies would have a matching colour headstock; most, like this example (below), have a headstock with the normal natural maple finish.

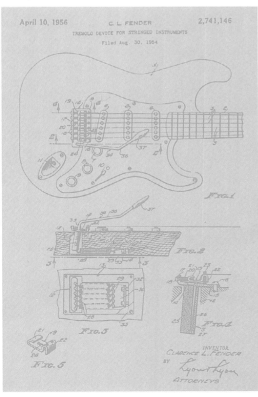

THIS PATENT (left), filed in summer 1954, concerns the Stratocaster's vibrato system, or 'tremolo device for stringed instruments' as it's described. The Fender team had been through much anguish to get the system (described by one insider as "Leo's pride and joy") to a manufacturable state, and at one stage they had to junk several thousand dollars' worth of tooling. Leo Fender, under his full name of Clarence L Fender, registered a number of other patents during the 1950s relating to various guitar parts and designs, including the bridge and pickup assembly of the Telecaster (patent filed in January 1950; see p14), and the Jazzmaster's offset-waist body (filed in January 1958).

cutaway in the back and the lopped-off front so you didn't have to move your arm. It had a lot of features you could talk about, and it did have the sound. We didn't have any trouble selling them. We sold them by the jillions."

The Stratocaster was the most refined guitar of its day, a masterful combination of aesthetics and functionality, and although it would be followed by more 'refinements' such as the Jazzmaster model, it would eventually emerge as an even greater achievement than its creators ever imagined. "I've watched this over the years," Carson says, "and a country player, a Western swing player, wouldn't be caught dead playing what a rock'n'roll player played, and vice versa. Finally the Strat just transgressed

all these things. It put to bed once and for all the fact that there is one guitar that will do it."

The Telecaster and Stratocaster are enough to qualify Fender as the leading light of the 1950s, but these models had a solid supporting cast – Fender amplifiers and the Fender Precision Bass – that allowed the guitars and the guitarists to break easily through conventional barriers, particularly in the area of volume. Fender guitars were louder than conventional hollow-body electrics … but 'loud guitar' is a bit of a simplification. The solid bodies gave Fenders an inherent capability for more sound with less feedback, but beyond that, 'loud guitar' really means 'loud amplifier'. Fender's amps – which were Leo's own real speciality – were the industry standard, regardless of what kind of guitar you played (Buddy Holly being the notable, ironic exception, playing his Strat through a Magnatone amp).

Amps, Don Randall says, "were the mainstay of the whole music business. It was through Fender amplifiers that all these bands became amplified. With the advent of the solidbody guitar and the amplifier it was the first time the guitar player could drown out the drummer. The amplifiers were the big factor. However, as it developed, the sales of guitars and amplifiers dollar-wise about paralleled each other after the initial period."

THE AUTO INDUSTRY *had a profound effect upon US guitar manufacturers during the 1950s, not least in its ability to enhance the look of an already stylish object with a rich, sparkling paint finish (like this Chevy Bel Air, right). Gretsch were among the first of the guitar makers to use Du Pont paints – the biggest supplier of paint to the automobile* factories – *to create instruments such as the 'Cadillac green' Country Club and 'Jaguar tan' Streamliner in 1954. Fender started making the occasional coloured guitar at this time, and from 1956 offered the option of 'player's choice' colours, renamed 'custom colors' the following year and including blonde as well as fiesta red.*

▽ FENDER STRATOCASTER
Produced 1954-current; this example 1957

Another rare non-standard coloured guitar, this instrument has a beautiful gold finish that accentuates the Stratocaster's flowing curves. The effect is further enhanced by the gold-plated hardware, which, together with the instrument's superb condition, make it a desirable and eminently collectible guitar.

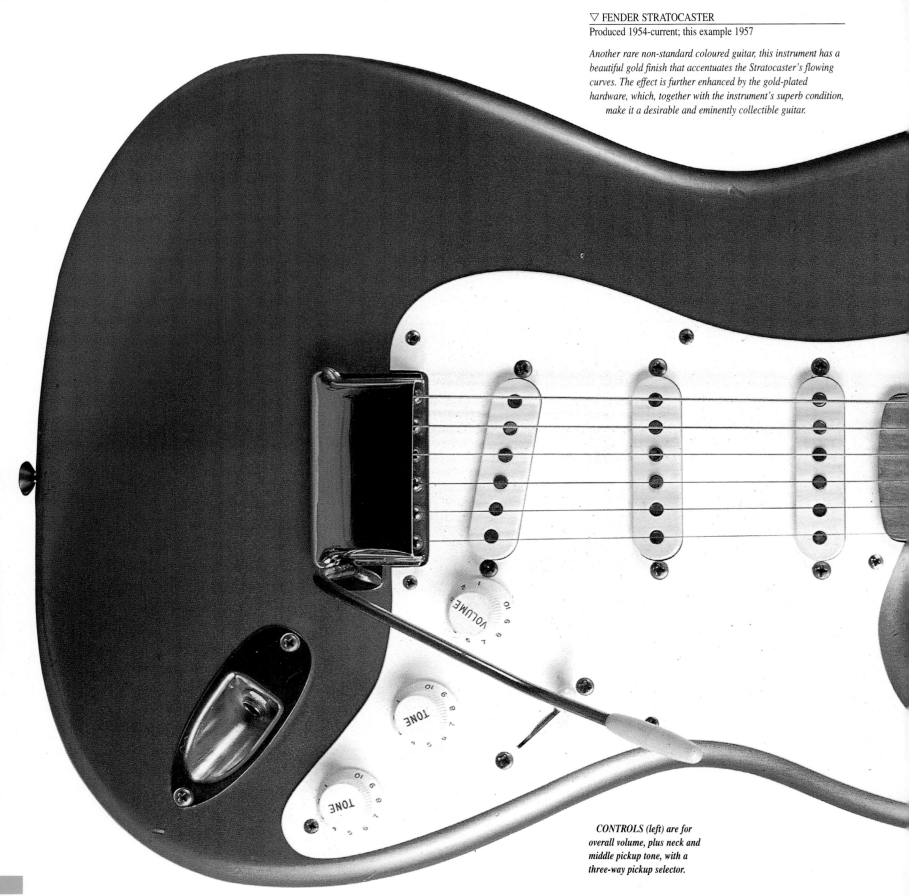

CONTROLS (left) are for overall volume, plus neck and middle pickup tone, with a three-way pickup selector.

1955

FRED GRETSCH Jr (left) had become president of the Fred Gretsch Manufacturing Company in 1948. Gretsch had been established in New York in 1883, but it wasn't until the 1950s that the company's guitars began to make an impact on the market, not least through the series of models bearing the name of top country guitarist Chet Atkins.

Fred Jr presided over a Brooklyn-based factory that poured out colourful instruments with eye-catching looks and great names. The stunning White Falcon (below) was at the top of the tree, and this together with guitars such as the Country Club, Duo-Jet and Country Gentleman made sure of Gretsch's place in the hall of 1950s guitar fame.

▽ GRETSCH WHITE FALCON

Produced 1955-1980, re-issued 1990; this example 1955

"Cost was never considered in the planning of this guitar," Gretsch boasted of the White Falcon, and at $600 it was by far the company's most expensive instrument. With a white paint finish, gold sparkle decorations and gold-plated hardware, the gleaming Falcon stood out like a beacon against the relatively drab sunburst and plain natural finishes of other guitars.

THE DISTINCTIVE tailpiece (left) has since been dubbed the 'Cadillac' by collectors because of the resemblance of its 'V' to the automobile company's logo. Also prominent in the metalwork is a 'G' for Gretsch.

COUNTRY GUITARS *by Thomas Goldsmith*

Country & Western music came to a crossroads in the 1950s. One way led to its old home of Nashville, Tennessee, where the round, warm tones of hollow-body electric guitars snuggled up to an increasingly pop-oriented sound. But at the end of the decade, over in California, the new twangy guitar-based Bakersfield sound took hold as players like Buck Owens & His Buckaroos began to draw the trebliest sounds yet from piercing, solidbody guitars.

ERNEST TUBB & His Texas Troubadours (above) helped the electric guitar gain ground in the conservative musical environment of Nashville in the early 1950s.

COUNTRY GUITARS

As the 1950s dawned, the electric guitar had for only a few years been allowed on the hallowed Grand Ole Opry stage, centre of the country music universe. Harold Bradley, one of the finest players of the era, and today president of the Nashville musicians' union, recalls: "The first guy they let play electric guitar on the Opry on a regular basis was Jimmy Short, with Ernest Tubb. Ernest had a hit with electric guitar on it and he would only come on the Opry if they let him bring the electric guitar."

A lean Texan with a homespun baritone that spoke of Western days and honky-tonk nights, Tubb had enjoyed a breakthrough record with 'Walking the Floor Over You', recorded in Dallas in 1941. Its single-noted melodic solo by Fay Smith, probably on a flat-top with a pickup attached to the soundhole, established the electric guitar at the centre of Tubb's many subsequent hits. Bradley went on to carry that particular torch in the year that Tubb joined the Opry, as he explains: "In 1943, I played the electric guitar behind Ernest Tubb. I travelled on the road with him between my junior and senior year in high school. I would play on a Gibson ES-150 with the old bar pickup," he says.

Bradley's use of a hollow-body Gibson with the famous 'Charlie Christian' pickup came out of his jazz orientation, something he shared with many of country's early electric players. Billy Byrd: "My first love when I was growing up was jazz, and I loved the big bands. There wasn't too many places in Nashville and around Middle Tennessee that played a lot of jazz.

"I had a family and I had three little girls," Byrd continues. "I had to stop playing for the kicks and I had to start playing commercial. When I went to work with Ernest in '49, it took me about two years of playing with him to feel free, because I would put a little jazz in there and it wouldn't fit. With Ernest you had to play a certain way or it wasn't Ernest Tubb."

Tubb rewarded Byrd by making him one of the best known guitarists in America, simply by calling: "Take it away, Billy Byrd!" before many of the solos. Byrd's appearances on records, radio and TV went a long way

GRETSCH were noted for finely engraved fingerboard markers (below), influenced by the work of top banjo makers.

FINE MATERIALS were used for the Falcon, such as ebony for the fingerboard (above).

GUITARS FOR MODERNS BY Gretsch

GUITAR CATALOGUES were dull and rather reserved until Gretsch's colourful 'Guitars for Moderns' brochure (right) burst on to the scene in 1955.

GRADY MARTIN (right) was one of the most prolific and original session guitarists on the Nashville scene, where he started as a teenage fiddler in the 1940s. Through the 1950s he contributed innumerable ground-breaking licks, solos and arrangements, from a lively twin-guitar sound with Jabbo Arrington on early Jimmy Dickens hits such as 'Sleepin

At The Foot Of The Bed' to the twanging bass lines of Johnny Horton and the vinyl-searing 'Knee Deep In The Blues' by Marty Robbins. His other work for Robbins ranged from the proto-fuzz of 'Don't Worry About Me' to the dancing Spanish figures of 'El Paso', and Martin's innovative playing was all over the enduring hits of Patsy Cline.

GRADY MARTIN

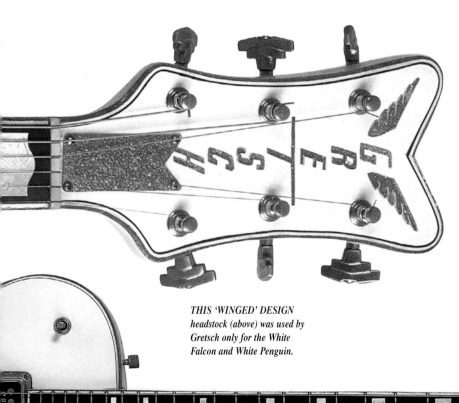

HANK GARLAND (above) won fame with his playing on Red Foley's 1950 'Sugarfoot Rag'. He played many sessions and crafted memorable guitar duet lines with Chet Atkins for Everly Brothers tunes like 'All I Have To Do Is Dream'. His career was cut short by a car crash in 1961.

in establishing the relatively new image of the stand-up, hot guitar man.

But country guitar and electricity go back much further than the 1950s. In 1934 steel guitarist Bob Dunn attached a pickup to a Mexican guitar and started cranking out imaginative and bluesy solos through a rigged-up amplifier. Dunn's role with Western swing pioneer Milton Brown and his Musical Brownies was echoed in Bob Wills' band a year later by a similarly electrified Leon McAuliffe. Country/swing historian Bob Pinson points to San Antonio's Jim Boyd as the first player to record using an electrified Spanish guitar, in a 1935 session with Roy Newman and his band. Then, in 1937, a stunningly adept, jazz-drenched Eldon Shamblin joined Wills on lead guitar, moving within a few years to early use of the Gibson ES-150

before adopting the electrified Super 400. The marriage of Western fiddle and improvised swing was itself electric, with the amplified instruments giving a country-based style for the first time an ability to compete amid the dim lights and thick smoke of the burgeoning honky-tonk scene.

With the electric guitar firmly established in mainstream country by Tubb, it started showing up everywhere. On the West Coast, with its own thriving country scene, electric guitar was primed to explode because of the innovations of Paul Bigsby and Leo Fender. Even though high-profile players like Byrd and Grady Martin played Bigsbys early on, a general division that would last for years was in the making: round warm tones from the hollow-body guitars of Nashville and trebly twang from the solids of California. "I don't remember the Tele being used much at the Opry," recalls Bradley, a Fender endorser by the 1960s. "I tried it and I couldn't stand it; I had one and I got rid of it. You had to learn to love it and play it and get used to the tone of it."

The players who shaped country guitar for most of the 1950s were in Nashville. Chet Atkins was the best known; he spent ten years at radio and road work before coming to stay at the Opry with the Carter Family in the late 1940s, and shows up playing graceful accompaniment on Carters' tunes like '(This Is) Someone's Last Day'. With a grounding in pop, jazz and blues as well as in country, the precise, innovative Atkins became immeasurably far-reaching, first as a player. His highly developed finger-stylings have made his influence felt from the 1940s to the present day on players as diverse as George Harrison and Lenny Breau. Atkins' careers as producer, solo artist and record company executive helped insure the role of guitar on Music Row throughout the decade and beyond. Nashville's top guitar

THIS 'WINGED' DESIGN headstock (above) was used by Gretsch only for the White Falcon and White Penguin.

FANCY TUNERS (below right) used on the Penguin and Falcon were Imperial models made by Grover of New York.

△ GRETSCH WHITE PENGUIN
Produced 1956-c1961; this example 1956

Launched at the 1956 National Association of Music Merchants trade show, the White Penguin was a solidbody-style companion to Gretsch's White Falcon. But the Penguin failed to take off, very few were made, and it is now a valuable collectors' item.

ROSA PARKS, a black bus-passenger in Montgomery, Alabama, defies a segregated seating rule when she refuses to give up her seat to a white person. Martin Luther King organises the year-long Montgomery bus boycott, which leads to the nullification of the bus-segregation laws, and establishes King as leader of the US civil rights movement.

JAMES DEAN is killed in a car crash; he had earlier in the year appeared in 'chicken run' crash scenes in Rebel Without A Cause. Meanwhile, a disaster at the Le Mans road race in France kills 82 onlookers.

DISNEYLAND is opened in Anaheim, Los Angeles. Walt Disney originally planned to call it 'Mickey Mouse Park'.

PHIL SILVERS debuts on US TV as Sgt Bilko. A commercial second station, ITA, starts broadcasting in the UK.

CHARLIE PARKER and Albert Einstein die. Einstein's "famous equation linking mass and energy pointed the way to the fission of uranium, and so to Hiroshima and Nagasaki," says a newspaper obituary.

CHUCK BERRY and Bo Diddley cut their debut records (on Chess and Checker). Bill Haley's 'Rock Around The Clock' is number one in the US and UK after it is featured in the movie Blackboard Jungle.

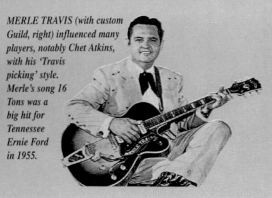

MERLE TRAVIS (with custom Guild, right) influenced many players, notably Chet Atkins, with his 'Travis picking' style. Merle's song 16 Tons was a big hit for Tennessee Ernie Ford in 1955.

JIMMY BRYANT (with Stratosphere Twin, left) came to fame during the early 1950s playing ultra-hot electric guitar solos on Cliffie Stone's Hometown Jamboree TV show in California, working with pedal-steel man Speedy West as The Flaming Guitars. Bryant was one of the first players to use Fender's Broadcaster solidbody, later experimenting with the unusual Stratosphere.

SPEEDY WEST and Jimmy Bryant recorded together; the 'take off' noted on the label of this 45 (above) meant a solo.

guns were friends as well as colleagues, as Byrd recalls: "I used to grab a rhythm guitar and Grady would grab a bass and we would back Chet up." The players' kinship and premium on creativity were at the heart of the Nashville studio approach, where players came up with their own arrangements instead of using standard notation. Their acquaintance with other styles gave an immediacy and accessibility to the country field. But as the 1950s progressed, too much pop perfection drained off some of country's lively, distinctive character in the name of going uptown.

One listen to former country picker Scotty Moore burning down an Elvis Presley side produced in Nashville in 1956 shows that the centre of the guitar universe had swiftly shifted away from the Grand Ole Opry. Moore's playing on 'Hound Dog' is sinister and violent, a glimpse into the void

THE BODY (below) is made from sap gum, an unusual choice for guitar building.

STRATOSPHERE's Twin (below) can hardly be said to have the flowing body lines of a Stratocaster, or the traditional reassurance of a Gibson Les Paul.

CONTROLS include two neck selector switches (between the two sets of strings), a three-way pickup selector for the six-string neck, and two on/off switches for the 12-string pickups alongside the volume and tone knobs for each neck.

36

NASHVILLE turned more pop in the late 1950s, and hard-core country with lots of high-end guitar sounds grew even more pronounced out West. Guitar slinger Joe Maphis had moved out in the early 1950s, and was soon wielding a flashy double-neck (below left) built by a young Semie Moseley (seen with custom triple-neck, left) whose Mosrite guitars went on to fame in the 1960s.

CHET ATKINS became one of the most famous guitarists of the 1950s through his domination of the Nashville studio scene and appearances on the Grand Ole Opry. In the middle of the decade he began an association with the New York guitar manufacturer Gretsch, whose Chet Atkins Hollow Body model (left) was the first of a long-running series of 'signature' models.

both during his solos and the fiercely rumbling 16ths he plays under Presley's vocal. You can even hear Moore making mistakes in 'Hound Dog' – and they work.

The youthful Fender company was building its name slowly, long-time Fender associate Bill Carson remembers: "There wasn't very many players on the West Coast. The best one that we had for Telecasters was Jimmy Bryant; he did a lot of albums with Speedy West." Bryant, playing an early Telecaster by 1950, was the ultimate California twangster, playing revolutionary, mile-a-minute stuff that went a long way towards getting the Fender name out front. Carson, himself a Western swing guitarist, worked with the company

getting players and clubs to try amps and guitars; Hank Thompson and Spade Cooley were early endorsers.

Fender had limited success attracting Nashville players to the Tele, but did snag an important one from Memphis, Carson says. "There was one guy that Leo [Fender] thought a lot of and that was Luther Perkins – he exposed the Telecaster to a lot of the audiences when he was playing with Johnny Cash."

Carson says he was also closely involved in developing the contour lines and other features of the Stratocaster. The Strat's capability of bending notes with a vibrato arm, he remembers, came about because steel players were in short supply on the West Coast. Revered Western swing guitarist Eldon Shamblin, who'd joined Bob Wills in 1937, got a special presentation from Leo Fender in 1954. "Eldon had the first experimental finish on a Stratocaster, a gold guitar," Carson says. "Leo gave it to Eldon himself and asked him to try it out. Eldon Shamblin has probably exposed the Stratocaster to more multitudes than anyone else, all the years he's been playing."

But the act that defined the Tele as the ultimate West Coast guitar was Buck Owens and the Buckaroos. Owens had come up with a treble-heavy sound on the low strings while pounding it out in the Bakersfield clubs. "When you're playing a honky-tonk – I played seven years in the

same one called the Blackboard – the bass strings in those days with the old amplifiers would get kind of lost, so I played with a lot of treble," Owens says.

Fender presented Owens and bandmates Don Rich and Doyle Holly with matching bound Telecasters and a Precision bass around 1959, all with an experimental sparkle finish made of ground glass and epoxy. "Leo was always a sucker for a country music band," says Carson. With major stardom for Owens close at hand by the end of the 1950s, he and Rich were about to return Leo Fender's favour by becoming two of the highest profile Telecaster blasters around. "There ain't nothing in this closet but twang," Owens says. "Don't play me nothing that ain't got no twang to it."

Harold Bradley, who spent the decade as a studio star of the first magnitude, is not the only player who well remembers the guitar-driven sound of country from those years. A host of current records, within and without country, echo the creative licks of the Nashville Sound and the energised, treble-happy sound of original West Coast country. In the end, the great country stars of the 1950s built much of their appeal on the creative use of electric instruments, and the relatively new field of electric guitar earned much of its early fame from the hot pickers of Nashville, Bakersfield and beyond. ■ THOMAS GOLDSMITH

NECKS (below) are of one-piece maple, and are bolted Fender-style to the body.

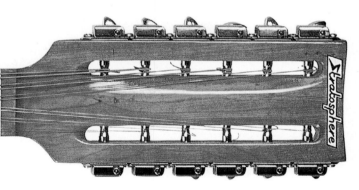

STRATOSPHERE said these standard necks could be replaced by bass or steel necks.

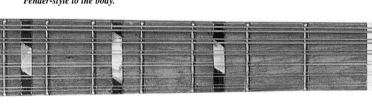

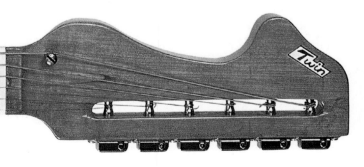

△ STRATOSPHERE TWIN

Produced c1955-1956; this example c1955

"The only twin-necked standard guitar on the market today," boasted the Stratosphere company of Springfield, Missouri, about their astonishing $330 six- and 12-string solidbody instrument – and with the exception of an earlier custom-built twin-neck or two made by Paul Bigsby in California, the claim was correct.

STRATOSPHERE also offered a single-neck guitar in six-string and 12-string versions. As the first company to market an electric 12-string (single- or twin-neck) they had to invent a tuning for the new instrument. One suggestion paired the doubled strings a musical third apart, rather than today's octave/unison mix, giving a novel twin-guitar sound.

THE TWO main US makers' stories were told earlier (Gibson starts on p16, Fender p26). This chapter deals with other US manufacturers, who ranged from huge Harmony to tiny Premier (left).

AMERICAN GUITARS *by Tom Wheeler*

One thing that made the 1950s decade so memorable was the juxtaposition of its freedoms against its rigidity. Compare the 1960s, for example: if the dominant cultural attitude is Do Your Own Thing, merely following that advice is hardly radical. But if the governing credo is Conform Or Else, then deviations from the norm are risky, even potentially revolutionary. And in electric guitar design, the 1950s was America's most revolutionary period ever.

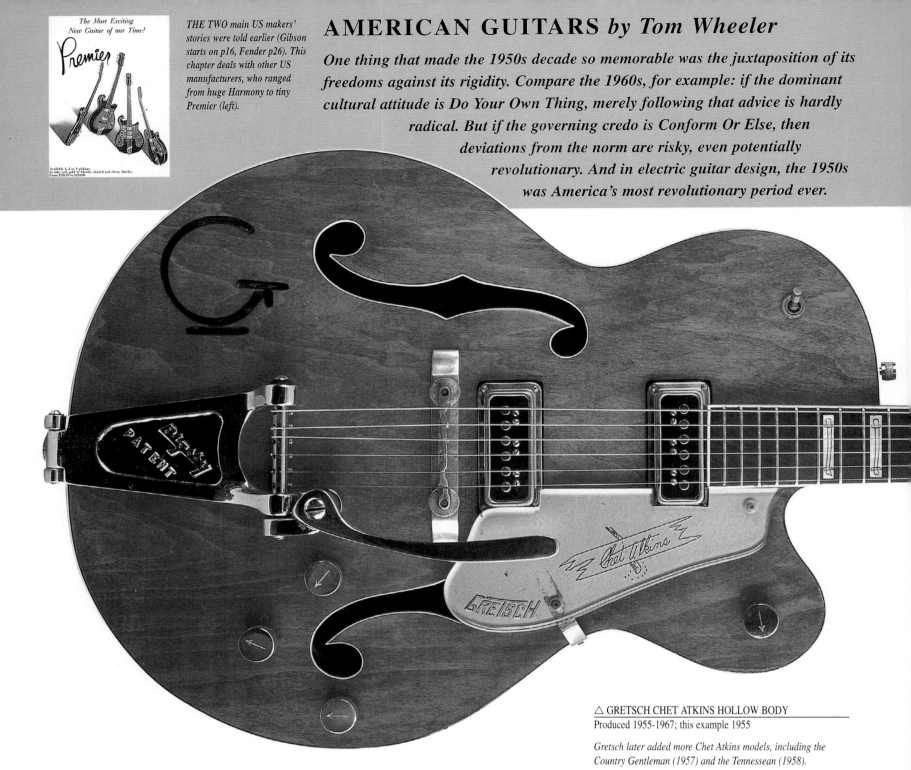

△ GRETSCH CHET ATKINS HOLLOW BODY
Produced 1955-1967; this example 1955

Gretsch later added more Chet Atkins models, including the Country Gentleman (1957) and the Tennessean (1958).

AMERICAN GUITARS

The 1950s left us with countless icons, from Coca-Cola bottles and capri pants to transistor radios and tailfins. One of my favourites is the boomerang-shaped ashtray in, say, tangerine. Its separation of form and function is so cavalier, so who-gives-a-damn, it perfectly typifies the playfulness in design that helped energise the period. It was a time when art seemed important enough to integrate into everyday products, when the squiggle-line influences of modernists like Kandinsky and Miró were seen everywhere: Formica counter tops, rec-room curtains, luncheonette menus, you name it. Almost as common were sketches of Our Friend, Mister Atom (nuclear particles apparently look like orbiting planets).

But there was more to 1950s design than amoeba-shaped coffee tables. While the wacky exuberance may have reflected an optimistic embrace of Sputnik-era technology, it co-existed with long-entrenched commitments to no-nonsense practicality. Handy-dandy

time-saver convenience was something of a marketing religion, as was affordability. Manufacturers responded with an assembly-line approach to everything from Tupperware to tract homes (think of those geometric Life magazine aerial photos of prefab subdivisions). Without this crank-'em-out mentality, the economic phenomenon of 'the American Dream' never would have materialised.

So the 1950s saw a contrasting mix of giddy art for the fun of it, rock-ribbed functionality, and an On To The Future optimism ("The Forward Look" as Chrysler called it), all of which made for a charged and challenging musical marketplace. To varying degrees, manufacturers rose to the occasion. Some of their products were wonderful, some were goofy, some were both.

Take Gretsch. Although they perfectly captured 1950s kitsch futurism with their stereo pickup description, 'Project-O-Sonic', their quirkiest ideas (snap-on back pads, unnecessary string mutes, semi-comprehensible circuits) were actually brainstorms of the following decade. Where I came from, Gretsches of the 1950s were considered

superior to practically all other guitars, something to which you might graduate after, say, an ES-350. That might surprise Gibson aficionados, but I was living in the US South at the time, and Gretsch was endorsed by Chet Atkins himself, and well, that was all anybody needed to know. These guitars were quintessential examples of thoughtfully designed and finely crafted instruments whose features would appeal to any thoroughly modern 'billy: Dynasonic or Filter'Tron pickups, Space Control bridge, StaTite tuners, and finishes more at home on flashy ragtops than flamey archtops.

Gretsch laboured to dazzle its customers but also to serve their needs. As the 1950s progressed, lovely and modest designs like the '51 Electro II and Art Deco masterpieces like the cat's-eye Synchromatics gave way to more extravagant creations, but even the late-1950s showboats were unflinchingly touted as guitars of the highest quality. The high-tack, gold-sparkle-trimmed White

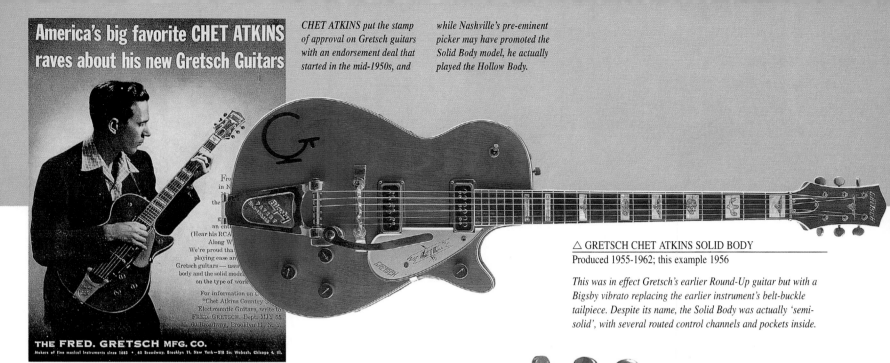
CHET ATKINS put the stamp of approval on Gretsch guitars with an endorsement deal that started in the mid-1950s, and while Nashville's pre-eminent picker may have promoted the Solid Body model, he actually played the Hollow Body.

△ GRETSCH CHET ATKINS SOLID BODY
Produced 1955-1962; this example 1956

This was in effect Gretsch's earlier Round-Up guitar but with a Bigsby vibrato replacing the earlier instrument's belt-buckle tailpiece. Despite its name, the Solid Body was actually 'semi-solid', with several routed control channels and pockets inside.

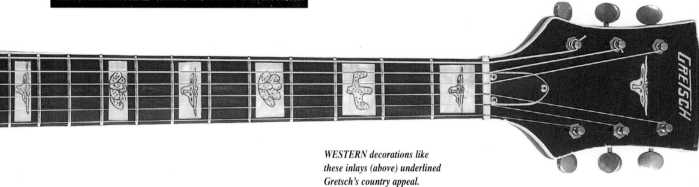

WESTERN decorations like these inlays (above) underlined Gretsch's country appeal.

ATKINS himself disliked the unrelenting cowboy trimmings such as the steer's head (left) and the body's 'G-brand', and gradually these were removed or toned down by Gretsch.

HARMONY was at America's instrument manufacturing hub, which for decades had been Chicago. A report on the company's 60th anniversary in 1952 noted that they produced "more than half of all the fretted instruments made in the US". Harmony made a few

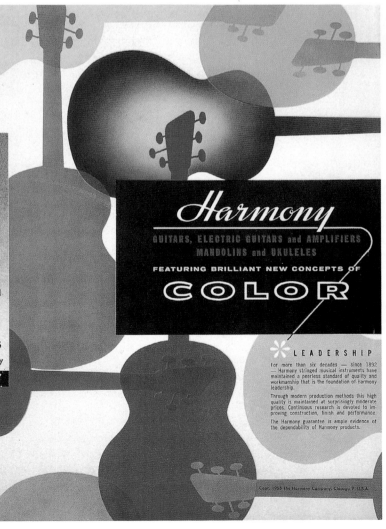

HARMONY was in something of a transition during the 1950s between its pre-war success, which was substantial, and its mid-1960s success, which was staggering. Aside from building guitars for mail-order operations such as Sears, Harmony offered everything from bargain flat-tops with stencilled cowboy paintings to electric archtops (as in this ad, left) and nifty little Stratotones.

admirable models of professional calibre, as well as huge quantities of moderately priced instruments that found their way into the hands of countless beginners.

Falcon may be the most outlandish instrument ever produced in quantity, the guitar's all-time Jayne Mansfield va-va-voom eyepopper, but Gretsch called it simply the best guitar ever, and they meant it. Another example of unapologetically over-the-top styling was the Chet Atkins Solid Body; with its longhorn logo, cows'n'cactus inlays and tooled leather trim, it was a Cadillac cowpoke's yee-haw vision come to earth.

Speaking of blending tradition, art, and The Forward Look: to gaze upon the Rickenbacker line from the 1950s was to see design aesthetics of every decade from the 1930s onwards rolled up into one grand parade. A hint of the Old World was found in Roger Rossmeisl's exquisite raised-ridge (or German Carve) top contouring. America's Depression-era industrial past was echoed in Rickenbacker's 1930s-style Frying Pan lap steel guitars, gigantic horseshoe-magnet pickups, tailpieces that looked like stamped metal, and Doc Kauffman-designed vibratos with fragile housings and exposed springs

UK GUITAR STAR Bert Weedon (above) plugs a hollow-body Hofner Club 50 electric.

HOFNER in Germany started making guitars in the 1920s, with electrics following in the 1950s. A special line was made from 1953 to be sold in the UK by Selmer, later including the small Clubs (far left) and the larger-body Committee, President and Senator (left).

DESPITE the lack of f-holes and general look, the Club models came with hollow bodies, making them comfortably lightweight.

HOFNER's Club 50 (above) was a cheap two-pickup hollow-body electric without f-holes. Along with the one-pickup Club 40 it saw great service on the UK beat scene of the late 1950s; a young John Lennon was an early 40 user.

(though less awesome than Doc's positively kinky motorised whammy, the standard vibratos were nonetheless idiosyncratic).

These plain Jane utilitarian items were mixed with a fabulous array of mechanical innovations and high-stylin' details – nameplates that looked like the one-piece chrome logos on cars; swept-wing bodies with scimitar soundholes, split-level pickguards, and whopper kitchen-oven knobs; laser-slim necks with double truss rods, triangle markers, and high-gloss fingerboards.

Several of Kay's guitars were well-made and boasted quality features like solid spruce tops, Melita bridges, and Grover Imperial tuners, and the backbone of the line was a series of reasonably good and very affordable guitars in many styles. Still, the company is best remembered for the stylistic boldness of selected models. Take the Barney Kessel's 'Kelvinator' headstock, so nicknamed because of

its heavy Kitchen Of The Future appliance vibe. Its mix of Atomic Age and Art Deco (Atomic Deco!), its lunch-counter gold dots on white plastic, the oversized V that would look right at home on an El Dorado landrocket – has there ever been a more evocative 1950s guitar icon?

An essential principle of Edsel-era guitar chic was that although expensive models were OK, an instrument didn't have to be costly to be cool. To wit: Danelectro. Nat Daniel founded his New Jersey company in 1946 and later cranked out thousands of guitars under the Silvertone (for Sears), Coral, and Danelectro brands. Many had hardboard tops and backs affixed to an interior skeleton of pine, as well as pickup casings made from lipstick tubes. These inexpensive but effective construction methods enabled the guitars produced by the Danelectro company to embody one of American commerce's most esteemed values: they were cheap, but they did the job.

But not all companies leapt into assembly-line production methods, Atomic Deco styling, or gonzo gizmo-mania. Some were concerned more with preserving traditions than breaking new ground. Epiphone's roots went back to the 1870s. By the 1930s it had as good a reputation as any maker in the world, and it extended several of its classic designs from the 1930s and 1940s into the 1950s. Although Gibson purchased the company in '57, the instruments of both incarnations of Epiphone were revered for their style, elegance, and artistry. The electric versions of its flagship, the Emperor, rivalled the best of Gibson, D'Angelico and Stromberg, and its early Sheraton was certainly one of the most distinctive and loveliest thin-bodies ever, with its faceted knobs, yellow pickup housings and Frequensator tailpiece.

Although Guild was founded in 1952 and did introduce some interesting innovations, it was concerned mostly

40

BERT WEEDON was the busiest UK session guitarist in the 1950s. He worked backing visiting stars like Frank Sinatra and Judy Garland, and in the studio helped create British rock'n'roll with acts such as Billy Fury and Tommy Steele. Despite starting his career with an English Abbot-Victor guitar, Weedon moved to Hofner, at first electrifying an archtop acoustic Committee (far left). In 1955 he started a solo career, overseen by A&R man George Martin (centre, left) who years later would achieve fame as the Beatles' producer. Weedon had his first hit in 1959 with 'Guitar Boogie Shuffle', a cover version of The Virtues' electric arrangement of Arthur Smith's late-1940s 'Guitar Boogie' instrumental.

Guitarist Bert Weedon (l.) checks over final details before recording his first solo sides for Parlophone on Wednesday watched by Sidney Torch (r.), whose orchestra accompanied him, and A&R chief George Martin.

▽ HOFNER CLUB 50
Produced 1955-1963; this example c1956

Hofner's Club 40 and Club 50 first appeared in 1955 as part of a UK-only line. Early examples have black-covered pickups and a distinctive oval panel; by 1958 the Clubs had a new rectangular 'flick action' control plate, and soon after adopted more conventional-looking metal-covered pickups. The better quality Club 60 model was added in 1958, at which time the Club 40 was priced at £29, the Club 50 was £35 and the Club 60 cost £44.

▽ SUPRO BELMONT
Produced 1955-1964; this example c1958

Never short of a snappy name, Valco dubbed the Supro Belmont's wild plastic covering the "No-Mar finish", and even managed to refer to the $99.50 guitar's plain ol' pickup as "the clean, clear-toned Melody Unit".

SUPRO (1959 catalogue, above) was one of the brandnames used by Valco, who also produced National guitars in the 1950s.

with traditional designs and built some of the decade's most stately and beautiful electric archtops. Several workers were former Epiphone employees, and their old company's heritage was recalled in pearl fingerboard blocks with abalone wedges, or in the Stratford 350's six-button tone selector panel, inspired by the Emperor. Other distinctive Guild touches included white plastic pickup covers and the lovely harp tailpiece.

National and Dobro introduced their most important designs in the 1920s and 1930s, and their post-war successor, Valco, made its biggest splash in the early 1960s. During the 1950s, though, Valco also made a variety of moderately priced electrics, some patterned after the Les Paul and some with bodies actually supplied by Gibson. For players not ready to spring for an ES-175, a Tele, or a Les Paul, Supro's Dual-Tone or Belmont (made by Valco) and

National's Glenwood, Stylist or Bel-Aire were fun and functional alternatives.

Of course, these are just a few of the decade's significant names, spotlighted here because they typified essential aspects of 1950s design. There were others, to be sure, like Paul Bigsby, whose instruments were historically important but very scarce and whose 'company' was a one-man operation; Mosrite, which started in the 1950s but was very much a 1960s phenomenon; and Carvin, a maker of terrific mail-order bargains even back in the 'I Like Ike, I Love Lucy' era.

Well, there's no single guitar that captures the spirit of the time. For me, the period's defining characteristic is its Danelectro-to-D'Angelico diversity, the clashing styles and personalities bumping up against each other like a tangerine boomerang ashtray sitting on a stately old rolltop desk. One thing those designers had in common, though,

was their foresight. After all, they were the ones who perfected the electric guitar's essential aspects. Players with a reverence for vintage instruments or simply an itch for kitsch can find faithful reissues of various models. But even aside from the re-creations, most guitars today borrow heavily from the 1950s pioneers.

Whether they were making double-neck rock-a-hula Rickenbacker lap steels, swingin' Epiphones with cloud markers and vine inlays, or Kay Old Kraftsman 'Jimmy Reed' twang buckets, the 1950s designers were certainly bold. By comparison, the faceless corporate committees responsible for many later innovations seemed timid. They'd never put a big honkin' G cattle brand right on top of a flame-maple guitar. But back in the Project-O-Sonic 1950s, designers weren't burdened by self-consciousness. They experimented, they took risks, they had fun. In other words, they had Style. ■ TOM WHEELER

ROCK'N'ROLL GUITARS *by Rikky Rooksby*

The popularity of the electric guitar was inextricably bound up with the birth in the mid-1950s of rock'n'roll. This was teen music: loud, rhythmic, aggressive, rebellious. And through amplification, the electric guitar could be all these things – as a host of players from Chuck Berry to Bo Diddley set out to prove.

ROCK'N'ROLL GUITARS

Electricity, in the form of pickups and amplifiers, gave the guitar the chance to dominate popular music. Unamplified, it had always been vulnerable to the sheer volume of piano or brass. With amplification, guitarists could play a single note and cut through a band's performance as effectively as the shrillest saxophone.

In most 1950s pop music the guitar had a background role as a chordal instrument, helping to fill out the sound and maybe playing some muted arpeggios – perhaps in a Perry Como or Eddie Fisher hit, for example. But a few talented guitarists like Chet Atkins and Les Paul were able to showcase their abilities and break into the charts.

Guitars like the Gibson Les Paul or the more daring Fender Stratocaster seemed futuristic, giving the instrument a new-fangled modernity that in many ways is difficult for us to capture now, since these designs are seen today as 'vintage classics'.

When rock'n'roll and rockabilly went mainstream in the mid 1950s, many hit tracks featured electric guitar. Few artists contributed more to the global profile of the guitar than Bill Haley and His Comets. They weren't the best, the rootsiest or the hippest, but they had over a dozen hits in 1955 and 1956 with which to spread the message, and were seen in films like Blackboard Jungle. Often in early

CHUCK BERRY is arguably the most influential rock guitarist of the 1950s. He's seen here in classic 'duck walk' pose (right) with the Gibson ES-350T on which he brought to life his fresh hybrid of boogie, country and blues.

THE 350T started life with these P90 pickups (left), later gaining humbucker types.

CONTROLS were standard: a volume knob (front) and tone knob (back) for each pickup.

GIBSON made fewer natural-finish examples of their archtop models (such as the ES-350T above) than they did sunburst, and collectors today will pay a premium for these rarer guitars. For example, in 1957 only 43 of the total of 147 ES-350Ts made at Gibson's factory in Kalamazoo, Michigan, had a natural finish to their laminated maple tops.

1950s pop if there was a lead break it would be taken by saxophone, but now the guitar was stealing up and would almost eclipse that instrument in solo territory. On Haley's waxings, guitarist Danny Cedrone or Frank Beecher would often double the saxophone, sometimes (as on 'Mambo Rock', recorded in 1955) harmonising a musical third above. Songs like 'Rock Around The Clock' (the recorded solo of which was played by an apparently country-influenced Cedrone), 'Rock The Joint', 'Shake, Rattle and Roll', and 'Razzle-Dazzle' had short but attention-grabbing guitar solos, and the playing is often quite fast for the time.

There's no doubt that Scotty Moore, who recorded with Elvis Presley throughout the decade, is another key figure. Presley's worldwide audience may not have known Moore by name, but the solos on early Sun tracks such as 'That's Alright' and on the RCA sides 'Heartbreak Hotel', 'Hound Dog' and 'Blue Suede Shoes' contributed much to the excitement of those cuts. And Moore, who was also Presley's original manager, usually didn't have to compete with a saxophonist. On 'My Baby Left Me' Moore's deft

△ GIBSON ES-5 SWITCHMASTER
Produced 1955-1962; this example March 1957

Gibson's ES-5 of 1949 was one of the first three-pickup guitars, but was difficult to control. The new Switchmaster version had a volume and tone control per pickup and a pickup selector switch.

picking comes through, and the guitar on 'Heartbreak Hotel' certainly holds its own with the tinkling piano. Moore's elegant and adaptable style owed something to the flatpicking of Les Paul and Tal Farlow and the fingerpicking of Merle Travis and Chet Atkins.

Moore's churning solo on 'Too Much' (recorded 1956) is infamous as one of the more anarchic moments in 1950s rock guitar, but as with other rock players of the era his breaks are more often based on chords rather than scales, as with the lead in 'Blue Moon of Kentucky', or the fret-shifting 'Good Rockin' Tonight'. On that track Moore also makes use of hitting the open E string against an E of the same pitch on the second string, because the available

string gauges of the 1950s were too heavy to allow players to get such unison effects by bending one of the strings (as they would go on to do in the 1960s).

Sam Phillips had recorded other strong guitar parts at Sun: before Presley and Moore came along there was Junior Parker's proto-rockabilly 45 'Love My Baby' with its blistering solo from guitarist Floyd Murphy. Working at the same time as Presley was Carl Perkins who was influenced by the choppy guitar riffs of T-Bone Walker. Perkins recorded his own song 'Blue Suede Shoes' in 1956 with a Gibson Les Paul, as well as later rockabilly tracks like 'Lend Me Your Comb' and 'Matchbox'. Meanwhile in Capitol's studios in Los Angeles, Cliff Gallup was kicking up

▽ GIBSON ES-350T
Produced 1955-1981; this example January 1957

Gibson launched three guitars during 1955 in their new 'thinline' style, in an attempt to produce more comfortable guitars than their existing deep-bodied electric archtops. The ES-350T (as well as the 225T and Byrdland) had a shallower body (around 2in deep), a shorter string-length and a shorter, narrower neck.

GIBSON's Byrdland was inspired by Ernest Tubb's guitarist Billy Byrd and sessionman Hank Garland, as publicised in this ad (right).

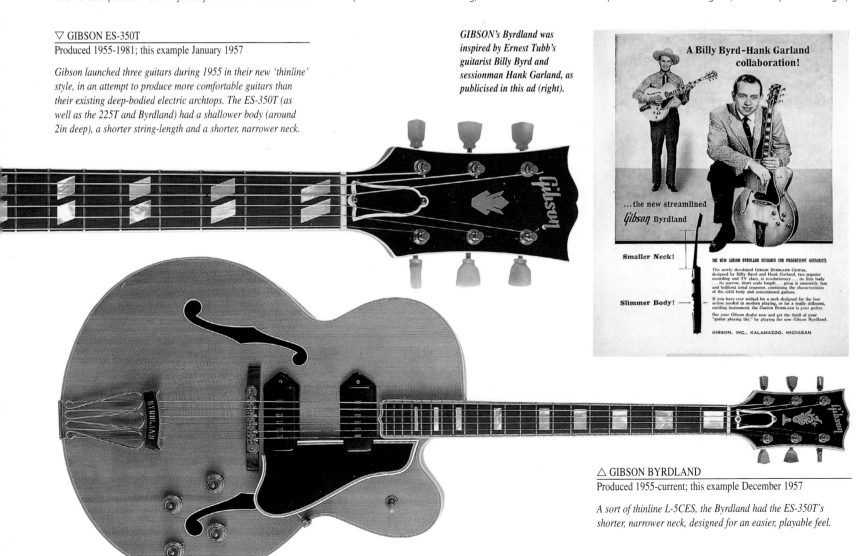

△ GIBSON BYRDLAND
Produced 1955-current; this example December 1957

A sort of thinline L-5CES, the Byrdland had the ES-350T's shorter, narrower neck, designed for an easier, playable feel.

1956

BRIGHT colours became hip in the 1950s, whether on the Technicolor movie screen or in the Formica world of the dream home. As we've seen, guitar makers like Gretsch and Fender quickly exploited this colourful trend. Danelectro's budget-conscious guitars were not far behind, as the New Jersey company's flyer (right) shows with its fuchsias, bronzes, peaches and sands.

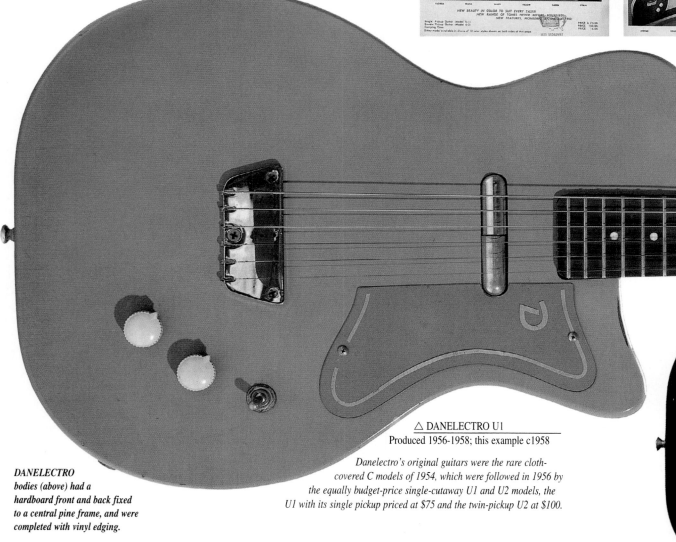

DANELECTRO's idiosyncratic 1950s metal pickup covers (left) were in fact made from lipstick tubes.

DANELECTRO
bodies (above) had a hardboard front and back fixed to a central pine frame, and were completed with vinyl edging.

△ DANELECTRO U1
Produced 1956-1958; this example c1958

Danelectro's original guitars were the rare cloth-covered C models of 1954, which were followed in 1956 by the equally budget-price single-cutaway U1 and U2 models, the U1 with its single pickup priced at $75 and the twin-pickup U2 at $100.

---

a storm. Although Gallup's time with Gene Vincent amounted to less than a year, his contribution to 31 Vincent recordings, including the tracks 'Be Bop A Lula', 'Race With The Devil' and 'Bluejean Bop' (1956), is now seen as seminal rockabilly guitar work, and his brilliant cameos at the heart of Vincent's 45s remain perfect lessons in brevity and style. Gallup dropped out of Vincent's band because he disliked touring, but Johnny Meeks stepped into his shoes with considerable aplomb, striding out on tracks such as the riff-laden 'Dance To The Bop' (1957).

In the 1950s one man became synonymous with the electric guitar, not least by writing the most famous song ever about a poor country boy who learns to play, takes his talent to the city and gets his name in lights. The song was 'Johnny B Goode' and the singer was Chuck Berry. By creating this folk hero for the amplified instrument Berry had an incalculable effect in mythologising it. He wrote the rule book for the fast shuffle boogie solo, and had a trademark intro – the guitar taking the first four bars of the twelve, the band coming in on bar five – as can be heard

on 'Roll Over Beethoven' among many, many others. A variant was 'No Particular Place To Go', which commences with Berry tootling an augmented chord, its dissonance mimicking a car horn. The songs had central solos where Berry would play a series of musical fourths, spiced up with 'bent' notes (from blues) and high descending thirds (from country). On 'Johnny B Goode' the guitar contributes

NEARLY FOUR DECADES after their biggest successes in the 1950s, two guitar-toting rock'n'rollers were included in a series of US stamps issued to honour outstanding American

individuals involved in the performing arts. Buddy Holly (above left) did not, of course, survive the 1950s, while Bill Haley (above right) lived until 1981 when he died aged 55.

little interjections, and has almost gained a voice in its own right: Berry had foregrounded the guitar to talk back at him. There's no doubt Berry is the man who more than anyone else 'invented' rock guitar, and his records remain a recurring source of renewal in rock music.

Listening to recorded rock guitar solos of the 1950s, certain typical features emerge. Heavy-gauge strings made string bending difficult, so it is employed more sparingly than it would be by the blues-rock players of the 1960s and 1970s. Semitone bends are therefore more typical, and at the time this toying with the pitch of a note helped to further rock guitar's rebellious image – the subtext being: we're rebels, because we don't care about your notions of what's 'in tune'.

The emphasis in guitar solos of the 1950s tends to be rhythmic rather than melodic or harmonic, again in contrast to lead breaks of later decades. Movement around the neck was limited, and broken chords were the order of the day.

NATHAN DANIEL's main business was the production of guitars and amps with the Silvertone brand for the Sears, Roebuck mail-order company, but in 1954 he began to put his own brand on a similar line of instruments, called Danelectro. The guitars were boldly styled and used inexpensive, basic materials. Daniel and his colleagues came up with a variety of designs based on this cheap and cheerful ethos, including a six-string bass (see p75). Daniel sold his company in 1967 to the MCA music company, who applied their record-label name Coral to some of the instruments.

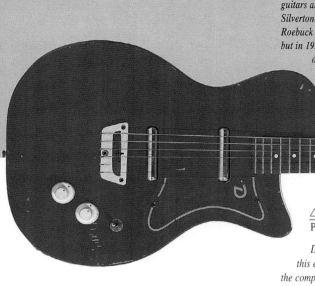

△ DANELECTRO U2
Produced 1956-1958; this example c1958

Danelectro's double-pickup partner to the U1 was the U2, this example finished in a dazzling red lacquer. In late 1958 the company replaced the U line with a series of twin-cutaway models, following the trend away from single-cutaway guitars.

TOPPING Danelectro's bolt-on poplar neck was a distinctive headstock (below right), the shape of which has given rise to the nickname 'Coke bottle' among collectors.

▽ FENDER MUSICMASTER
Produced 1956-1980; this example 1957

Fender's two new 1956 guitars, the Musicmaster and two-pickup Duo-Sonic, had a shorter string-length than usual; the company said they were "ideal for students, and adults with small hands".

FENDER began a series of ads in the 1950s where an odd scenario is tagged with the phrase 'You Won't Part With Yours Either'; these two (right) feature the Musicmaster.

▽ FENDER DUO-SONIC
Produced 1956-1969, re-issued 1993; this example 1959

Like its single-pickup ally the Musicmaster, the Duo-Sonic too featured an anodised aluminium scratchplate during the 1950s.

THE FIRST underwater transatlantic telephone cable linking the US and the UK opens for service.

SOUTHDALE CENTER "the world's biggest shopping town" opens in Minneapolis, with 72 stores on a 10-acre site. It becomes the model from which most other malls are cloned.

ROCK Around The Clock becomes a movie and defines the standard rock movie plot about a manager who discovers an unknown group (Haley & His Comets) and hits it big. Meanwhile, Hollywood deals with drug addiction for the first time in Otto Preminger's The Man With The Golden Arm.

THE HUNGARIAN uprising is quelled by invading Soviet tanks as martial law is imposed.

BOXER Rocky Marciano retires undefeated having won every one of his 49 professional fights, all but six by a knockout.

THE BRITISH parliament votes to end the death penalty.

THE SUEZ CRISIS develops when the UK, France and Israel retaliate against Egypt for nationalising the Suez Canal. Air attacks on Egypt ensue, and the USSR threatens a nuclear response. A ceasefire in November at last calms a tense, fearful world.

45

The guitar tone was generally clean, although it wasn't too long before players started to experiment with a little distortion. One short echo ('slapback') was popular to thicken the sound.

While Chuck Berry was cutting hits for Chess in Chicago, its sister label Checker was releasing the R&B records of Bo Diddley. Both Diddley and Berry would have a significant later influence on the career of the Rolling Stones. Diddley had nothing like the same commercial impact as Berry, but his forceful rhythm was another advance for the guitar, and he pioneered tremolo and distortion. He was one of the first players to approach the electric guitar as an instrument in its own right, rather than a means of playing acoustic ideas louder.

His 1955 cut 'Bo Diddley', for example, is a thumping monochord of sound, with the guitar just occasionally breaking out from his insistent signature rhythm, while on 'Pretty Thing' from the following year Diddley plays an arresting intro quite different to Chuck Berry's dial-ins, as well as a brief chordal break which sounds like he's imitating the harmonica. 'Bo's Guitar' (1958) is an instrumental that

RICKENBACKER's unusual body shape (below) did not survive the 1950s; it's the company's more elegant designs from later in the decade (see p74) that have come to be considered as Rickenbacker's true classics.

RICKENBACKER's Combos featured anodised metal scratchplates (left), as did some Fender guitars in 1956.

SKIFFLE was an amateur folk music, ideally made on homemade instruments, that had a burst of fame in 1950s Britain. The Vipers Skiffle Group (right) included future members of The Shadows, but the big name to emerge was Lonnie Donegan: his 'Rock Island Line' was a hit on both sides of the Atlantic in 1956.

AMONG THE GLUT of movies put out in the 1950s to try to capitalise on the huge popularity of rock'n'roll , Frank Tashlin's 'The Girl Can't Help It' from 1956 (see poster, below) was unusual: it had acting, a plot, colour, stereo sound, and great cameo performances from acts like Gene Vincent (right), Eddie Cochran and Little Richard.

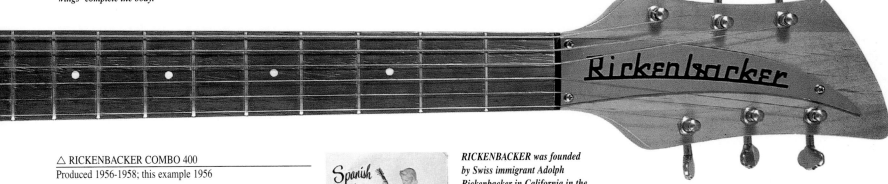

reveals a little more of Diddley's tone than most of the early cuts, and he uses lots of strange noises by scraping the lower strings with a pick. In the same year his tremolo'd lower-string riff ·even gets to lead in the doo-wop 'I'm Sorry', and the break on 'Crackin Up' (1959) is a good example of the chordal nature of much 1950s soloing. The vehicle for Diddley's music was a series of strikingly shaped guitars built by Gretsch.

Mainstream pop continued to have less room for the guitar than rock'n'roll. In a genre like doo-wop, for example, the emphasis was on vocal harmony, and teen ballads needed orchestral arrangements. Although the first wave of rock'n'rollers died – some were burned out, others were jailed, found the Lord, or joined the army – the electric guitar carried on.

The popularity of guitar instrumentals showed that rock'n'roll had put the electric guitar firmly and permanently on the musical map, exemplified by such original cuts as Link Wray & His Ray Men's sinister 'Rumble' (1958), or the more popular work of Duane Eddy whose first hit instrumental, 'Rebel Rouser', came along in 1958 with sax-man Gil Bernal in hot pursuit.

Eddy made his low-pitched guitar melodies into a trademark, sometimes playing them on six-string bass, with lots of reverb and a tremolo unit to help colour the sound. Eddy mostly used a Gretsch Chet Atkins Hollow Body because he liked its tone, though he was never completely comfortable with its construction and had to stuff the body to minimise feedback. Meanwhile in Britain Bert Weedon became the first guitarist to break the Top 40,

with 'Guitar Boogie Shuffle' in 1959 (it had been a hit earlier in the year for The Virtues in the US). In 1957 Weedon had put together the 'Play In A Day' teaching book which would have an immense influence in the UK.

The main player associated with the Fender Stratocaster in the 1950s was Buddy Holly. His fast strumming, coupled with the guitar work of Niki Sullivan, was an integral part of their hits. Ricky Nelson's 45s were enlivened by the fluent Telecaster bending of James Burton, and another important player was Eddie Cochran, whose rhythm work on 'Summertime Blues' (1958), 'C'Mon Everybody' and

'Something Else' (1959) was an essential element. Favouring a Gretsch, Cochran could turn in rhythmic Berry-like solos on 'Completely Sweet', use musical thirds in 'Don't Ever Let Me Be', or play typical chordal breaks.

By the end of the 1950s rock'n'roll was ebbing as a commercial force. Many of its leading practitioners were out of action, out of time, or out of luck. But the seeds of rock guitar were planted in a generation who would come through in the 1960s, taking these ideas and playing them through bigger amps at greater volume. The rock'n'roll sound would live on, turned up to 11. ■ RIKKY ROOKSBY

THE THROUGH-NECK style has a neck (below) extending the length of the guitar, and added 'wings' complete the body.

△ RICKENBACKER COMBO 400
Produced 1956-1958; this example 1956

The Combo 400 was one of the first Rickenbacker guitars to point the way toward the success that the company would enjoy in the next decade. It replaced Rickenbacker's earlier and ungainly 'horseshoe' pickup with a modern-looking unit, and featured a through-neck construction that was practical and cost-effective.

RICKENBACKER was founded by Swiss immigrant Adolph Rickenbacker in California in the 1920s, at first as a small tool-and-die operation. Rickenbacker soon grabbed guitarists' attention by introducing one of the first electric lap-steel guitars of the early 1930s, moving to conventional electric Spanish guitars after Adolph sold out to businessman FC Hall in 1953.

RICKENBACKER's stylish logo (above) with its interlinked letters recalls automobile logos of the 1950s that were designed as one continuous strip of chrome.

JAPANESE guitars of the 1950s often muddled the form and function of the American instruments they copied. Guyatone's designers, for

instance, made visual allusions to a resonator guitar with the three-pickup EG-300's metal body plates (below), but these were purely decorative.

JAPANESE GUITARS *by Hiroyuki Noguchi*

Despite the fact that a small, modest electric guitar industry had started to grow in Japan following World War II, Japanese guitarists of the 1950s desired nothing less than American instruments upon which to play American-inspired music. Japanese guitar makers learned quickly that they had to export in order to survive.

TOKYO SOUND (catalogue, right) was set up by Mitsuo Matsuki in the late 1940s to manufacture Guyatone guitars.

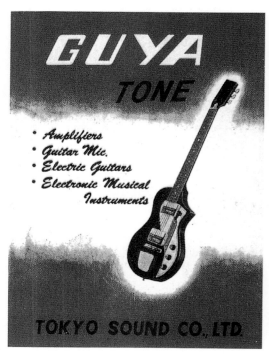

GUYA
TONE
• *Amplifiers*
• *Guitar Mic.*
• *Electric Guitars*
• *Electronic Musical Instruments*

TOKYO SOUND CO., LTD.

JAPANESE GUITARS

Dance halls grew in popularity in mid-1930s Tokyo, with Western-style bands playing jazz, fox trot, tango and Hawaiian music. One such Hawaiian musician on the dance hall scene was guitarist Buckie Shirakata (1912-1994), a second-generation Japanese-American who had arrived at Yokohama port from Hawaii in 1935 with a Rickenbacker 'Frying Pan' guitar. It is said that this was the first electric guitar to be brought into Japan.

At the same time, electric guitars were being developed by the Japanese. As in America, this began with steel guitars. Among those who had heard about the invention of the electric guitar in the US was Atsuo Kaneko (1916-1993), and he began independent research into the making of electric guitars (and would later became one of the founders of the Teisco company). Kaneko loved Hawaiian music and jazz, playing in a Tokyo band. Around

1934, he got to know Mitsuo Matsuki, who owned a hardware store near his home. Matsuki, too, was hooked on Hawaiian music and fascinated by the idea of electric guitars. Kaneko and Matsuki got on very well with one another, and made a couple of prototype electric steel guitars together. Matsuki would later go on to set up the Guyatone company (see top of facing page).

Kaneko continued to play in his band, and developed a prototype electric guitar with Hiroyoshi Hashimoto (born 1915) who in 1948 would join Teisco. Kaneko and Hashimoto performed in various dance halls and small theatres using their own steel guitars and amplifiers, but in October 1940 the authorities forced the closure of dance halls, which they regarded as symbols of frivolity and pleasure. Gradually, it became difficult to perform jazz and Hawaiian music in public places. In December 1941, when war broke out between Japan and the USA, English was

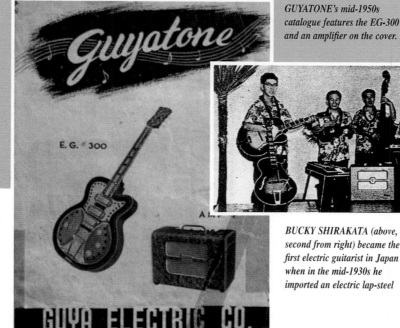

GUYATONE's mid-1950s catalogue features the EG-300 and an amplifier on the cover.

▽ GUYATONE EG-300

Produced c1956-1958; this example c1956

Early Japanese makers of electric guitars, such as Guyatone, began to develop hollow-body electrics during the first half of the 1950s, primarily as a reaction to the expensive imported American models that became available at the time. Guyatone's EG-300 model was one of the earliest to reach production.

BUCKY SHIRAKATA (above, second from right) became the first electric guitarist in Japan when in the mid-1930s he imported an electric lap-steel guitar from Hawaii. Here (above) he plays at an event in Tokyo in 1952 to celebrate Gibson's appointment of a Japanese distributor.

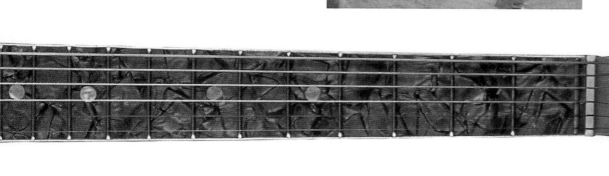

▽ TEISCO J-1

Produced 1954-c1960; this example c1956

Just as Gibson had their Les Paul and its Junior model, so Teisco had their solidbody Les Paul-inspired TG-54 and its junior version, the J-1, both issued during 1954. The J-1's pickup was also used by Teisco on some steel guitar models.

THE DESIGN of the J-1 is clearly American-inspired, even if Teisco did manage to incorporate one more fret than Gibson's Les Paul Junior.

totally forbidden. There was a military atmosphere everywhere in Japan, and the atmosphere was heightened in January 1943 when the Japanese government announced a ban on Western music, under which overseas music was completely forbidden.

Military defeat in August 1945 turned all the values in Japan completely upside down. Jazz and Hawaiian music, previously banned as enemy music, inundated the radio waves, and people were comforted by bright and cheerful Western music. Even worn-out records or guitars with a few missing strings sold well. The era of oppression had ended and the democratic age had arrived.

Musicians became free too, able to perform their favourite music on their favourite instruments without any restrictions. Demobilised servicemen formed bands and played in clubs built to offer entertainment to the 400,000 occupying troops. In 1946, Atsuo Kaneko returned to

Tokyo and started playing again. He started once more to make pickups and steel guitars, and approached the Fuji Onkyo sound company in Tokyo about producing steel guitars. Kaneko and Dohryu Matsuda (born 1921), an engineer with Fuji Onkyo, collaborated successfully together, and in the summer of 1946 they established the Awoi Sound Research Institute (later renamed Teisco Co Ltd) in Minato-ku, Tokyo, with the aim of manufacturing a line of electric guitars and amplifiers.

Guyatone and Awoi (Teisco) were located close to one another in Tokyo, and at first in the 1950s there was contact between the two companies, and probably some influencing of each other's products. Both produced steel guitars, amplifiers, and pickups. Later, when the businesses were in competition, they became rivals.

In the 1950s, thanks to the special procurement orders for the Korean War, Japan saw a remarkable economic

recovery. In 1952, the Peace Treaty and the US/Japan Security Treaty came into effect, putting an end to the occupation. At once there was an unprecedented Western music boom in Japan. Live performances at big theatres played to full houses, and jazz and Hawaiian music gained new popularity, as did country music. Later, rockabilly appeared on the scene, as well as Japanese versions of Elvis Presley and other rock'n'roll acts.

As the 1950s developed, hollow-body electric guitars drew much attention. Every Japanese guitarist aspired to have an f-hole Gibson or Epiphone guitar – and Gibson, for example, appointed a Tokyo-based distributor in 1952. But imported guitars were extremely expensive. Not everybody could afford to buy one. Teisco and Guyatone could see that this style of electric guitar would be in demand and started to develop their own hollow-body electric models. Teisco unveiled the EO-180 in 1952, the EP-6 in 1953 and

1957

THE THIRD GUITAR in Gretsch's Chet Atkins series, the Country Gentleman (shown in a 1959 catalogue, left) was from its launch in 1957 produced with a single-cutaway body. It would move to twin-cutaway style in 1961.

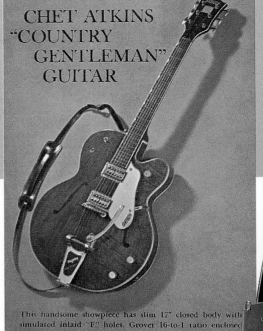

CHET ATKINS "COUNTRY GENTLEMAN" GUITAR

This handsome showpiece has slim 17" closed body with simulated inlaid "F" holes. Grover 16-to-1 ratio enclosed gears. Bigsby Tremolo and Tailpiece. Adjustable rod — Actionflo neck. Satin ebony Neo-Classic fingerboard. Heavy 24-karat gold plating and rich mahogany-grained country style finish. Gretsch Filter'Tron twin electronic heads. Trim, fine-quality leather shoulder strap.

PX6122 Chet Atkins "Country Gentleman" Electric Guitar $575.00

▽ GIBSON LES PAUL CUSTOM
Produced 1954-1961, 1968-current; this example 1957

In 1957 Gibson changed the layout of the Les Paul Custom model by installing three new humbucking pickups to replace the previous pair of single-coil types, as well as a modified three-way switch to provide what Gibson described as a "much wider range of tone coloring". Humbucking pickups reduce the hum and electrical interference that can afflict standard single-coil pickups, by wiring two coils together out of phase and with opposite magnetic polarities. Players and collectors especially seek out Gibson's early humbuckers with 'PAF' (patent applied for) labels fixed to the base, used between 1957 and 1962.

THIS NEW three-pickup layout (below) was probably prompted by Fender's Strat.

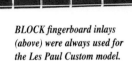

BLOCK fingerboard inlays (above) were always used for the Les Paul Custom model.

SALES hit a peak during 1956 and 1957 of Gibson's Les Paul series, which included six models: the $375 black Custom, by 1957 in revised three-humbucker guise (above); the $247.50 gold-top; the $179.50 beige Special; the $132.50 beige TV; and the $120 sunburst Junior, which was also available at the same price in a 'three-quarter' format with a shorter neck, designed for beginners. Les Paul himself often favoured the black Custom for live work, as he explains: "When you're on stage with a black tuxedo and a black guitar, the people can see your hands move, with a spotlight on them: they'll see your hands flying." Paul was an incorrigible tinkerer, rarely able to leave a guitar the way it came from the factory. The Custom he's seen using in 1957 (right) has had a body built specially for him with the flat, uncarved top he preferred.

the EP-4 and EP-5 in 1955, and Guyatone developed the EG-300 in the early 1950s. Around this time, instrument importers in Western countries became interested in Japanese-made electric guitars. Buyers from the United States placed orders with both Teisco and Guyatone, and exports came to occupy a large part of their business.

Thanks to electric guitars, the position of the guitar in bands was largely improved in 1950s music. However, except for Hawaiian music, guitars rarely played a central role in Japanese bands. It was not until the 1960s, with the advent of solidbody instruments, that electric guitars took their place at the heart of the music.

During the 1950s Mitsuo Matsuki of Guyatone received a 45 record from an American friend. Matsuki says he doesn't remember the title of the tune, but remembers that it was by Les Paul and Mary Ford. It included a clear guitar sound he had never heard before. He says he was mesmerised by the sound, and that while he realised that it must be an electric guitar, he didn't think it was the sound of a hollow-body instrument. Matsuki says he instinctively felt that it was not a steel guitar, but a guitar with a solid body. This marked the beginning of Matsuki's

CHET ATKINS and Jimmie Webster, Gretsch's main guitar ideas-man, are seen (right) at a trade event in 1958. Atkins holds his new Gretsch signature model, the Country Gentleman, the name of which he says was inspired by the title of one of his records. "When 'Country Gentleman' had been a hit I guess it was probably Gretsch's idea to put out another model. They were selling so many of the orange Chet Atkins they wanted to put out a little more expensive guitar, with good tuning pegs, better wood selection, and a body that was generally larger and thinner." Jimmie Webster, a musician who became responsible for many of Gretsch's guitar designs and novel features, is holding an early version of the company's White Falcon Stereo guitar.

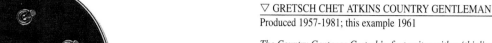

▽ GRETSCH CHET ATKINS COUNTRY GENTLEMAN
Produced 1957-1981; this example 1961

The Country Gent was Gretsch's first guitar with a 'thinline' body, as established by Gibson, and the first with their new Filter'Tron humbucker pickups, devised by engineer Ray Butts and launched in 1957, the same year as Gibson's humbuckers.

GIBSON reserved their fancy split-diamond headstock inlay for top-of-the-line guitars, such as the Les Paul Custom (below), or the Super 400CES (right) that Scotty Moore (far right) is playing with Elvis Presley in a scene from the 1957 movie Jailhouse Rock.

THE SOVIET UNION launches within a month Sputnik I and II, the first artificial satellites to orbit the earth. Sputnik II has a dog, Laika, on board, proving that life can survive in space. A subsequent attempt to launch a satellite by the US in December fails. The space race begins.

IN THE UK, the Wolfenden Report calls for homosexual acts between consenting adults to be decriminalised.

NUCLEAR TESTS in the Pacific are condemned by mass protests in Tokyo, but the demos fail to stop Britain explode its first H-bomb near Christmas Island. Nevil Shute's On The Beach, a horrific vision of worldwide nuclear devastation, is published.

ELVIS PRESLEY stars as Vince Everett in his third film, Jailhouse Rock (poster above, and still above left), with a set of songs 'mostly' composed by Jerry Leiber and Mike Stoller.

RADIO FANS listen to hits such as 'Come Go With Me' (Dell-Vikings), 'Peggy Sue' (Buddy Holly) and 'Bye Bye Love' (Everly Brothers).

TV DEBUTS include Wagon Train, Perry Mason, and Zorro in the US, and Emergency Ward 10, Pinky & Perky, and Six-Five Special in the UK.

JACK KEROUAC launches the Beat Generation with his novel On The Road, as Sal Paradise and Dean Moriarty roam America to a jazz soundtrack.

research into solidbody guitars. After much trial and error, a prototype was completed, and in 1955 a model called the Les Paul Guitar was released on to the market. Into the late 1950s, solidbody guitar models such as the LG line (30, 50 and 60) were developed by Matsuki and Guyatone. These models were primarily intended for export, and some were sold in the UK with brandnames such as Antoria as well as Guyatone.

Teisco's engineers had also seen an early 1950s Gibson Les Paul, which gave them the opportunity to develop a solidbody electric guitar. Noboru Arai, a jazz guitarist and good friend of Hiroyoshi Hashimoto, started to use a Les Paul gold-top around 1953. Hashimoto fell in love with it at first sight. He wanted to make the same guitar, so he borrowed the instrument from Arai.

The engineering team at Teisco thoroughly researched Arai's Gibson, and after great efforts completed their first solidbody electric guitar, the TG-54, in March 1954. Three months later a 'junior' J-1 version was unveiled. Between that time and the end of the decade several more models were developed, and as with Guyatone all were basically intended for export. With the exception of steel guitars,

Japanese guitarists of the 1950s did not use Teisco or Guyatone electric guitars. In Japan at that time everyone had great faith in anything American. Nobody paid much attention to domestic products when American products were of such high quality. Teisco and Guyatone were searching for a major breakthrough, but their products were inferior compared to the instruments that were being produced in the United States at the time.

However, combined with the remarkable expansion of electric guitar exports in the later 1950s, technology advanced and mass-production systems were established. It was not until the mid-1960s that electric guitars became available to the ordinary Japanese, triggered by the sweeping popularity of the instrumental American guitar group The Ventures. Many electric musical instrument companies suddenly appeared, like mushrooms after rain, all trying to follow Teisco and Guyatone. But for Japanese electric guitar manufacturers the 1950s had been a gradual learning period in which they grew in size and strength, making steady progress that would in later decades allow them to catch up with and overtake American guitar makers. ■ HIROYUKI NOGUCHI

MAIL-ORDER GUITARS *by Michael Wright*

CHICAGO-based Kay and Harmony were among the main suppliers of guitars to mail-order companies. Kay's own lines included the up-market Barney Kessel series, previewed by the jazz guitarist in a 1957 ad (left).

For many American guitarists in the 1950s without a fortune to spend on a first instrument, the great mail-order catalogues provided just what was needed... and all delivered directly to your door, whether you were in a big city or stuck out in the middle of nowhere. Best known of all were the basic, affordable Silvertone brand instruments made for the Sears, Roebuck catalogue.

IT'S THE YEAR FOR

KAY AND KESSEL

Exit flowery phrases. Enter this simple announcement, yet tinged with deep pride, that Kay and the nation's number one jazz guitarist Barney Kessel—winner of the Down Beat, Metronome, and Playboy polls—have together developed a professional guitar which will establish new standards in quality of sound, workmanship and design.

You are invited to see the gold ribbon untied at the NAMM convention where Barney himself will play in the 'K' CLUB, in Kay's Music House.

And speaking of 1957, the Kay's Music Club.

ALL THREE of Kay's Barney Kessel models – the Pro, Artist, and Jazz Special – came with options of one or two pickups (below) and in natural or sunburst finish. The Artist and Special had a Melita bridge, as seen on some Gretsch models.

BARNEY KESSEL's signature (above) was removed from the pickguard of later versions when the guitarist switched his endorsement to the Gibson company.

SEARS, ROEBUCK's 1954 catalogue (left, with cover shown below left) displays their Silvertone brand version of the Kay Thin Twin (top left) alongside Harmony- and Kay-made hollow-body electrics.

Sears' first solidbody electric, their version of the Harmony Stratotone, is shown centre left. Below this are a couple of Harmony-made Hawaiian electric guitars as well as a Silvertone amplifier.

THE MOST CELEBRATED Les Paul Sunbursts, or 'bursts' (right), are those whose bodies exhibit the most outrageous wood patterns ('figure' or 'flame'). Figure is a random fluke in wood: some Les Paul Sunbursts are highly attractive, others extremely plain.

1958

SEARS' 1959 catalogue shows six electrics (left to right): Danelectro-made 'solid center body'; Kay-made Les Paul-like hollow-body; Danelectro-made bass; Kay-made hollow-body; and Harmony-made 'thinline'.

Kay Musical Instrument Company. Harmony was begun in 1892, and in 1916 was actually purchased by Sears to provide its stringed instruments. Harmony was sold to a group of its own executives in 1940, but continued to be Sears' largest and principal source. Danelectro was started in 1946 by Nathan Daniel, the man who designed Epiphone's Electar amplifiers of the late 1930s. From 1954 Danelectro was one of the largest manufacturers of Sears' catalogue electric guitars.

Some of the brandnames that appeared on these catalogue guitars of the 1950s included: Silvertone, for Sears (earlier Sears guitars had been called Supertone); Sherwood and Airline, for Montgomery Ward; Penncrest, for Penney's; Old Kraftsman, for Spiegel; and 'A', for

Alden's. The brandname belonged to the retailer, and could be applied to guitars from different suppliers.

The catalogue guitars were value-priced but that does not necessarily mean they were poor instruments. At the top end, many of these guitars were actually quite good, although often catalogue guitars were not quite up to the same quality as the equivalent brandname instrument. For example, when Sears began to sell the Kay Thin Twin (see page 22/23) its Silvertone version had cheaper and hence thicker necks as well as just slightly less fancy cuts of wood than the Kay-branded guitar. At the bottom end the guitars were more humble, but still with some quality – remember, they could be returned if customers were not satisfied.

Working in tandem with the guitar mass manufacturers, the mass merchandisers followed market tastes like a shadow. As the 1950s began the styles of music in which electric guitars were most visible included Hawaiian, which had had a remarkable run of popularity for nearly half a century, and country & Western. Hawaiian music demanded little lap steels, which in some ways can be said to have fathered the electric guitar itself, while the country & Western bands were picking pedal steels and

'electrified' archtops, still top dogs of the guitar world. In response, early 1950s catalogues offered mainly Hawaiian lap steels and a few full-bodied, non-cutaway archtops with one or sometimes two pickups.

When in 1952 Kay introduced the cutaway electric to its archtop line, the catalogues very quickly incorporated it into their offerings. In around 1954 another Kay innovation, the Thin Twin, began to show up in the catalogues as well. Size-wise, the Thin Twin was somewhere between Gibson's ES-175 hollow-body and the new Les Paul. While it was hollow, it did have wood down the middle to reduce the feedback of its pickups. The Thin Twin was sold through the Sears, Montgomery Ward and Spiegel catalogues, carrying their house brandnames.

The solidbody electric guitar started on a slow curve in the early 1950s, eventually taking off mid-decade with the success of rock'n'roll. The first 'Spanish' solidbody electrics appeared in the Sears catalogue in the spring of 1954, the Silvertone version of the Harmony Stratotone, a sort of mini-Les Paul with one or two pickups. These were offered only briefly, and by the fall 1954 catalogue, Sears had switched to single-cutaway Danelectros, the presence of which increased as the decade progressed.

RHYTHM
TREBLE

Gibson
Les Paul
MODEL

- GREATER TONAL RANGE
- MORE BRILLIANT PERFORMANCE
- LONGER SUSTAINING QUALITY
- EASIER PLAYING ACTION

GIBSON's tag (above) noted the Les Paul's "long sustain", which would endear it to later generations of guitarists.

WHEN A GUITAR is as highly prized as the Les Paul Sunburst, even the tags (right) originally attached to the guitar become collectible. The orange label promotes Gibson's Sonomatic strings; the brown booklet offers care tips.

Gibson
hand made
SONOMATIC STRINGS
POWERFUL · DURABLE
MAGIC TONE
GIBSON, INC.
KALAMAZOO, MICH.

INSTRUCTIONS
GIBSON STRINGS
GIBSON POLISH

FOR TOP PERFORMANCE OF YOUR NEW GIBSON

Framus

"Billy Lorento" Model

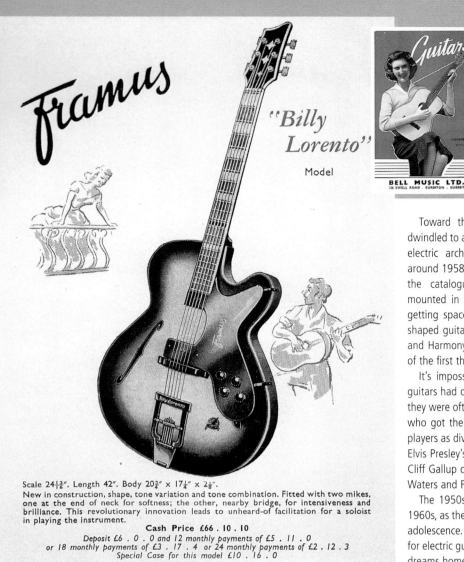

BELL MUSIC were the leading mail-order suppliers of guitars in the UK in the 1950s, with a catalogue (left) that introduced guitars to many fledgling stars. Bell's various imported lines included Framus guitars of Germany, with one model (far left) designed by guitarist Billy Lorento, better known later as pickup designer Bill Lawrence.

Toward the end of the 1950s Hawaiian lap steels dwindled to a single offering, and where once non-cutaway electric archtops dominated, cutaways now ruled. By around 1958 or so, in response to the growing folk boom, the catalogues were offering flat-tops with pickups mounted in the soundholes. By 1959, Danelectros were getting space pressure from other hollowbody Les Paul-shaped guitars, including versions of Kay's Thinline series and Harmony's Jupiter. Finally, 1959 saw the introduction of the first thin-body electric, a three-pickup Harmony.

It's impossible to underestimate the impact catalogue guitars had on the development of popular music because they were often the first guitars of many future stars. Those who got their start on a guitar from a catalogue include players as diverse as Duane Allman of the Allman Brothers, Elvis Presley's guitarist Scotty Moore, slide king Ry Cooder, Cliff Gallup of Gene Vincent's band, and bluesmen Muddy Waters and Freddie King, among a host of others.

The 1950s were just a prelude to the guitar-drenched 1960s, as the cresting post-war Baby Boom swept into high adolescence. But it was the 1950s which created the desire for electric guitars, and the 'wish books' that brought those dreams home. ■ MICHAEL WRIGHT

A GREAT YEAR for guitar-fuelled records: Duane Eddy's 'Rebel Rouser', Eddie Cochran's 'Summertime Blues', Link Wray's 'The Rumble'... and Chuck Berry's 'Johnny B Goode' plays his guitar like ringing a bell.

JAPAN and India change to the metric system; America launches a moon rocket that misses; blues populariser W.C. Handy dies; the artist to be known as Prince is born.

PRIVATE EYE Peter Gunn begins his TV investigations amid a moody jazz soundtrack.

THE CAMPAIGN for Nuclear Disarmament (CND) is started in the UK, with its first protest march from London to the Atomic Weapons Research Establishment at Aldermaston. Over 9000 scientists from 44 countries petition the UN to end nuclear weapons tests.

THESE 'CROWN' inlays (below) had first appeared on Gibson's revised ES-150 model in 1950.

RECORDING companies decide to adopt the Westrex 45/45 stereo system, and some of the big labels release the first stereo records in the summer.

TV OWNERSHIP in the US is rocketing, with sets in over 75 per cent of homes. And TV makers like Philco encourage viewers to move the TV around the house, advertising new portable models such as the Slender Seventeen (left).

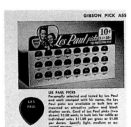

GIBSON managed to exploit the name of their most famous endorsee in many ways, as demonstrated by this retailer's counter display for picks, allegedly "personally selected and tested by Les Paul".

△ GIBSON LES PAUL 'SUNBURST'
Produced 1958-1960; this example 1959

While mail-order catalogues churned out budget-price guitars, makers of more up-market instruments reassessed their lines. Gibson's gold-top Les Paul model had dipped in popularity, so in 1958 the company tried to regenerate interest by giving it their more traditional cherry sunburst finish. Production did increase modestly during 1959 and 1960, but the Sunburst model was dropped during 1960 after fewer than 2000 had been made. Years later, this 1958-1960 Sunburst has become the most valuable vintage guitar, with prime 'flamed' examples regularly fetching high five-figure sums today and often consigned to bank vaults.

THE SUNBURST has Kluson Deluxe tuners with 'tulip' plastic buttons (above) that tend to deteriorate with age.

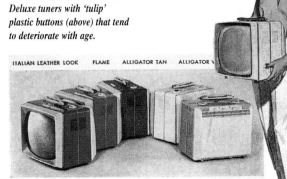

Most slender of all ... even the back is beautiful!

the best of **MUDDY WATERS**

CHESS LP 1427
HIGH · FIDELITY · ·

BLUES GUITARS *by Paul Trynka*

As the 1950s unfolded, the old generation of acoustic blues players gave way to a new wave of players who were electric in every sense. In just a few years musicians such as Big Bill Broonzy or Memphis Minnie became outmoded, and in their place came a brash, extrovert troupe – Muddy Waters, Guitar Slim, Howlin' Wolf – with the sound and image of the electric guitar at the heart of their appeal. They would change the sound of popular music forever.

DESPITE CHESS's failure to sign the hugely commercial Jimmy Reed, Chess ruled as Chicago's premier blues label in the 1950s, releasing influential and commercially successful recordings by Muddy Waters (above), Howlin' Wolf, Little Walter, Sonny Boy Williamson II and many more. The label made full use of Chicago's overflowing pool of

talent, and the city's guitarists became accustomed to midnight calls from the Chess studios asking if they could perform a particularly tricky part. Although Muddy Waters and Howlin' Wolf both ran legendarily tight outfits, in the studio they would regularly call on the likes of Freddie King or Buddy Guy to augment their usual band.

BLUES GUITARS

In many respects the electric blues scene of 1950s Chicago was born in the more rural surroundings of Helena, Arkansas, where Robert Lockwood Jr, adopted son of Robert Johnson, could be heard playing the electric guitar alongside Sonny Boy Williamson every week on the influential King Biscuit Time radio show, from 1941. Lockwood single-handedly converted seemingly all of Mississippi's guitarists to the electric instrument, and it would be these players – Muddy Waters, Jimmy Rogers, Elmore James – who would in fact go on to form the backbone of the emerging Chicago scene.

Over the same period T-Bone Walker evangelised for the electric guitar over on the West Coast, with the result that by 1947 or 1948 practically every young blues musician was converted to the sound of the new instrument. The electric guitar was hip, it was loud, it was better for single-string lead work... and if you were working on the street it helped you earn more tips. That was the reason that Jimmy Rogers fitted a DeArmond pickup to his Sears acoustic, and when he took his Mississippi bandmate Muddy Waters down to

the Chicago Musical Instruments store to get a pickup for his own guitar, a musical revolution was born. Waters' first electric hit, 'I Can't Be Satisfied', dates from 1948, the same year that John Lee Hooker cut 'Boogie Chillen'. These two flagbearers for a new electric era were joined by musicians such as Gatemouth Brown in 1949, BB King in 1951, Howlin' Wolf in 1952 and Guitar Slim in 1953, and with the huge explosion of new talent, guitar playing developed at a dizzying pace.

Looking back at evocative old black-and-white photos of blues performers of the late 1940s and into the 1950s, it's hard to believe that many of them were at the cutting edge of technology. But that was exactly the case. From the moment the Fender Telecaster first rolled out of Fullerton, California, it appeared in the hands of blues players: for example, a 1950 photo of Clarence Gatemouth Brown and his brother James 'Widemouth' Brown shows them both sporting Telecasters – Clarence's a black model with studded decoration that could even be one of the two-pickup Esquires which preceded the Tele. At a time when the industry derided the new-fangled Telecaster as a toilet seat with strings attached, blues guitarists embraced it. The

GIBSON's double-cut Junior was the company's first with their new cherry finish.

GIBSON's Les Paul guitar, overlooked in many musical quarters, was a favourite of many Chicago blues guitarists, including Muddy Waters (right). Others who played a Les Paul in the 1950s included Hubert Sumlin and Jody Williams from Howlin' Wolf's band, Freddie King, and Buddy Guy, who went on to popularise the Strat after his Gibson was stolen from a club.

same would be true of other pioneering guitars throughout the 1950s, as blues musicians were at the forefront of those exploring the sounds of solidbody instruments, semi-solid guitars such as the Gibson ES-335, and the sonic possibilities of over-driven amplifiers.

Blues of the 1950s boasts many musical mavericks, but it's fair to say that the music can generally be divided into three distinct schools. First comes Chicago blues, as epitomised by Muddy Waters or Elmore James – in its early form, essentially the Mississippi blues of Robert Johnson but cranked up and electrified. Then there was the BB King or Lowell Fulson school of blues: increasingly sophisticated, with more gospel influence and single-string guitar soloing, largely derived from T-Bone Walker and Louis Jordan. Thirdly, Texas blues was best exemplified by

HOWLIN' WOLF (above) learned guitar from Delta blues pioneer Charley Patton in the 1920s. Wolf later formed one of the South's first electric blues bands when he teamed up with Willie Johnson, who'd adopted an electric guitar after seeing Sonny Boy Williamson. Wolf's genius for spotting talent was confirmed by his subsequent recruitment of the mercurial Hubert Sumlin, who would craft memorable guitar riffs on classic Wolf tracks such as 'Wang Dang Doodle' and 'Killing Floor'.

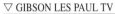

▽ GIBSON LES PAUL TV
Produced 1955-1959; this example 1958

The TV model was a light-coloured version of the Les Paul Junior. The name may have been an attempt to gain from Les Paul's mid-1950s TV outing, 'The Les Paul & Mary Ford Show'.

THE JUNIOR and TV were the simplest solidbody models in the Gibson line of the time, with basic hardware, single pickup and plain decoration.

△ GIBSON LES PAUL JUNIOR
Produced 1954-1961; this example 1960

Nineteen fifty-eight was Gibson's year of the double-cutaway. The company reacted to the requests of players who wanted more room at the top of the neck to reach the higher frets for lead playing. Not only did Gibson introduce the entirely new double-cut ES-335 and 345 semi-hollow models during 1958 (see p69) but also in that year the company radically modified the shape of the solidbody Les Paul Junior and TV models to the new style shown here. The Junior's fresh look was also enhanced with a new cherry red finish. The design lasted until 1961, when the Les Paul models would be produced with the 'SG' shape.

TV, JUNIOR and Special had started life with a single-cutaway body (still on view in this 1957 catalogue, left). During 1958 and '59 a revised double-cutaway style (as seen above) was introduced.

EPIPHONE

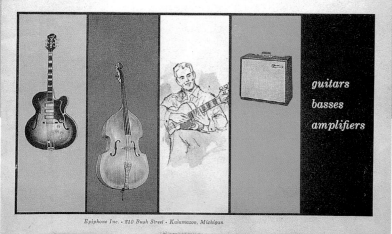

Epiphone Inc. · 210 Bush Street · Kalamazoo, Michigan

EPIPHONE were bought by Gibson in May 1957, and while Gibson had expected only to get Epiphone's upright bass business, they actually ended up with virtually the entire company: guitars, basses, amps and more (as reflected on the Gibson-Epiphone catalogue shown, left). Production of Gibson's revised line of Epiphone models was underway by 1958.

THE STANDARD tailpiece on Epiphone hollow-body guitars was the company's unusual 'Frequensator' unit (see p8), but along with makers such as Gibson and Gretsch, Epiphone also offered the Bigsby vibrato tailpiece (below) as an option.

Gatemouth Brown: open-E tunings, the use of the capo, and picking with the fingers were all typical Texas techniques used by the likes of Brown, Johnny Guitar Watson, and Guitar Slim. As the 1950s progressed, these different growths cross-pollinated.

When electric blues first hit Chicago the music essentially derived from 1930s blues. Both Muddy Waters and John Lee Hooker (based in Detroit but hugely popular in Chicago) offered updated versions of down-home Mississippi blues. Their music was therefore completely appropriate for a northern, urban, African-American audience which had only recently moved from the rural South. In some respects, if you ignore the electric guitars, the music seemed something of a throwback compared to the sophisticated urban music purveyed by Lonnie Johnson, Big Bill Broonzy or even Louis Jordan.

'NEW YORK' pickups (below; the name refers to Epiphone's original home) continued to be used until around 1961.

EPIPHONE's eccentric early multi-button pickup switching system was replaced with these conventional controls (above).

△ EPIPHONE EMPEROR
Produced 1958-1969; this example c1959

'Emperor' was a model name from Epiphone's pre-Gibson years when production was based in New York (see p8), but under the new owners this Kalamazoo-made version received a more conventional control layout. Other hollow-body electrics in the new Epi line included the Sheraton, Broadway and Century.

electric guitar, which would reach a new plateau as a lead instrument over the same period.

BB King exemplifies the progression in electric guitar styles throughout the 1950s. Starting out as a strictly Delta player, influenced by his cousin Bukka White, King absorbed the jazzy soloing of Lonnie Johnson, the single-note lead technique of T-Bone Walker, and the laid-back jump blues-influenced sound of Lowell Fulson. His work with Robert Lockwood, a fan of jazz saxophone as well as a great Robert Johnson exponent, must also have exerted a profound influence. King's first recordings for the Bullet and RPM labels were spikey-sounding affairs, many of them boasting the distinct solidbody tones of a Fender Esquire or Stratocaster.

However, when Gibson's ES-335 debuted in 1958, King immediately purchased the radical and often under-rated semi-solid instrument. Asked why, King concisely runs through every one of the 335's sales points: light weight, combination of solid and acoustic tone, thin body, and good upper-fret access. Just as the ES-335 brought the

But as the decade progressed, Chicago blues became more diverse and sophisticated, as perhaps best exemplified by Waters' harp player, Little Walter.

Walter was really the first player to explore the possibilities of the amplified harmonica, which he termed the 'Mississippi saxophone'. Amplified, the harp sounded fatter, jazzier, and more suited for solo or lead work, and when Walter teamed up with the musically-educated Myers brothers in 1952, he helped change the musical emphasis from the rhythmic Delta slide sound to a more open, melodically-led form of music. Exactly the same progression would take place in the sound of the

the unequalled tone of
EPIPHONE

...in exciting new
GUITARS
AMPLIFIERS
BASSES

World-famous quality
since 1873

▽ EPIPHONE CRESTWOOD
Produced 1958-1970; this example 1959

Gibson introduced solidbody models to the Epiphone line when they took over the brand in the late 1950s, including this attractive two-pickup Crestwood model as well as the single-pickup Coronet. Both featured a stylish metal logo plate on the headstock, and for the first few years had 'New York' pickups.

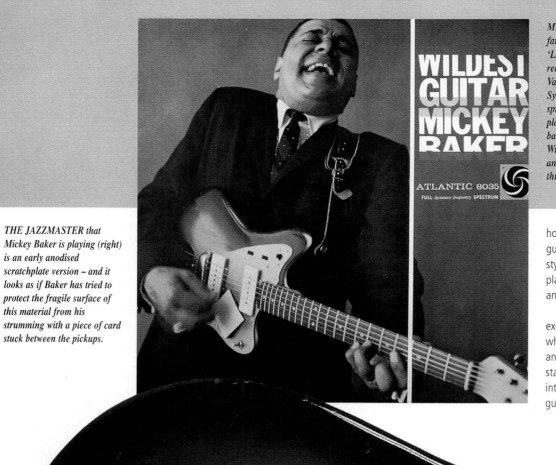

THE JAZZMASTER that Mickey Baker is playing (right) is an early anodised scratchplate version – and it looks as if Baker has tried to protect the fragile surface of this material from his strumming with a piece of card stuck between the pickups.

hollow-body jazz guitar up to date, King brought blues lead guitar up to date, perfecting a fluid, almost vocal guitar style which would influence countless numbers of blues players including guitarists such as Buddy Guy, Otis Rush, and Freddie and Albert King.

In the early 1950s King's fame as a guitar hero was far exceeded by a much brasher and more extrovert character who would change the sound of blues and R&B guitar in an equally profound way. Modern guitar history often states that it was the likes of The Kinks or Eric Clapton who introduced distortion and overdrive techniques into the guitarist's armoury, but Guitar Slim's huge 1953 crossover

CONTROLS on the Jazzmaster (left) were intricate. A small slide-switch above the front pickup selected between two individual circuits, intended to allow the player to preset a rhythm sound and a lead sound, and then switch at will between the two. This dual-circuit idea was adapted from a layout that Fender's production manager Forrest White had designed back in the 1940s when he built guitars as a hobby. The sound of the new Jazzmaster was richer and warmer than players were used to from Fender, and the guitar had what many felt were 'un-Fender' looks. The fact that the Jazzmaster was so different when compared to other Fenders may explain its relative lack of success.

FENDER JAZZMASTER
Produced 1958-1980, re-issued 1986; this example 1959

The Jazzmaster was launched in 1958 as Fender's top solidbody, at $329 some $50 more expensive than the Strat. At that sort of price Fender could not resist tagging their new Jazzmaster as "America's finest electric guitar... unequalled in performance and design features". Immediately striking was the unusual offset-waist body shape and, for the first time on a Fender, a rosewood fingerboard. The 'lock-off' vibrato system was new, too, aimed at preventing tuning problems if a string should break, and the Jazzmaster had an elaborate new control layout.

EARLY EXAMPLES of the Jazzmaster came with an anodised aluminium scratchplate, but this was soon replaced with a plastic unit in white or tortoiseshell (above).

CLARENCE 'Gatemouth' Brown has a Gibson L-5 here (about 1949, left) but soon switched to a Telecaster. His use of Fender's new guitar would influence Albert Collins and Guitar Slim to play a Tele.

GUITAR SLIM's outrageous stagecraft, characteristic guitar sounds and gospel-influenced songwriting anticipated much of rock'n'roll, soul and R&B, even the work of Jimi Hendrix. Although not the first player to put a distorted electric guitar on record, Slim was the first to use distortion as an integral part of his style. He also stood out from other players thanks to his distinctive personal style: he would flaunt red suits, green shoes, hair dyed any colour from silver to blue, 120-feet guitar leads, and a guitar strap made from fishing line. When Gibson launched the Les Paul guitar Slim bought one instantly (he is seen with a gold-top in the photo, left), but he's also known to have played Fender Strats and Teles.

hit 'The Things I Used To Do' boasted a distinctive, heavily distorted guitar sound. The influence of innovators such as Guitar Slim and BB King meant that by the end of the 1950s Chicago blues became more and more technically sophisticated. The Chess company, particularly their in-house songwriter Willie Dixon, pioneered many influential techniques. Dixon in particular was intent that each prospective single should boast a catchy title and vocal hook, a distinctive guitar riff, and an individual rhythm, and he experimented with different guitarists for a particular feel. In the competitive Chicago circuit new techniques spread like wildfire, aided by the Chicago Musical Instruments retail store on 18th and Halsted which reportedly would lend instruments to influential players in prototype 'endorsement' deals. Their tactics worked: lending a Fender Precision to Little Walter and Muddy Waters' bassist Dave Myers helped establish the electric bass in the city, while the store's regular customer, Earl Hooker, was almost without fail the very first on the block with the newest, latest and shiniest instrument. As Otis Rush recalls, "Earl Hooker always used to be coming by with all kinds of gimmicks. All the musicians I knew didn't

have any stuff, but Earl was always coming by with new guitars, he had a guitar with two necks, and he sorta turned me on to the Strat."

According to Buddy Guy, Earl Hooker was the first player to realise that the Fender Bassman amplifier, on which the later Marshall units would be based, gave a fatter and more overdriven sound than the company's other guitar combos. Take into account the fact that by the later 1950s many of the city's guitarists were exploiting the inherently fat sound of Gibson humbuckers or the typically cutting sounds of the Strat's 'in-between' pickup-switching options, and it becomes obvious that in many ways the development of blues guitar playing throughout the 1950s anticipated that of white rock in the 1960s. It's no coincidence that the commercial but powerful sound of late-1950s guitarists such as Howlin' Wolf or Muddy Waters, based on distinctive rhythms and catchy, over-amplified guitar riffs, would effectively become a primer for late-1960s Led Zeppelin. Sadly, by the time that Chicago blues were taken up by the so-called British Invasion of the early 1960s, the music would be regarded as outmoded in its heartland. ■ PAUL TRYNKA

FENDER introduced a new, enlarged headstock design (above) for the Jazzmaster from its inception. This same larger shape would be adopted by the Fender company for use on the Stratocaster model during the mid-1960s.

WITH THE JAZZMASTER as their most expensive model in 1958, Fender emphasised in ads of the time (left) that the company was able to appeal to a wide range of players with their full line of guitars, from the cheapest 'student' models such as the $119.50 Musicmaster or $149.50 Duo-Sonic up to the 'professional' Jazzmaster at $329.50. As a comparison, Gibson's electric solidbody line at the time went from the $120 Les Paul Junior to the $375 Les Paul Custom.

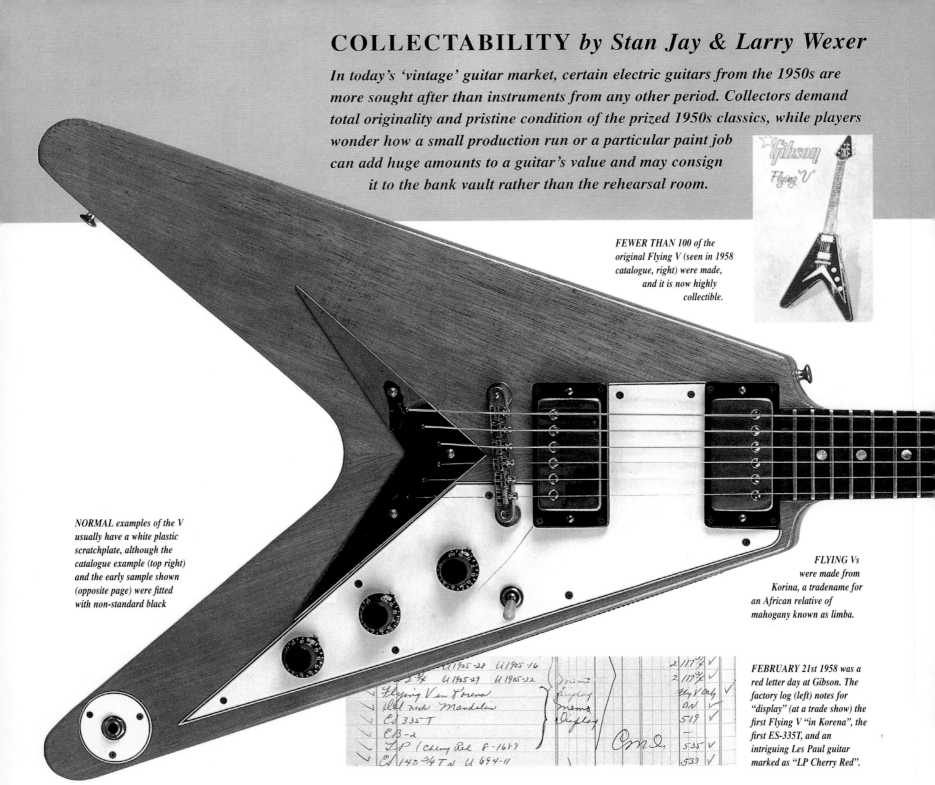

COLLECTABILITY *by Stan Jay & Larry Wexer*

In today's 'vintage' guitar market, certain electric guitars from the 1950s are more sought after than instruments from any other period. Collectors demand total originality and pristine condition of the prized 1950s classics, while players wonder how a small production run or a particular paint job can add huge amounts to a guitar's value and may consign it to the bank vault rather than the rehearsal room.

FEWER THAN 100 of the original Flying V (seen in 1958 catalogue, right) were made, and it is now highly collectible.

NORMAL examples of the V usually have a white plastic scratchplate, although the catalogue example (top right) and the early sample shown (opposite page) were fitted with non-standard black

FLYING Vs were made from Korina, a tradename for an African relative of mahogany known as limba.

FEBRUARY 21st 1958 was a red letter day at Gibson. The factory log (left) notes for "display" (at a trade show) the first Flying V "in Korena", the first ES-335T, and an intriguing Les Paul guitar marked as "LP Cherry Red".

COLLECTABILITY

The post-World War II era became an American cultural crucible in the 1950s. This was a time of economic prosperity, technological advancements, and the beginnings of social rebellion and introspection as a reaction to stifling conformism. Cultural icons of the period included larger-than-life personalities teeming with sexual energy, as well as objects which represent bold statements of the American aesthetic self-image.

The post-war era was characterised by many as a fresh start – a 'year one' – in which to begin anew and stumble headlong into the modern age. This feeling became an underlying current in 1950s culture. People sought to move ahead and to embrace new technologies. They perceived change as positive, and new things were considered an improvement over the old.

Many of the previous generations' household devices and fixtures were literally thrown away. The Tiffany style lamps which hung in the dining room were, unbelievably by

today's sensibilities, relegated to the attic, or, more shatteringly, tossed without thought into the trash heap.

The automobile market is symptomatic of how the commercial marketplace behaved during the 1950s. Redesigned models came out every year or two, which helped engender the desire for the constantly newer, improved style. Some of these shapes were replete with sexual innuendo. As Americans felt more secure of their world position, the collective ego was expressed by these large two-ton luxury liners of the road. With each passing year cars had more gadgets, louder radios, bigger fins, more horsepower, and longer chassis. The aesthetics of the 1950s automobile and other modernistic designs – the vertical vacuum cleaner, abstract shaped coffee tables, lamps, and even Tupperware – saw a further expression in electric guitar designs of the period.

When we think of our idols, there is usually a guitar in hand (their hand, not ours; well, maybe ours). In wishing to emulate our heroes, we seek to own their original

equipment. We see Elvis with his blond 1950s J-200 acoustic and Scotty Moore with his Super 400CES, and Chuck Berry with the ES-350T. The 1950s was the period when all of these Gibson models originated, and they came into being at the same time that the confluence of the major streams of American traditional musics came to form rock'n'roll.

Unlike previous decades, the 1950s saw successful American musicians using the latest equipment – part of the ethos of the 1950s was to be shown in pictures with shiny new stuff. When these new instruments became worn they were seen as 'used' replaceable guitars, not worthy of great reverence beyond their utility value.

Trends in popular music from the late 1950s onward resulted in individuals buying instruments that enabled them to create music of their own. In the 1940s you bought the records and listened to the radio. By the late 1950s you went out and got a guitar and a bass and soundproofed the garage. Manufacturers were pressured

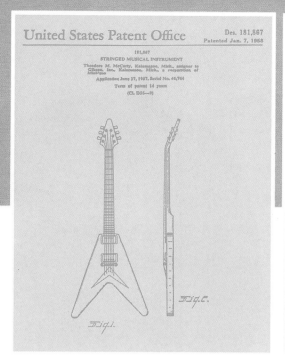

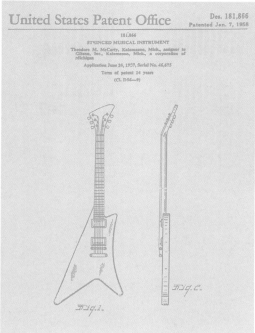

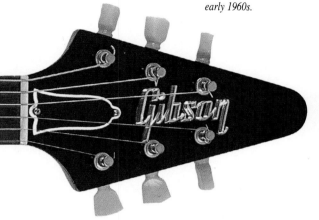

GIBSON decided that Fender's generally more flamboyant solidbody guitars were beating their traditional instruments in visual appeal, and launched two new 'Modernistic' models in 1958. The Flying V and the Explorer (see p66) abandoned conventional style, featuring original, boldly adventurous designs. But the guitars proved too radical: public response was negative, and very few were sold. Result: a prime 'vintage' rarity today, worth a fortune. A third Modernistic Gibson, the Moderne, was planned but never made it into production, even though a patent for the design was filed in summer 1957 (left, alongside Flying V patent).

▽ GIBSON FLYING V
Produced 1958-1959, various re-issues; this example 1959

Publicised by Gibson as "an asset to the combo musician with a flair for showmanship", the Flying V failed in fact to excite any kind of musician, and sales were poor. Gibson shipped 81 of the $247.50 Flying V in 1958 and 17 in 1959, while an estimated 20 more were assembled in the early 1960s.

▽ GIBSON FLYING V
Produced 1958-1959, various re-issues; this example c1957

This is a pre-production Flying V sent by Gibson to their case supplier, Geib of Chicago, in 1957 so that a special fitted case could be designed for the unusual new instrument. In return for their industriousness, Geib were allowed to keep the guitar – a valuable gift, as it turned out.

CARS had a major effect on most American designers of the 1950s. No doubt Gibson's team would have drawn inspiration for the Flying V from the showy tailfins of grand creations like this 1956 Pontiac Convertible (right).

America's Number 1 Road Car...

THIS early V (above) has a gold logo; most models, like the one in the main picture, have a silver-coloured version.

much as major companies have, recently, tried to reproduce these originals, today's copies are very close, but are not exact replicas. The intangible qualities which are so evident to knowledgeable players and discerning collectors are what set the fine vintage instruments apart from their latter day counterparts.

The original electric guitars of the 1950s were made in limited quantities. Many models were newly introduced and met with only limited success. Manufacturers kept producing new ideas, some of which were accepted by the buying public, and some of which were not. A classic example is the Gibson Modernistic guitars. In trying to escape Gibson's stodgy image, Ted McCarty and his colleagues designed rocket-shaped guitars which didn't take off in the marketplace, including the Flying V, the Explorer and the mythical Moderne which is seen even more rarely than Howard Hughes hitchhiking on the highway. Less than 150 Modernistic guitars were produced in total, making this unsuccessful endeavour into what

to build many times the numbers of instruments that they had leisurely made before. (Gibson, for example, made 317 natural and sunburst ES-335s in 1958, and in 1967 they built 5718 of them.) As the companies continued to make minor model changes, at a certain point these changes were no longer improvements. And as we reached the late 1960s musicians began to realise that the quality of contemporary instruments was in many cases no longer equal to the quality of those that had been made in the

past. This, in conjunction with musicians trying to recapture the sounds of their heroes, caused players to look for the older guitars, and since then the 'vintage' market has come into being.

But why are some instruments considered 'vintage', and others just 'used'? Vintage guitars are made of materials, or with a degree of workmanship, not exhibited on current models. A vintage guitar is an original, having specific characteristics stemming from its time of manufacture. As

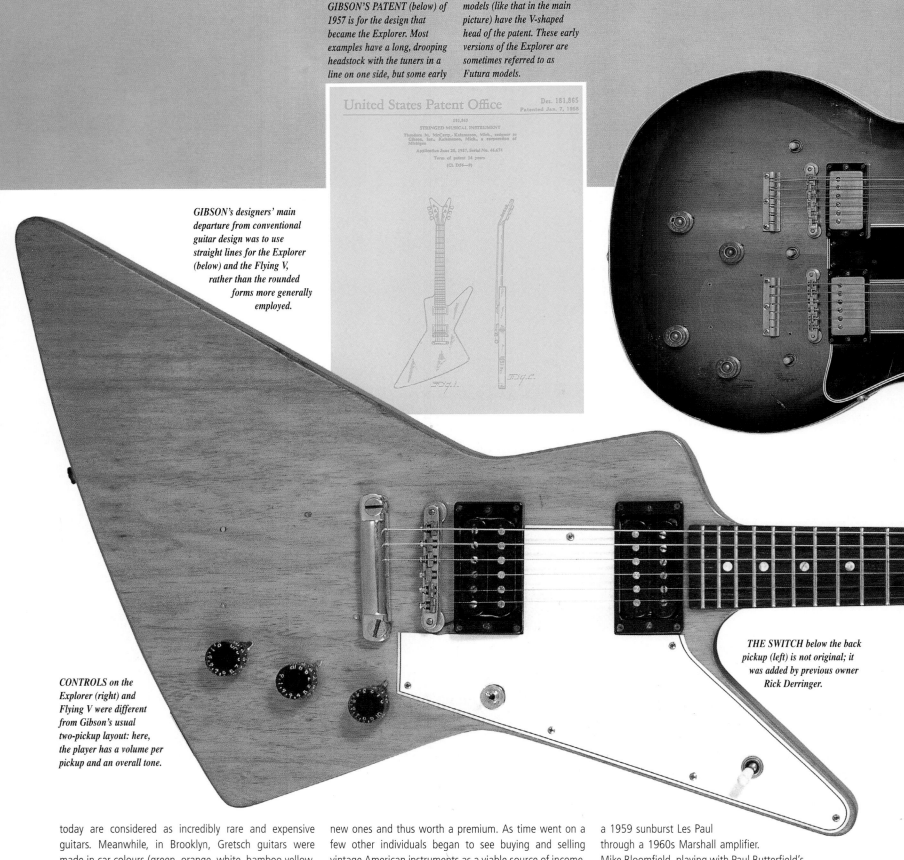

GIBSON'S PATENT (below) of 1957 is for the design that became the Explorer. Most examples have a long, drooping headstock with the tuners in a line on one side, but some early models (like that in the main picture) have the V-shaped head of the patent. These early versions of the Explorer are sometimes referred to as Futura models.

GIBSON's designers' main departure from conventional guitar design was to use straight lines for the Explorer (below) and the Flying V, rather than the rounded forms more generally employed.

CONTROLS on the Explorer (right) and Flying V were different from Gibson's usual two-pickup layout: here, the player has a volume per pickup and an overall tone.

THE SWITCH below the back pickup (left) is not original; it was added by previous owner Rick Derringer.

today are considered as incredibly rare and expensive guitars. Meanwhile, in Brooklyn, Gretsch guitars were made in car colours (green, orange, white, bamboo yellow, copper mist) with Cadillac tailpieces and western motifs (dead cows, cacti, cattle brands, and leather-tooled side-covers and cases). These kitsch accoutrements are, oddly, typical of the 1950s.

Even the most modest and affordable old guitars, like those sold at the Sears, Roebuck store or through their mail-order catalogue under the name Silvertone, had a primitive, wacky quality and unique tone which endear themselves to us, even now.

Pioneering dealers such as Harry West and Izzy Young in New York and Jon & Deirdre Lundberg and Marc Silber in California established between the late 1940s and the late 1960s the idea that old guitars were potentially better than

new ones and thus worth a premium. As time went on a few other individuals began to see buying and selling vintage American instruments as a viable source of income, and set up businesses whose purpose it was to find, restore, market and actually sell these fretted jewels of American craftsmanship to an eager and hungry audience. Today there are over 250 dealers advertising their inventories every month in magazines such as Vintage Guitar and 20th Century Guitar.

In folklore there has always been a feeling that the true lore is something that is rapidly disappearing. In vintage guitars, the same feeling has caused people to become collectors, and amass and hoard their favourite six-string babies, lest they become unobtainable. At the same time as this occurred with acoustic instruments in the late 1960s, one began to see a recording artist like Eric Clapton playing

a 1959 sunburst Les Paul through a 1960s Marshall amplifier. Mike Bloomfield, playing with Paul Butterfield's Blues Band, was seen with black-guard, early 1950s Telecasters, then P-90 gold-top Les Pauls, and ultimately with a PAF-equipped 'burst. In this way visibly prominent artists defined the instruments which would be taken seriously by professionals, and this engendered vintage lust in musicians at large. Clapton still exerts a tremendous influence on the market, even today. His appearance on a TV show in the mid-1990s with an early-issue dot-neck ES-335 spurred a rash of phone calls to dealers and, in fact, resuscitated the resale value of a model that many considered undervalued.

What makes some instruments more desirable or more in fashion is a cyclical process, in part due to which models

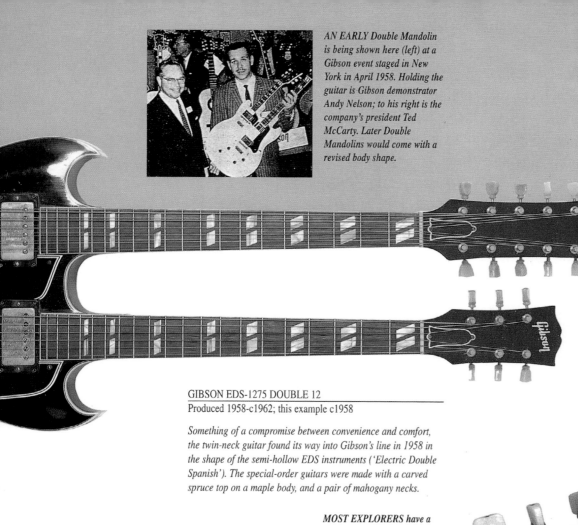

AN EARLY Double Mandolin is being shown here (left) at a Gibson event staged in New York in April 1958. Holding the guitar is Gibson demonstrator Andy Nelson; to his right is the company's president Ted McCarty. Later Double Mandolins would come with a revised body shape.

Custom-built Doubles

DOUBLE 12
A completely new and exciting instrument . . . the Double 12 combines the conventional six-string guitar neck with a twelve-string neck—six strings double strung which can be tuned either in thirds or an octave apart for reinforced resonance and unusual tonal effects. The Florentine double cutaway design provides easy access to the entire fret range of both necks. Has arched top of fine-grained spruce, back and rims of select maple, attractive laminated pickguard, and nickel-plated metal parts.

- Two slim, fast, low-action necks
- One-piece mahogany necks, adjustable truss rod
- Rosewood fingerboards, pearl inlays
- Adjustable Tune-O-Matic bridges
- Twin, humbucking pickups on each neck with separate tone and volume controls for each neck
- Three-position toggle switch to activate either or both pickups
- Neck selector switch to activate either neck

Custom-built to order only
17¼″ wide, 20″ long, 1⅝″ thin . . .
24½″ scale, 20 frets
Double 12 Sunburst, solid white,
  or solid black
  75 Faultless plush-lined
  oblong case

DOUBLE MANDOLIN
Tailored to meet specific unique requirements, the Gibson Double Mandolin lends conspicuous quality to any performance . . . character that commands attention. Combining a six-string guitar neck and a mandolin neck with six strings tuned an octave higher than the regular guitar tuning, this instrument offers solid tonal brilliance with many unusual and interesting effects. The Florentine double cutaway design provides easy access to entire range of both necks. Made with arched top of fine-grained spruce, back and rims of select maple, attractive laminated pickguard, and nickel-plated metal parts.

- Two slim, fast, low-action necks
- One-piece mahogany necks, adjustable truss rod
- Rosewood fingerboards, pearl inlays
- Adjustable Tune-O-Matic bridge on guitar neck
- Special combination, adjustable bridge on mandolin neck with rosewood base and nickel-plated saddle
- Twin humbucking pickups on guitar side and one on mandolin side with separate tone and volume controls for each neck
- Toggle switch to activate either or both pickups
- Neck selector switch to activate either neck

Custom-built to order only
17¼″ wide, 20″ long, 1⅝″ thin . . .
Guitar neck, 24½″ scale, 20 frets
Mandolin neck, 15½″ scale, 24 frets
Double Mandolin Sunburst, solid white,
  or solid black
  1235 Faultless plush-lined oblong case

GIBSON EDS-1275 DOUBLE 12
Produced 1958-c1962; this example c1958

Something of a compromise between convenience and comfort, the twin-neck guitar found its way into Gibson's line in 1958 in the shape of the semi-hollow EDS instruments ('Electric Double Spanish'). The special-order guitars were made with a carved spruce top on a maple body, and a pair of mahogany necks.

GIBSON offered two twin-neck models (shown in the 1960 catalogue, above). The Double 12 (left) mixed 12-string and six-string necks, while the Double Mandolin (right) had a standard six-string plus a short-scale six-string neck tuned an octave higher than normal. Gibson's special-order twin-necks came in solidbody style from 1962.

MOST EXPLORERS have a long, drooping headstock rather than this V-shape head (right).

◁ GIBSON EXPLORER
Produced 1958-1959, various re-issues; this example 1958

Gibson's Explorer found even less favour when it was launched in 1958 than its companion Modernistic guitar, the Flying V. While factory records are not entirely clear, the best estimates put the original 1958-59 Explorer production at 22 units, with a further 16 assembled from leftover parts in the early 1960s.

GIBSON's move to weird shapes in 1958 influenced other makers to loosen up at the drawing board. Kay's Solo King (below, and in 1960 catalogue, right) in single-pickup guise was less than a third of the price of Gibson's Modernistic axes, and twice as ugly. Kay optimistically described the Solo King as "compact, easy to hold".

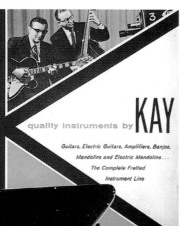

quality instruments by KAY

Guitars, Electric Guitars, Amplifiers, Banjos,
Mandolins and Electric Mandolins . . .
The Complete Fretted
Instrument Line

action

Action is the precise adjustment of strings, frets, nut and bridge. Kay action is sensitive to your lightest touch. Kay action lets you make beautiful music for hours on end . . . with the greatest of ease!

$139⁵⁰ $105⁵⁰ $175⁵⁰ $79⁵⁰ $59⁵⁰

$99⁵⁰ $79⁵⁰ $75 $95

KAY ELECTRIC GUITARS

△ KAY SOLO KING
Produced 1958-1960; this example c1958

As if to prove that anything Gibson can do Kay can do worse, the Solo King was Kay's attempt to jump the weird-shape bandwagon. Wisely, they jumped off again very quickly.

are being used by musicians who are currently famous. The 1970s are considered by many to be a time of 'death by keyboard' (you know, disco – rhythm & blues for people who have neither). Most of the major manufacturers were sleepwalking through their own production processes. This general lack of attention to detail and corporate complacency made guitarists long for products constructed at the same quality level as the 'originals'. For most players and collectors, this would mean that they had to look for vintage instruments: the genuine articles.

So what is it that makes a 'vintage' instrument a 'collectible'? It is more than its being good sounding and having great playability. It is rarity, originality and condition. Lest we overstress this concept, the difference between (1) a completely original 1954 Strat in near mint

GIBSON's 335 appeared to be a hollow-body thinline guitar, but it effectively combined a hollow-body guitar with a solidbody by incorporating a solid block of maple running from neck to strap button through the centre of an otherwise hollow body. This made the guitar much less prone to the screeching feedback that afflicted many hollow-body electrics when played at high volume.

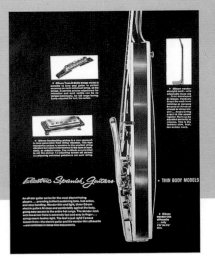

GIBSON's thinline body style (explained in this 1960 catalogue feature, left) was by 1958 used on five instruments: the Byrdland, ES-350T, 335TD, 225T and 125T. That same year the company also had five full-depth electric hollow-body guitars in the line: the Super 400CES, L-5CES, ES-5 Switchmaster, ES-295, and the ES-175.

△ GIBSON ES-335TDN
Produced 1958-1960; this example October 1959

The 'dot-neck 335' has become a prime collectible guitar. The original production of the ES-335TD with dot-shape fingerboard markers lasted only from 1958 to 1962, when Gibson replaced the dots with block-shape markers. The earliest 335 models were officially named ES-335T (the T stands for 'thinline') but soon a D was added by Gibson (D means 'double' pickups). The extra N on the model shown stands for 'natural' finish; ES-335TD alone indicates the sunburst variety. From 1960 the 335 was also available in a cherry red finish, known as an ES-335TDC.

COLLECTORS *prefer 335s with 'dot' necks, but also with 'long' pickguards that extend beyond the bridge (as on all the 335s shown here), a type used until late in 1960. Early the following year a shorter pickguard that stopped level with the bridge was adopted.*

WHEN GUITARS themselves become expensive collectors' items, the associated memorabilia becomes collectible too. Catalogues and other advertising material from the 1950s have long fetched a premium on the 'vintage' market; this 335 entry (right) comes from a much sought-after example, Gibson's classic guitar catalogue of 1958.

△ GIBSON ES-335TD
Produced 1958-current; this example September 1959

The sunburst 335 was always made in greater numbers than the natural version, which was dropped in 1960. For example, in 1959 Gibson shipped 521 sunburst but only 71 natural 335s.

THE 335 was Gibson's first thinline model to feature a pair of symmetrical cutaways (left) for easier high-note playing.

MANY GIBSON ES thinline models feature this so-called 'crown' inlay on the headstock (above right), although the ES-355, for example, boasts a split-diamond, while the ES-330 has a plain head with only the Gibson logo.

△ GIBSON ES-335TDN
Produced 1958-1960; this example November 1959

When a Bigsby vibrato was factory-fitted, tailpiece holes were covered with pearl (as here) or a black 'Custom Made' plate.

condition with original form-fit brown case and 'tags' (meaning warranty, and other manufacturers' informative blurbs), strap, lead and key to the case, and (2) a refretted '54 Strat with one non-original pickup and the Bakelite replaced with more modern plastic, can be a loss of 50 per cent of its value. And if the instrument has also at some stage been 'refinished' – in other words if the original finish has been replaced – then the guitar will be worth even less on the vintage market.

The one exception to the general rule of all collectibles is the flame-driven market of the original Les Paul Sunburst, or 'Standard'. In this singular instance a highly tiger-striped example with a repaired headstock and new tuners can still fetch its maximum potential, while a Plain Jane with virtually no 'figure' (the visible pattern) but in clean original condition will be worth 30 to 40 per cent less. We marvel at the forgiving myopia of the Les Paul collector in allowing for such a lapse in condition when searching for the eternal flame.

The custom-colour phenomenon of Fender guitars asserts the primacy of the iconographic value of a custom paint job in ways which were never realised in the automotive market. A rare, cool custom colour such as fiesta red or shoreline gold, or the 'Mary Kaye' combination of transparent blonde with gold hardware, dramatically enhances the price of a Stratocaster so equipped. When one perceives these factors as having discernible market value it becomes readily apparent that the vintage guitars under discussion have a representational and artistic worth that goes beyond what they are as functional objects. This, in essence, is exactly what qualifies them as 'collectible'.

The guitar industry has sought, today, to internalise this phenomenon in creating "collectors' edition" guitars and limited runs of guitars with specific appointments. In most instances these are produced in larger quantities in one year than many of the original vintage instruments were made during their entire production runs. But this phenomenon has had a laudable side effect in that it has caused the major manufacturers to re-examine the construction of their own vintage guitars and to at least attempt to reproduce in contemporary instruments the qualities which made the originals great.

We cannot go back in time like Michael J Fox did in his De Lorean, but we can still own the beloved artefacts of the past. Part of the beauty of the vintage guitar is that these old instruments continue to be playable, so that we can still create new music from old technology. Guitars as collectibles have taken on a life of their own (would that we could, also). With their great increase in value, some guitars are no longer suitable to drag to the local bar to play the Friday night gig, as much as we might like to. While many may bemoan the state of affairs, arguing that guitars are made to be played, the fact that collector-grade instruments will be preserved in glass-walled aggregations means that this musical heritage will, at least partially, be preserved for our descendants.

On the other hand, as long as there are mirrors and electric guitars, flea markets and pawn shops on the back roads, and accepting spouses and local taverns, there will be weekend warriors who preserve the rock'n'roll culture of the 1950s. ■ **STAN JAY & LARRY WEXER**

RADIO & TELEVISION *by Michael Wright*

In the warm glow of memory, radio and television in the 1950s have an image of being innocent Happy Days, of Ricky Ricardo yelling "Lu – cy!" or Jack Warner signing off with a cosy "Evenin' all". But with the emergence of radio and television as primary vehicles of entertainment, the reality was much more turbulent, involving inter-media struggle and inter-generational strife. Often, an electric guitar would hover somewhere near the centre of that controversy.

TV WAS invented in the 1920s, but it wasn't until the 1939 New York World's Fair that the medium really caught the imagination of the American people. In 1946, NBC established the first TV network, and by the end of the 1940s there were four competing US networks: NBC, CBS, ABC and DuMont. Television was instantaneously

successful, and by 1956 more than 70 per cent of all US homes had TVs. For most of the first half of the 1950s, when ads like this (above) appeared, US television programming was essentially a transference of 1940s radio to the new medium, with variety shows, quiz shows, crime dramas and comedies being taken straight off the radio.

CONTROLS (below) are a volume for each pickup and overall tone (although a volume knob is missing here).

RADIO & TELEVISION

As the 1950s began, the medium of television was doing its best to kill radio. Commercial radio broadcasting had been around in the US since the early 1920s, with the big networks NBC and CBS forming in 1926. From the early days on, radio thrived as a live medium, with live variety shows and big orchestras. However, big changes in taste occurred after 1945, as war-weary citizens settled into suburban domesticity and began to create the baby boom. Radio audiences preferred to hear quiz shows and dramatic productions: 'Gangbusters', 'The Lone Ranger', and 'I Love Lucy'. Instead of big bands, listeners favoured singers. National radio networks were becoming fiscal dinosaurs. As a result they started to look for new outlets, and where they looked was television.

Guitars had a presence on 1950s television programming, but except for a few big highlights their role was limited. Actually, two guitarists had their own network shows just as the decade dawned. Folk singer Paul Arnold hosted American Song in 1948, and later a folk and country programme The Paul Arnold Show which lasted until 1950, while tenor jazz guitarist Eddie Condon hosted Eddie Condon's Floor Show into 1950.

One of the longest running of the new variety shows that also debuted in 1948 was The Perry Como Show, which frequently featured Les Paul and Mary Ford. It was undoubtedly this exposure which helped propel the duo to superstardom, leading in 1953 to their own daily five-minute Les Paul & Mary Ford Show

sponsored by Listerine, although after that year's No.1 summer smash, 'Vaya Con Dios', which stayed on the chart for 31 weeks, the brilliant guitarist's sun would set far faster than it had risen.

Perhaps the biggest and most influential of the early variety shows were Arthur Godfrey's Talent Scouts (1948) and Arthur Godfrey And His Friends (1949), which led the ratings and introduced many new artists to the public, including Roy Clark (although both Elvis and Buddy Holly would fail to succeed at auditions for Godfrey).

Indeed, as an illustration of the power of this new medium, it was Godfrey who almost single-handedly started the craze for ukuleles. Godfrey, between sips of Lipton tea, would occasionally strum a uke and, in fact, actually had an instructional TV show in 1950. When Godfrey discovered an inexpensive but good plastic uke and promoted it on his show, he sparked a run on plastic instruments designed and made by the great Mario Maccaferri. Countless little baby boomers started playing ukes. For many, this led to a lifelong addiction to guitars.

British TV goes back to John Logie Baird's pioneering tests in the mid-1920s, but the first official broadcasts, from the BBC, began in 1936. By 1950 the BBC was still the lone TV broadcaster, but showing the Queen's coronation in 1953 did much to boost the medium. In 1955 a commercial station, ITA, started broadcasting.

Most forms of popular music were poorly served by British TV and radio as the 1950s began, and when rock'n'roll took off later in the decade the response

BODIES and necks for Guyatone's solidbody guitars were manufactured by Maruha Musical Instruments in Kyushu and assembled in Guyatone's Tokyo factory.

MAGNA Electronics began making Magnatone amplifiers in the late 1940s, adding solidbody electric guitars to the line in 1956. Based in California, Magna found that their guitars were never as popular as their amplifiers, of which Buddy Holly was the most famous 1950s user.

MAGNA's first Magnatone guitars appeared in 1956. Assistance came from fellow Californian Paul Bigsby, who provided hardware for several models, including the Mark V of 1957. A new Rickenbacker-like line was launched in 1959 when ex-Rickenbacker man Paul Barth briefly came on board. The Magnatone brand lasted into the 1960s, also used on organs and hi-fi gear.

△ MAGNATONE MARK V
Produced 1957-1960; this example c1959

As well as the obvious vibrato, the pickups and control panel are typical of the work of Magna's collaborator Paul Bigsby.

▷ MAGNATONE MARK III DELUXE
Produced c1957-1960; this example c1958

A typical budget concoction of the 1950s: note the enormous Formica scratchplate covering the whole of the front, the Bakelite knobs, and the unmistakable 'M' logo on the tailpiece.

▽ GUYATONE LG-30
Produced c1958-c1963; this example c1959

Exported from Japan under Guyatone and Antoria brandnames, models such as this were staples of the British beat scene of the late 1950s and early 1960s, being cheap, electric and available.

HEADSTOCKS might be plain (above right) or bear a brandname logo (below).

GUYATONE
SOLID
Electric
GUITARS
Unexcelled Value - Quality - Performance

DESPITE the presence of a truss-rod cover on the headstock (right), the LG60B's truss-rod was not adjustable.

△ GUYATONE LG-60B
Produced c1958-c1963; this example c1958

Guyatone in Japan enjoyed clear US influences on their first solidbody electrics: the LG of the model name stands for Les Paul Guitar, while the body shape was in fact influenced by 1950s Supro models such as the Belmont (made by Valco in Chicago). Guyatone's LGs, developed around 1958 for export, soon featured Fender-style heads with six-in-a-line tuners.

BRITISH Guyatone distributor J&I Arbiter issued this leaflet (right) in 1959. It showed an LG-50 (£25), and listed LG-30 (£20) and LG-60 (£30) models.

remained sluggish. The top variety show, Sunday Night At The London Palladium (1955 onwards), would stick to untrendy artists such as Gracie Fields or Guy Mitchell.

It was left to a handful of programmes to help fledgling beat-boomers spot a hip chord-shape or two. Six-Five Special (1957) was the first teenage music show, with a jiving audience circling the likes of Tommy Steele and Adam Faith. Jack Good's Oh Boy! (1958) was the pick of a small bunch, an atmospheric version of audience mayhem that might pitch the John Barry Seven against Marty Wilde or a young Cliff Richard, while on Juke Box Jury (1959) a panel that mixed stars and punters voted new records a hit ('ding!') or a miss ('bzzz').

While people were beginning to see more guitars on TV, most often either acoustic or electric archtops, radio — remember radio? — was preparing a counter-assault in America that would make absolutely sure folks heard guitars, and change the course of known civilisation.

FENDER instruments are promoted in a CBS TV studio setting in this 1958 ad (right). No doubt the ad agency were pleased with the coup of placing Fender in the studio of one of the leading American TV networks of the day. But ironically it was CBS who, just seven years later, would buy out the Fender companies in a spectacular deal that would see $13 million change hands.

GRETSCH's Country Club Stereo was available in Cadillac green (below) or normal sunburst finish.

STEREO PICKUPS on Gretsch guitars (left) were modified versions of the company's normal Filter'Tron pickups. Each pickup was split so that one would feed treble strings and the other bass strings to separate amps.

GRETSCH used the Melita bridge (above) for much of the 1950s. It was the first bridge to offer independent intonation adjustment for each string.

GUITARS appeared in many unexpected places on American TV of the 1950s. In 1955, The Lawrence Welk Show hit the air to almost universal critical scorn. A relic of the accordion craze that was already over by the time it aired, Welk's show did nonetheless feature solos by (smiling) guitarist Buddy Merrill. Sessionman and

Gibson endorser Tony Mottola made 'original descriptive music' for something called Danger (right). Even Desi Arnaz would occasionally strum an axe for bits of I Love Lucy. And who could forget Jane Davies on the Ina Ray Hutton Show or Jimmy Dodd picking a rodent-shaped guitar on The Mickey Mouse Club?

sparks the danger television show

An innovation in background music—Tony Mottola and his Gibson! The original and unusual themes, composed and played by this talented artist, set and sustain the mood of the "Danger" T.V. program Tony Mottola and his Gibson are a well-known duo... his guitar has been carefully chosen for its consistent dependability and tonal perfection. For music in the "Danger" manner, or for more standard guitar rhythms—Gibson sets the pace.

Now available to guitarists, the original arrangements of the themes from the "Danger" show.

GIBSON, INC., Kalamazoo, Michigan

Back when the US networks divested themselves of radio, a number of developments began to coalesce which would redefine the medium and eventually re-establish its cultural importance. For one thing, in the late 1940s American radio stations increasingly relied on recorded music to replace the disappearing 0network programming. In 1949 Todd Storz, owner of KOWH in Omaha, Nebraska, invented the Top 40 radio format, playing the most popular tunes in rotation. The idea swept the radio industry like wildfire. In around 1950, New York's WNEW was the first to mix recorded music with news. Radio was ready to find its modern voice.

Simultaneously, momentous changes in music began to occur, for which radio provided the ideal outlet. In 1948, losing money hand over fist, WDIA in Memphis, Tennessee, made a desperate decision and became the first-ever all-black format radio station. They hired a young guitarist to perform, who became known as Blues Boy King. In 1950, not far from WDIA, Sam Phillips opened Sun Studios. That same year WDIA's BB King had a national R&B hit with 'Three

DISC JOCKEYS (right) came to personify the shift of emphasis that started during the 1950s from live music performance to the broadcasting of records.

o'clock Blues'. A local young truck driver was listening. His name was Elvis. Meanwhile up in Cleveland, Ohio, in 1951 a disc jockey named Alan Freed began to notice that kids were buying so-called 'race' records — a record business term for uptempo R&B songs by black artists — with a beat they could dance to. The records featured electric guitars.

Freed started playing this music on his show and called it 'rock and roll'. All the kids started listening, and of course the radio business noted the ensuing buzz. In 1954, Freed was hired by New York's WINS to do Alan Freed's Rock & Roll Party. WINS quickly led the New York radio pack, and the rest of radio followed.

The older generation reacted with fear and trembling to the arrival of rock'n'roll. Radio stations were besieged with callers demanding that the 'nigger music' be stopped, or pointing to a Communist conspiracy. The kids just kept buying it up. In 1956 the Memphis truck driver Elvis Presley, backed by Scotty Moore's archtop

electric, copped three No.1 hits. Rock and its electric guitars never looked back, and by 1958 the US Top 40 was dominated by rock'n'roll.

Which brings us back to television — remember television? With American radio fomenting a revolution starring guitar-toting teen idols, TV couldn't ignore the top of the pops. Ironically, it was two stalwarts of the big band era, Tommy and Jimmy Dorsey, who gave the new music one of its early breaks. It was on their programme Stage Show that Elvis made his TV debut in January 1956, hips swivelling, many months before his more famous appearances on The Ed Sullivan Show when the camera pulled back to censor his dance in 'Ready Teddy'.

The controversy surrounding Elvis' TV performances turned out to be a tempest in a teapot. Television never did fully warm up to rock'n'roll in the 1950s, and really didn't have to. By the later 1950s, tastes had shifted again and musical variety shows began to give way to Westerns.

Electric guitars show up on a few more American TV programmes in later years, including four shows that were produced during 1957 by Alan Freed, called The Big Beat, with Chuck Berry and Mickey (Baker) & Sylvia, as well as 1959's The Music Shop, with Ritchie Valens.

The decade itself was winding down, and was about to enter the radio 'payola' scandals (which would end Freed's career) and the swinging sixties. But it was the 1950s which laid the foundation, bringing the sounds of electric guitars on to the radio and those censored, swivelling hips on to the television. ■ MICHAEL WRIGHT

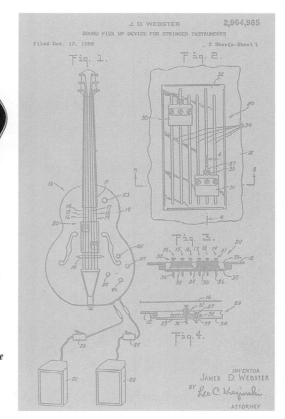

GRETSCH COUNTRY CLUB STEREO
Produced 1958-1965; this example 1958

'Stereo' became a magical word in the late 1950s. Pre-recorded stereo tapes first appeared in 1956, LPs a few years later, and in 1958 the first stereo guitars were launched: the Gretsch Country Club Stereo and White Falcon Stereo. They worked by splitting the output of the strings and feeding them to two separate amplifiers.

JIMMIE WEBSTER (right) was Gretsch's guitar ideas man, and he's pictured here with the stereo guitar system he developed for them in 1958.

WEBSTER's original patent (right) for the first practical stereo guitar system, filed in 1956, shows a stylised drawing of a large pickup with two individual elements positioned on sliders. In fact, the type put into production had two static, modified pickups, sensing either the three highest or three lowest strings, "whereby tones produced from each of said groups of strings may be selectively controlled".

J. D. WEBSTER 2,964,985
SOUND PICK UP DEVICE FOR STRINGED INSTRUMENTS
Filed Dec. 12, 1956 2 Sheets-Sheet 1

Fig. 1. Fig. 2.

Fig. 3.

Fig. 4.

INVENTOR
JAMES D. WEBSTER
BY Leo C. Krazinski
ATTORNEY

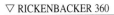

THE COMPANY which made Rickenbacker guitars was the Electro String Instrument Corporation, formed in Los Angeles in 1934. In 1953 founder Adolph Rickenbacker sold Electro String to businessman FC Hall. The following year Rickenbacker's first conventionally shaped electrics began to appear, and in 1958 the classic Capri style (left) hit the market.

▽ RICKENBACKER 360
Produced 1958-current; this example 1959

Rickenbacker introduced a series of models during 1958 that formed the basis for the company's success during the 1960s. These thinline hollow-body electric guitars, known for the first few years as the Capri series, were largely the responsibility of Roger Rossmeisl, an inspired German-born guitar designer and maker who had come to work for Rickenbacker around 1954.

STYLISH and arrestingly different, the new models that Rickenbacker released in 1958 had a set of classic features, including 'toaster' pickups (above) and 'stove' knobs (left). Also in evidence was Rickenbacker's striking 'slash' scimitar-shaped soundhole, cut into a large body that had beautifully curved cutaways and designer Roger Rossmeisl's distinctive carved-out tailpiece area, topped off with the unusual two-level scratchplate. In 1958 the 360 cost $309.50, or with vibrato (model 365) for an extra $20.

1959

STEREO was a buzz word in the late 1950s not only in studios but also with guitar makers. Gibson's ES-345 (below) was their first stereo guitar, as proudly stamped on the tag (left) that came with this instrument.

▷ GIBSON ES-345TDN
Produced 1959-1981; this example October 1959

After Gretsch had introduced the first stereo guitar in 1958 (see p72), Gibson came up with a simpler stereo system for their ES-345 and 355 models which sends each pickup to separate amps.

CHERRY RED (below) was the colour in which most ES-355s were finished, apart from a few custom jobs, until a walnut option was offered by Gibson in the late 1960s.

△ GIBSON ES-355TD-SV
Produced 1959-1981; this example November 1959

Gibson's ES-355 was a deluxe version of the 335, and the SV suffix of this example identifies it as a stereo model with Varitone. The large Varitone control, developed by Gibson's pickup expert Walt Fuller, is situated above the usual knobs, and is used to select from six preset tonal settings. It proved unpopular with players and is often disconnected.

GIBSON STEREO

TONY MOTTOLA (left) demos a stereo ES-355 through Gibson's GA-88S stereo amp outfit "enabling the guitarist to create a symphony of warm, full stereophonic sound".

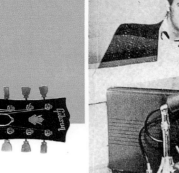

SUN STUDIOS, Memphis, Tennessee, 1954 (right). Elvis Presley, bassist Bill Black and guitarist Scotty Moore grin as producer Sam Phillips poses by the studio's disc-cutting lathe.

songwriters and producers Leiber & Stoller and Atlantic's chief engineer Tom Dowd, working with The Coasters in New York. But the spread of multitrack was not universal. The Beatles used only two-track – voices on one channel, instruments on the other – as late as 1963.

The frequency range and balance captured by the best studios in the 1950s was little different to that boasted by modern facilities, at least until the invention of digital recording. The sheer simplicity of the methods used, straight from microphone to tape with a minimum of processing, was capable of producing sounds of

breathtaking realism and presence. Only in the high levels of ambient noise (which were an inevitable consequence of the valve electronics employed) do some of these recordings betray their age.

But while the major studios were capable of technical excellence, they were not at the forefront of musical developments. The 1950s saw the rise of independent recording labels and small studios which were ideally placed to discover and record new types of music. These studios were often run by a single engineer and/or proprietor, and would survive from week to week by

recording mundane local events, while using the income generated to subsidise their real musical interests.

Sam Phillips's Memphis Recording Service, better known as the Sun studios where Elvis Presley made his first records, was typical. Sun had a single recording room 18ft by 30ft, with a control room at one end and an office at the other. Phillips had no more than eight microphones and a five-into-one mixing desk. And he had a pair of Presto disc-cutting lathes, one of which made the first known recording of Elvis Presley who called at the studio to make a demo, ostensibly to play to his mother.

Phillips also had two good Ampex tape machines, the second of which was used to provide the primitive 'slapback' echo that is the Sun recordings' trademark. A feed was taken to the machine, probably from a microphone in the recording room: its placement would account for the way the effect varies from track to track. Once recorded, it was immediately picked up off the monitor head and fed back into the final mix: the delay inherent in this process created the initial echo. With

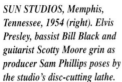

Gibson thin-body guitars feel just right

ANDY NELSON (left), described as Gibson's "artist-enthusiast", poses with a mono ES-355 in this 1959 ad. Gibson offered the 355 in mono and stereo formats, the mono variety also lacking a Varitone control. As the 355 continued in production during the 1960s, Gibson produced more stereo than mono models.

▽ GIBSON LES PAUL SPECIAL
Produced 1955-1959, various re-issues; this example 1959

After a weakness was revealed at the neck/body joint, later examples have the neck pickup moved further down the body.

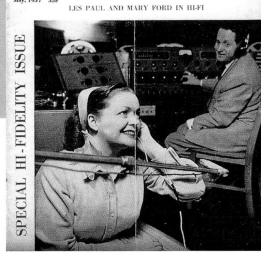

METRONOME

MUSIC USA

May, 1957   35¢

LES PAUL AND MARY FORD IN HI-FI

SPECIAL HI-FIDELITY ISSUE

LES PAUL (at the controls in his home studio, left, with Mary Ford at the microphone) had an eccentric, self-taught grasp of the recording process that inspired some great ideas. While guitarist Paul wasn't the first to use overdubbing, his multi-guitar piece 'Lover', recorded in 1947 and released by Capitol the following year as

Les Paul's 'New Sound', did much to attract attention to the potential of overdubbing, as did his subsequent hits with Ford such as 'How High The Moon'. Later, Paul came up with the avant-garde idea of an eight-track tape recorder, and commissioned the Ampex company to build him the very first such machine in 1957.

PLANE CRASH KILLS STARS

NEW YORK, Wednesday.—The world's pop fans were shattered this week by the tragic deaths of three top disc stars—Buddy Holly, Big Bopper (J. P. Richardson) and Ritchie Valens.

Harriott

BUDDY HOLLY is killed in a plane crash in Iowa along with Ritchie Valens and the Big Bopper.

RUSSIA launches Lunik I into planetary orbit around the sun, lands Lunik II on the moon, and uses Lunik III to take the first photographs of the dark side of the moon.

CALIFORNIA passes the first exhaust emissions law in the United States.

equipment so basic, Phillips' fundamental resource was time itself. While engineers who worked in major studios were tied to rigid session schedules and union agreements, not to mention technical standards and textbook procedures, those in independent studios had the time and freedom for experimentation.

Phillips, for instance, permitted levels of distortion that would not have been acceptable in the large studios of the time. For example, he would place guitar amplifiers in the bathroom to get a harder sound. And he had his famous echo effect. All these things were the lifeblood of early

rock'n'roll, eagerly copied at hundreds of small studios across the country. Independent engineers were expected to take an active part in recording, pushing up the faders to make drumbeats distort for extra impact, fading in and out echo at appropriate points, riding the faders to smooth out uneven vocal performances. At the same time, the rudimentary nature of recording during the 1950s meant that musicians were naturally adept at playing together in small spaces, listening and reacting to one another, and producing a genuine performance.

Phillips used no overdubbing or splicing. Each section of tape produced in the Sun studios represents a single moment in time. Other independent studios and producers were adept at tape editing, often splicing several takes together to make one finished song, and at overdubbing by copying from machine to machine. This clumsy technique was used to great effect on many of Buddy Holly's recordings, starting with 'Words of Love' in spring 1957. The independents undoubtedly led the way in pop, while the majors tried to catch up. ■ JOHN MORRISH

WIZARDRY ON WHEELS

The Revolutionary

MORRIS Mini-Minor

▽ GIBSON LES PAUL SPECIAL
Produced 1955-1959, various re-issues; this example 1959

A shortlived variant, the double-cutaway Junior replaced the single-cut version early in '59, and was renamed SG Special later in the year. Only a small number would have been left-handed like this rare example.

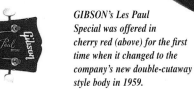

GIBSON's Les Paul Special was offered in cherry red (above) for the first time when it changed to the company's new double-cutaway style body in 1959.

BMC's MINI, "the people's car", is launched on the UK market. Designed by Alec Issigonis, the £500 Mini is described by one newspaper as the vehicle "for which tens of thousands of economy motorists have been waiting". Meanwhile the initial section of Britain's first motorway, the M1, is opened for traffic.

IN CUBA, dictator Fulgencio Batista's government is overthrown by a revolutionary movement under Fidel Castro.

THE WORLD's population is estimated at 2800 million, and is said to be increasing at the rate of 45 million every year.

DEAD: Guitar Slim, Cecil B De Mille and Billie Holiday. Born: Richie Sambora, Emma Thompson and Bryan Adams.

SOVIET leader Nikita Kruschev visits the United States; his main complaint is that for security reasons he is not allowed to tour Disneyland. Later he observes: "The people are for peace." Quite right.

EUROPEAN GUITARS *by Paul Day*

In contrast to the United States, Europe in the early 1950s was still deep in the age of post-war austerity, and young people were not yet afforded their own identity nor the luxury of an independent lifestyle. While rock'n'roll was beginning to make waves across the Atlantic, it had yet to have any impact in the UK, where the guitar often literally took a back seat and the electric variety was still far from common.

THIS GOLDEN Hofner from the early 1960s was presented by Hofner to UK guitar star Bert Weedon, who still owns it today. The rectangular control panel was used from 1958.

GOYA (below) was a brand applied to guitars imported into the US by Hershman. From 1959 some were made by Hagstrom in Sweden, with distinctive touches including colourful plastic finishes and multiple control layouts.

EUROPEAN GUITARS

The British skiffle craze of the mid-1950s inspired thousands to take up the guitar, leading to increasing numbers of cheap and cheerful instruments in circulation. From these humble but fun beginnings many aspiring musicians made what seemed to be a natural progression to rock'n'roll. As the new sounds which reflected the fast-changing face of American popular music began to filter across the big pond, so too came a growing awareness that the guitars used on US records must be very different from those found in Britain and the rest of Europe.

Record albums and theatre or TV appearances by visiting American artists provided a tantalising taste of futuristic Fenders, exotic Epiphones, glossy Gibsons, Gretsches or Guilds, and radical Rickenbackers. Despite their undoubted desirability, such tools of this new trade were beyond the reach of most British guitarists, not just financially and

geographically, but also politically, as a 1951 UK government embargo on foreign instrument imports would not be lifted until summer 1959.

So it was that in the 1950s choice and availability remained very limited in Britain, despite the increasing popularity of the instrument. Rock'n'roll was becoming a major player in the music business, with the electric guitar considered de rigueur. Of course, both rock'n'roll and its electric exponents were despised by 'real' musicians, many of whom were nonetheless still required to play this dreaded devil's music on the new instruments – which does much to explain the low standards of British recorded re-creations of contemporary US hits in the 1950s.

The West German maker Hofner assumed a high profile in the UK quite early on, thanks to importer Selmer, at first with electrified big-bodied archtops, then smaller-bodied Club models and, in 1956, their solidbody Colorama. In the

WEST GERMAN maker Hofner made a big impact in 1950s Britain, as shown in importer Selmer's 1959 ad (right) that features an eccentric mixture of the top UK bandsmen, session players and embryonic rock'n'rollers.

SELMER were the biggest UK importer of electric guitars in the 1950s. The 1957 catalogue (above) features a Hofner.

SUCCESS STORIES START WITH *Hofner*

BERT WEEDON · TOMMY STEELE · ROY PLUMMER · JEFF ROWENA · JIM DALE · FRANK DENIZ · JUDD PROC · BOBBY CORAM · DENNIS NEWE · DENNY WRIGHT · ERIC KERSHAW · DICKIE BISHOP · DON FRASER · BILL SHEARER

CUT HERE AND ...DAY!

TOMMY STEELE SAYS

TOMMY STEELE was Britain's first rock'n'roll star, before becoming the dreaded 'all-round entertainer'. His first hit was 'Rock With The Caveman' (1956), and in '57 he made No.1 with 'Singing The Blues'. Steele is pictured (left) with a Hofner Committee and is seen in the big ad (far left) with a Hofner President.

▽ HOFNER GOLDEN HOFNER THIN
Produced 1959-1962; this example 1961

The West German Hofner company added the Golden Hofner model to the top of their line at the end of the 1950s. Described by Hofner as "a masterpiece of guitar perfection", it was certainly the company's most ornate and attractive electric hollow-body guitar. By 1959, as well as an extensive line of domestic-market guitars, Hofner offered nine UK-only models: the Golden Hofner, Committee, President, Senator, Club 40, Club 50 and Club 60 hollow electrics, plus a pair of Colorama solids with one or two pickups.

HOFNER's unique headstock shape (left), used on the Golden Hofner and Committee models, was appropriately described by the company as 'frondose', meaning leaf-like.

HOFNER used some beautiful fingerboard inlays, including the Golden Hofner's pleasing

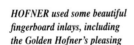

floral pattern (above), bounded by the typically German device of parallel lines.

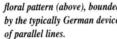

△ HARMONY STRATOTONE JUPITER H-49
Produced 1959-1965; this example c1960

In the US, Harmony continued to produce electrics such as this Jupiter (in the same line as a Mars and a Mercury model). Controls included a volume and tone per pickup, plus a tone control for the three-way selector's centre 'out of phase' position.

HARMONY's colourful catalogue of 1958 (above) detailed their competitively priced electric models, ranging from the Mars H-45 at $70 to the Espanada H-63 at $199.50.

infant days of the electric guitar market in the UK such solid 'planks', as they were often derisorily described, were not numerous in comparison to hollow-body electrics. Hofner's original solidbody had few partners in Britain at the time, although one of its first competitors was also handled by an obviously aware Selmer.

The Grazioso solidbody was made by the Neoton company in Prague, Czechoslovakia, an unlikely origin for a guitar so heavily influenced by Fender's still-recent creation, that most ultra-American of all electrics, the super-streamlined Stratocaster. Although clumsy styling guaranteed that it was far from a copy, the Neoton Grazioso came with bolt-on maple neck, two-tone sunburst contoured body, triple pickups, built-in bridge/vibrato unit and a front-recessed output socket. This array of features, strongly suggestive of Fender, guaranteed instant appeal and, accordingly, impressive sales to numerous nascent

pluckers such as George Harrison and Albert Lee. Selmer soon realised that the 'Grazioso' name was uncommercial, and swiftly changed it to the more American-imaged 'Futurama' (see p83).

The late 1950s brought the first Japanese-made electrics to British shores, imported to swell the still thin ranks of solids. These early efforts were primitive and poor in quality, but at least offered an interesting alternative. Most originated from the Tokyo-based Guyatone factory, although these were later imported bearing other logos, including Antoria or Star. Unusually, styling was derived from Valco, a less familiar name on the US solidbody scene and responsible for the National and Supro brands, some models of which featured a single sloping cutaway shape. Guyatone's version employed a smaller body, probably to match the comparatively diminutive stature of Japanese guitarists, and blithely ignored the real needs of a western

export market which was looking for guitars that more closely matched the models made by American companies such as Gibson, Fender, Gretsch and the like.

Despite reductions in dimensions and inherent quality, these oriental imports proved popular in the UK as they certainly embodied a more modern image than many, along with favourably affordable prices. Players such as a young Hank Marvin suffered their shortcomings while awaiting the opportunity to acquire a Fender or Gibson dream machine. Although the former brand certainly took over later as the main influence on guitar design, Gibson's more traditional stance tended to dominate the 1950s.

By the late 1950s the influence of electric guitars had spread worldwide, evidenced by other countries' contributions to the cause, and some of these did make their mark on a pre-beatboom British market. In Sweden, accordion maker Hagstrom decided they wanted a piece of

△ FRAMUS HOLLYWOOD 5/132
Produced 1959-1961; this example c1959

Framus, a German maker, initially dabbled in big hollow-body
electrics, entering the solidbody market in 1959. The Hollywood
name had an American air, and as the nearest thing to Les Paul
lookalikes in Europe at the time they sold well, complete with a
choice of one, two or three pickups plus fancy paint jobs.

GRETSCH influence is evident
(below) not just in the stereo
idea, but in the Melita bridge
and the sparkle finish of
the double pickguards.

VEGA's control layout for the
model 1200 includes a normal
volume and tone per pickup
(far left), a three-way pickup
selector (above the neck) and
a two-way selector (left) for
mono/stereo operation.

△ VEGA 1200 STEREO
Produced 1959-c1960; this example c1959

In the US, Vega of Boston decided to get themselves noticed in
the new stereo scene with this spectacular 12-pickup instrument,
which retailed for a steep $1000. "For stereo use with two
amplifiers," explained Vega, "a flick of the switch projects all of
the treble notes through one amplifier and all the bass notes
through the other. Electronic vibrato is also provided."

VEGA's 12 pickups (above) are   designed to sense treble tones
split into two groups of six, two   and the six nearest the neck are
for each string. The rear six are   for bass response.

82

▽ FUTURAMA 3
Produced 1959-1963; this example c1959

'Futurama' was the brandname that UK importer Selmer applied from around 1959 to the previously-named Grazioso solidbody electric from Czechoslovakian instrument manufacturer Neoton.

SALESMAN Robert Nielsen holds Vega's stereo guitar at its summer 1959 launch (right), as company president William Nelson looks on.

EARLIEST VERSIONS of the Futurama (above) had 'Resonet' on the scratchplate,

'Grazioso' on the headstock. Each of the three switches turns a pickup on and off.

the electric guitar action and launched two- and four-pickup solidbody models in 1958. These visually arresting guitars boasted banks of pushbuttons and chromed panels plus abundant sparkle and pearloid plastic – all unsurprisingly appropriate in view of their accordion-derived ancestry. Such exercises in excess even fared well in the US where Hagstroms bore the Goya brandname.

Similar cosmetics would also adorn the offerings from contemporary guitar makers in Italy, as that country countered the dwindling appeal of the accordion by turning to the increasingly popular electric guitar. East Germany and Holland were perhaps less obvious sources, but they too turned out assorted oddballs and budget boxes in the 1950s, while UK makers, although still small in number and size, had not been idle.

Some traditional British brands like Abbott-Victor chose to stay safely staid, but the long-established Grimshaw

company adopted a more adventurous attitude. Their Short-Scale Deluxe model ventured into new stylistic territory, marrying American influences to distinctly English eccentricity. The result was an electric archtop ideal for UK rockers, with teardrop soundholes, curving control panel and innovative six-coil twin pickups. Little wonder that modern-minded players such as Bruce Welch, Joe Brown and Alvin Lee appreciated these advanced-style attributes.

There were virtually no British-built solidbody guitars in the 1950s until Burns-Weill debuted late in the decade. This alliance of Jim Burns and Henry Weill produced a line of solid oddities, some featuring very daring design ideas. In contrast, their Fenton model was afflicted by a small body similar to that found on Japanese electrics, although this was not by accident or coincidence but merely a compliance with UK distributors' requests that Burns-Weill should copy their Far Eastern competitors in terms of size

and shape – a neat twist on future trends. This then was the somewhat restricted electric guitar scene in Britain, until the time when guitarists gained the ultimate freedom of choice. By November 1959 the first official imports of American instruments since the import ban hit UK shores – and the British guitar business would never be the same again. Such competition obviously hit hard at the hitherto insular established brands, but the industry was expanding rapidly as demand for affordable beginner instruments increased in ratio. In the face of this new, long awaited, ultra-attractive opposition, many makers survived and even flourished, often because they were able still to compete on price advantage if not quality.

British guitarists finally had all the options – from basic to best, from frugal to flamboyant – and the future looked rosy for all, manufacturers and music makers alike. The beatboom had begun. ■ PAUL DAY

The 1950s was a truly influential era for rock'n'roll as we know it today. Not only were the first American guitarists emerging but the likes of Joe Brown, Hank Marvin and Bert Weedon were beginning to influence their fellow British players. To illustrate that fact, when Thames TV did a This Is Your Life programme with Weedon as the subject, the assembled audience included a roll-call of famous guitarists headed by Eric Clapton and Brian May.

The birth of the Fender Telecaster in 1948 sowed the seeds of a musical revolution. Now that the solid-bodied electric guitar was a reality, it wouldn't be long before the first guitar heroes arrived to write their names in history.

With Elvis Presley the biggest name in rock'n'roll, it followed that his guitarist should be the man most aspiring six-stringers looked to for inspiration. Scotty Moore was that individual, and it's a tribute to his influence that Alvin Lee, a major UK guitar hero with his band Ten Years After, regards recording with Moore in 2003 as one of the highlights of his life.

"I joined the Elvis Presley Fan Club just to get a photo of Scotty Moore and his guitar," he revealed. "Like a lot of Nashville guys he's incredibly modest, and a lovely man as well. He's a very mellow dude, and some of those early solos are classics: they stand up as songs in their own right. You can actually sing them. To be honest, just to sit with the guy was a privilege: I said show me this solo, that solo…taking advantage of the situation, both being in the studio with guitars in our hands. It was a schoolboy's dream come true."

Moore's stint with Elvis started in 1954 as part of a bass-less trio with drummer DJ Fontana, Presley himself supplying rhythm guitar. The recordings made by Presley and Moore in the Sun Studios (a 'hole in the wall' measuring barely ten metres by six) were clearly groundbreaking, and all the more impressive when you consider Sam Phillips' equipment list ran to no further than five microphones, a mixer and two tape recorders with echo units attached. It was that tape echo that was the key to the so-called 'Sun sound', adding a depth and distance to Elvis's first singles. Then RCA bought out his contract…after which Phillips continued with Johnny Cash, Jerry Lee Lewis and Carl Perkins.

One of Sun's soon-to-be-developed trademarks was a solid bedrock of sound supplied by a combination of amplified double bass and drums which would survive the poor pressing quality of early singles. The bass strings would sometimes even be whacked with a drumstick rather than plucked with fingers to emphasise the rhythm. The result was overlaid with the sparse but clear sound of the guitar and, of course, a distinctive vocal. It's hard to remember any Sun performer whose style was anything less than unique – but, then, they were writing on a blank page of history.

The Sun Studios on 706 Union Avenue became a National Historic Landmark in 2003, the year Sam Phillips died. "The history and culture of this little studio often reflected the mood of America through music," said Secretary of the Interior Gale A. Norton. "It was a popular hub for the recording of diverse musical styles and traditions that transcended several decades. National historic landmarks are our country's most important places that illustrate our American story. It would be impossible for us to tell the story of rock'n'roll in America without Sam Phillips and Sun Records."

Scotty Moore continued to add echo to his guitar sound after Presley's switch to major label RCA, improvising where necessary. He recorded his utterly memorable part for the chart-topping 'Heartbreak Hotel' by

BERT WEEDON became the first guitarist to break the Top 40 in Britain, with 'Guitar Boogie Shuffle', in 1959. His teaching books, including 'Play In A Day', had a tremendous influence.

SCOTTY MOORE was Presley's first manager and guitarist. He recorded with the King throughout the fifties, and was an undoubted influence on thousands of young rock'n'roll guitar players.

LES PAUL 'How High The Moon' 1951
"The Beatles used to start out gigs with the opening riffs from 'How High The Moon'. Everybody was trying to be a Les Paul clone in those days." That testimony from (Sir) Paul McCartney is just one reason why Les Paul should be remembered for more than just his signature Gibson guitar. This was the sound of the future, as another notable bassist agrees. "Les Paul was the first person to turn me on to the guitar," said one-time Rolling Stone Bill Wyman. "'How High The Moon' had terrific verve, proof at last that pop could provide stylish, instrumental inventiveness."

T-BONE WALKER
'I Walked Away' c1952
Aaron Thibeaux 'T-Bone' Walker lived and played in Texas until his late thirties, but it wasn't until he moved to California in 1947 that he started having much success. His influence ranged from BB King through Buddy Guy to Stevie Ray Vaughan and beyond. The impact of Walker's eloquent single-string work is felt in the blues up to the present day, and this track illustrates why.

ELVIS hit the music world like a tidal wave – upsetting traditionalists, some of whom believed his brand of music could turn teenagers into "devil worshippers, stimulate self-expression through sex, provoke lawlessness, impair nervous stability and destroy the sanctity of marriage." Elvis fans said, "Bring it on!"

CHUCK BERRY made a trademark out of the Gibson blond ES-350T, which originated in the 1950s. Some commentators regard Berry as arguably the most influential guitarist and songwriter of the entire rock genre.

ELVIS PRESLEY 'That's All Right' 1954

Any of Presley's first hits could be cited as milestones, but this began as a studio knockabout between Scotty Moore, Bill Black and Elvis that producer Sam Phillips saw the potential of. "I don't know what it is you're doing but just keep on doing it," he gasped as he reached for the record button, while a second treatment of the number had him expostulating: "God, they're gonna run us right outta town when they hear this." Backed with rocked-up bluegrass favourite 'Blue Moon Of Kentucky', this Arthur Crudup composition would light the blue touch paper for a generational explosion.

together at the somewhat rudimentary Chess Recording Studios in Chicago. He recalled in his autobiography that "each musician had one mike excepting the drummer, who had three. I had one for my guitar and one for my vocal. There was a stack of throw rugs, a giant slow-turning ceiling fan and two long fluorescent lights over a linoleum tile floor. Leonard Chess was the engineer and operated the Ampex 403 quarter-inch monaural tape recorder. We watched him through the control-room window instructing us with signs and hand waving to start or stop the music."

All basic stuff, but an arrangement that came up with some classic sides. Indeed, the studio at 2120 S Michigan Avenue was also the creative home for the likes of Muddy Waters, Willie Dixon and Howlin' Wolf between 1957 and 1967. The studio's notoriety also attracted other musicians, including the Rolling Stones, Fleetwood Mac and the Yardbirds in the 1960s. It was designated a Chicago Landmark in 1992.

If the guitar was the leading instrument in rock'n'roll, then Duane Eddy was arguably the leading instrumentalist. His style of playing the melody line on the bass strings of his semi-acoustic Gretsch was unique, but it was the studio know-how of Lee Hazlewood, owner of the Audio Recording Studio in Arizona, that ensured Eddy stamped his distinctive mark on rock.

Having recorded Eddy's debut hit 'Movin'N'Groovin", Hazlewood discovered when he took the tape from his own sparsely equipped studio to Goldstar in Hollywood that he could achieve a sound with a deeper, longer echo by halving the speed of the tape. The addition of an abrasive sax solo by Plas Johnson cemented the track's hit status.

Recording in the pre-rock era had been a relatively simple affair: jazz was cut 'live' in the studio onto acetate discs using perhaps a couple of strategically placed microphones, any mistakes dictating the whole song be recorded again. The advent of the reel-to-reel tape recorder allowed mistakes to be cut out and the tape 'spliced' back together. Just as importantly, there was the

putting his amplifier at one end of a hallway at the RCA building and the microphone at the other. His choice of guitar was a Gibson ES-295 for the early Sun sessions and, from 1957, a Super 400 CES. Surprisingly, perhaps, he never built on his career with Elvis and slid from the limelight as Presley joined the US Army and, on his return, set his sights on the silver screen.

Elvis's drafting in 1958 stopped his runaway train in its tracks, or at least shunted it into the sidings for a couple of years. And it should come as no surprise that Rick Nelson, Elvis's intended 'replacement', boasted a guitar-player to rival the King's in James Burton. Ironically, Burton would take Moore's place at Presley's shoulder when he finally kicked Hollywood into touch in 1968 and returned to the concert stage. However, it was Burton's work a decade earlier that had put him in line for the job.

Burton's finger-picking bridged Country and R&B styles and, combined with his concise soloing style, was ideally suited to the pop single format and much copied by others. His choice of guitar was the Fender Telecaster, a workhorse instrument with just two pick-ups and not offering a great deal of variation. Just like Burton, though, it was right for the job.

Interestingly, even though Ricky Nelson dropped the 'y' and, as Rick Nelson, went on to become a 1970s country-rock pioneer, everybody still remembered his breakthrough hits. So in 1985 he took a step back in time, re-cutting his early rock'n'roll classics with the benefit of modern technology, producer Jimmie Haskell and vocal backing group the Jordanaires he'd shared with Presley. "I'd tried to play the old songs many different ways," he said, "but it's kind of nice to go back to the sound I started with."

Yet as Haskell revealed it wasn't quite as easy as that. "Ricky, with all his brilliance, mistakenly thought that, to accomplish the original, we should do it the way we recorded it in the old days." Nelson had in fact found a studio in North Hollywood run by surf-punk band the Unknown and equipped with a three-track recorder, an old-fashioned tube console and a tape echo. Unfortunately the expertise needed to get the most out of the equipment appeared to be absent, and Haskell had to be brought in to rescue the project using contemporary technology. (Nelsons' death at the end of 1985 in an air crash made these his last recordings.)

Chuck Berry's classic slices of teenage angst came

Written by bass player and producer Willie Dixon, as were so many Chess hits of the time, the song was recorded twice in '52 and '54, the second time with its composer on string bass. UK bandleader Chris Barber heard it and persuaded Waters to tour the UK in 1958 – the start of a chain of events that would lead to the formation of the Rolling Stones, not to mention naming Long John Baldry's backing group, the Hoochie Coochie Men. File under influential.....

DUANE EDDY focused attention on his unique guitar sound with the album 'The "Twangs" The "Thang"' released in 1959.

DUANE EDDY developed his "twangy" sound by tuning his normal six-string guitar down an octave and playing melody on his bass rather than top strings. With raunchy raw solos of Rebels backing group members Steve Douglas and Jim Horn, and the rebel yells of Ben De Moto, the overall effect was a potent blend of rock'n'roll, R&B and Southern States' influences.

LES PAUL created the Gibson Les Paul model guitar beloved by countless musicians while in hospital in 1941 recovering from a car crash. In the fifties, he and then-wife Mary Ford notched up four million-sellers – 'Mockin' Bird Hill', 'How High the Moon', 'The World Is Waiting For The Sunrise', and 'Vaya Con Dios'.

LES PAUL was rightly proud of the range of acoustic and solid body guitars he developed with Gibson. He (with his wife and TV show) was a major factor in the guitar overtaking the saxophone in popularity among musicians in the early 1950s. He later became a much-in-demand tutor.

GENE VINCENT (second from the left) was a charismatic musician whose career was painfully short. He recorded some classic tracks at Capitol Studios, particularly in the fifties, while his brief road career the Blue Caps was regarded as the wildest rock'n'roll act on and off stage.

possibility of overdubbing another instrument without erasing the original recording: hence a backing track could be recorded and a guitar solo superimposed upon it. Unlike the live environment, this could be tried again and again until a satisfactory result was achieved. Last but not least, the tape could continue to roll for its complete length rather than recording being restricted by the length of the gramophone disc: thus an informal spontaneity could yield better results.

It was a guitarist, Les Paul, who had created the first working multi-track recorder, multiple recording heads allowing the width of the tape to be divided between instruments or microphones. He used this to make a chorus of then-wife Mary Ford's voice and filled the gaps

with his overdubbed country-jazz licks. Later in the decade, he began developing the concept of sound-on-sound recording, overdubbing part after part on a 78 rpm record-cutting machine, and later on magnetic tape. Virtually all popular music recorded since has been made with the methods he developed. Jimmy Page of Led Zeppelin was a major Les Paul fan and it's no coincidence that Zeppelin's albums feature layer upon layer of overdubbed, multi-tracked guitars.

The next innovation to work with the tape recorder was the mixing desk, which would be used by the producer and engineer to mix and balance the input of the microphones to produce what was still then a mono (monaural) recording.

As with all innovations, however, these advances were not universally hailed as progress. Multi-tracking arguably downgraded the importance of instrumental virtuosity – what was the world coming to if you could play a solo until you got it right? Technically inferior musicians could have their deficiencies masked, but as it transpired this threw the doors open for a wider range of performer and was much to rock'n'roll's benefit.

Much of the more innovative guitar music of the 1950s was created by independent labels in small studios rather than by the so-called 'majors'. The big labels' recording facilities might have been impressive, but the ability to get the best out of the big bands and orchestras of the time didn't necessarily do much for small rock'n'roll combos who could easily get lost. Gene Vincent found this when he was forced to use the Capitol Tower in Hollywood after rival label Decca bought his usual recording venue, Bradley's Barn in Nashville.

Whereas producer Owen Bradley had recorded his vocals in the hallway, the musicians in the small studio

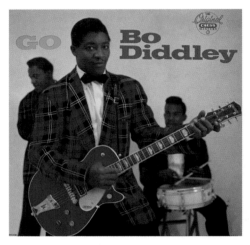

BO DIDDLEY 'Bo Diddley' 1955
The Bo Diddley beat is a foundation stone of rock'n'roll, borrowed by such unlikely bedfellows as Buddy Holly, the Rolling Stones and the Police. This was Diddley's first single, coupled with the equally impressive, harmonica-driven 'I'm a Man', and fused futuristic tremolo guitar to a nursery-rhyme lyric. "I got the name Bo Diddley from the kids in grammar school," said the former Ellas McDaniel, "and the name and the beat go together. I had the name, and then I made the beat with it. I came up with that beat." No-one's arguing…

BILL HALEY'S *classic single 'Rock Around The Clock' (arguably the all-time anthem of rock music – and its biggest and most consistent selling single with sales far exceeding 20 million) triggered off the rock'n'roll revolution when it was featured in the 1955 movie 'The Blackboard Jungle'.*

BUDDY HOLLY *impressed musicians on his tours from Australia to the UK: they hailed his guitar style and the then little known Fender Stratocaster which, together with his horn-rimmed glasses, became his trademark.*

being protected from inter-microphone leakage by circular baffles, Vincent and his Blue Caps were dwarfed by the opulent Capitol studio: the sound's focus was lost, while the engineers could not cope with the volume. Small was clearly better in cases like this.

Bill Haley recorded in a converted New York ballroom called the Pythian Temple, a former live music venue that illustrated the difficulties artists of the era faced. Whereas proper studios had sound-deadening insulation on the walls to avoid reflection, there was little attempt to dampen the room's natural acoustics. Yet producer Milt Gabler managed to use several of the Temple's features to his advantage. "We put drapes on the balcony to kill the sound," he revealed, "and recorded the bands on the stage because the ceiling there would be lower behind them and act as a natural shell." Haley would stand on the dance floor looking up at his band on the four-foot-high stage, singing towards them rather than away as in live performance. Another trick Gabler employed was to place a mic out further in the room to pick up some natural reverb "so that the sound would just 'crack'; you'd get that edgy ambience."

The death of Buddy Holly in the infamous plane crash of 1959 robbed the world of not only a gifted singer-songwriter but a highly underrated guitarist. His best work was done with producer and co-songwriter Norman Petty in the studio that was constructed in New Mexico. Petty's studio techniques ranged from the sublime – vocal and instrumental double-tracking on Holly's 'Words Of Love' – to the unconventional but effective hands-on-knees percussion effect on the same artist's 'Everyday'. After Holly's death Petty would overdub new backings onto demo tapes, creating commercial records from Buddy's primitive song sketches – another example of how studio technology could be used.

Down in New Orleans the J&M studio run by Cosimo Matassa was turning out records with a sound every bit as distinctive as Sun in its own rhythm and blues-orientated way. As with Sun, a limited range of equipment used to its utmost resulted in a distinctive sound, reinforced by a riffing style that found instruments doubling up in unison. Such regional variations would struggle to outlast the 1950s, however, as music increasingly sought to run with the cutting edge of sound recording.

Many innovations in sound occurred quite by accident: for instance, Rock'n'Roll Trio guitarist Paul Burlison accidentally dropped his amp and knocked a 'tube' loose (this was, of course, in the pre-transistorised era). The resulting fuzzy, distorted tone added to the musical mystique and originality of his Telecaster-playing. "Whenever we wanted that fuzz sound," Burlison remembered, "I simply pulled a tube loose." However it came about, the fuzz sound revolutionised both rockabilly and rock'n'roll music – even though it usually came in the shape of an effects pedal!

Not that this 'jiggery-pokery' pleased Bert Weedon, Britain's premier guitarist who'd served his apprenticeship in the big-band era: "After practising so hard to achieve a good pure tone it was a bit of a bringdown to play some of the things that were asked of me," said the man whose session-man solos enlivened discs by Tommy Steele, Marty Wilde and Terry Dene. "However I always try to give the public what it wants – and if it wants a clangy guitar, then I'll oblige!"

As production techniques became more sophisticated, a divide naturally occurred between live performance and recorded music. The raw live impact of rock'n'roll was inevitably diluted as the likes of Buddy Holly and the Everly Brothers concentrated on perfecting their sound with a relative disregard of stage image. Certainly, the post-Elvis wave couldn't hope (and mainly didn't try) to emulate the King's impact.

The Nashville sound which still exists today can be traced back to 1954, when producer Owen Bradley was

JOHNNY BURNETTE'S backing group The Rock 'n Roll Trio created an innovative fuzzy, distorted tone – by accident, when guitarist Paul Burlison knocked a "tube" loose on his Telecaster.

BERT WEEDON wasn't what anyone would call the quintessential rock guitarist. He was definitely of the pre-Presley age. But his playing talent was acknowledged by his peers, albeit mainly in the UK, and his influence on wannabe rockers of the fifties was tremendous.

BERT WEEDON definitely proved an exception to the old saying, "Those who can, do; those who can't, teach…". He showed with his books that he could and did teach a generation of rock guitarists. And with his fingers he showed he could perform, on stage, or as a recording session musician.

THE ROCK 'N'ROLL TRIO 'Train Kept A-Rollin' 1956 Talented singing brothers Johnny and Dorsey Burnette were the supposed stars of the Rock'n'Roll Trio, who appeared on US TV's famed Ted Mack's 'Amateur Hour' several times during 1956, winning each time. Yet when they secured a recording contract with Coral Records and entered the studio, it was guitarist Paul Burlison, the man who made up the numbers, who proved their secret weapon. Burlison had found a 78 rpm record of Tiny Bradshaw's 'Train Kept A Rollin' in a Nashville record store. The trio's version with its rough, raw edge inspired the Yardbirds, Aerosmith and others to take it to a new generation.

BUDDY HOLLY 'Peggy Sue' 1957 This song, featuring coruscating Stratocaster runs from its author, was initially titled 'Cindy Lou', but Crickets drummer Jerry Allison had a crush on a girl named Peggy Sue and convinced Buddy to change the title just before the recording session. The rest is history. When Holly was posthumously awarded a Grammy for Lifetime Achievement, the presenter proclaimed 'Peggy Sue' "the first international rock anthem", while the Rock'n'Roll Hall of Fame honoured the song as "one of the most popular and influential rock classics".

MICKEY & SYLVIA 'Love Is Strange' 1957 Best known bizarrely for its inclusion on the 'Dirty Dancing' soundtrack over two decades after its release, 'Love Is Strange' had meanwhile inspired countless guitarists. Although the duo recorded together as late as 1965, they never approached the Top 20 again, which may be to do with the fact that Bo Diddley reputedly wrote this tune for them under an alias.

CLIFF RICHARD, seen with The Shadows, not long after he had recorded 'Move It', his first single, produced with session musicians, and now regarded as Britain's first rock'n'roll record. Richard's career seems as if it will never end; he has recorded chart hits in every decade since it began.

CHUCK BERRY 'Johnny B Goode' 1958

This was an autobiographical song from the master. "My mother repeatedly said I'd be a millionaire one day...Johnny is more or less myself," claims Berry in his autobiography. Created with the aid of his semi-acoustic Gibson, it has entered space on Voyager 1 thanks to Dr Carl Sagan, inspired a film 'Go Johnny Go' and a follow-up song 'Bye Bye Johnny', yet remains the quintessential Berry creation. The guitar introduction has been copied a thousand times, yet never with quite the same effect.

DUANE EDDY 'Rebel Rouser' 1958

As with most of Duane Eddy's hits, 'Rebel Rouser' was assisted by a fair degree of studio trickery. His distinctive guitar was recorded in Arizona with a miked-up grain silo acting as a massive echo chamber. As well as overdubbing a sax in a Hollywood studio, producer Lee Hazlewood added handclaps and 'rebel yells', crediting the result to 'Duane Eddy, his Twangy Guitar and the Rebels'. It shot to Number 6 (19 in Britain) and established the instrumental as a recognised pop genre.

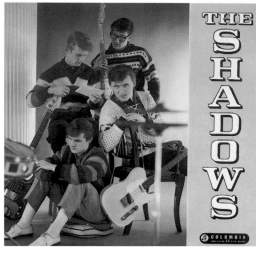

CLIFF RICHARD 'Move It' 1958

Cliff Richard's first hit single was cut at Abbey Road in July 1958 with session guitarist Ernie Shear shadowing Ian Samwell, Cliff's first guitarist. At this stage his backing band were known as the Drifters (soon to be renamed due to the more famous US R&B vocal group) and Hank Marvin had yet to be recruited. Samwell's composition was originally scheduled to be the B-side, but the results were so encouraging the disc was flipped before release. Samwell would bow out in October to concentrate on songwriting, but never bettered this.

TOMMY STEELE had a career, albeit brief, in the rock music business, albeit soft rock, before ever he cared a name for himself as an all-round musical entertainer and movie star. In the fifties he showed he could play a bit, although some of his recordings were much the better for having Bert Weedon and his Hofner on side as a session guitarist.

ROCK with TOMMY STEELE

DECCA'S DYNAMIC RECORDING STAR singing his best sellers — "Rock with the Caveman", "Doomsday Rock" and "Singing the Blues".

Presented by HAROLD FIELDING

ALL NEXT WEEK!
FINSBURY PARK EMPIRE

Twice Nightly at 6.25 & 8.40 p.m.
...e's Great, Great, Great ".
...er Robertson, 'Daily Sketch'

Chet Atkins GUITAR METHOD In Diagrams and Notes

CHET ATKINS was another tutor/player who, during the fifties, was the best known (some say the best) guitarist on the Country scene, especially in Nashville studio sessions. Atkins was one of the prime movers in graduating the guitar as merely a chordal instrument backing-up the vocal, to the main sound on many recordings.

EDDIE COCHRAN 'C'mon Everybody' 1958

Along with 'Summertime Blues', this is the greatest moment from a man whose star blazed all too briefly prior to his fatal road crash in 1960. Both songs were written by Cochran and mentor, manager and co-writer Jerry Capehart, and both saw Eddie playing the Gretsch semi-acoustic with a Gibson pickup and added Bigsby tremolo that gave him such a distinctive sound. It was his third and last US Top 40 hit.

CHAMPS 'Tequila' 1958

One of today's best-selling mobile phone ringtones, this infuriatingly catchy instrumental written by pianist Danny Flores (credited as Chuck Rio) topped the US chart in 1958. Guitarist Dave Burgess recorded it as a novelty B-side to one of his releases, but liked the result so much he invented a group and released it under the nickname of singing cowboy Gene Autry's horse, Champion! Glen Campbell and duo Seals and Crofts passed through the Champs' ever-changing ranks and, though too late to play on the recording, undoubtedly pounded out the riff many times.

CHAN ROMERO 'Hippy Hippy Shake' 1959
Chan Romero's electrifying Latino rock'n'roll smash influenced the Beatles (whose version appears on 'Live At The BBC') and was a Top 3 hit for fellow Merseybeaters the Swinging Blue Jeans some five years after Chan recorded it. Chan was inspired by the late, great Ritchie Valens and was on his recording, accompanied by the same studio musicians that recorded with Valens, most notably Rene Hall who played both lead guitar and six-string bass. The track, which lasted just one minute and 43 seconds, has since appeared on several film soundtracks.

JOHNNY KIDD & THE PIRATES 'Please Don't Touch' 1959
Most people recall Mick Green as the Pirates' lead guitarist but it was future Tornados member Alan Caddy who did the business (with Tony Doherty on rhythm) on a 1959 recording that was still getting covered over two decades later when Girlschool took it back to the charts. Kidd (alias Freddie Heath) co-wrote the song at age 18, too. It deserves more than to be overshadowed by the bigger hit 'Shakin' All Over' that followed, though he penned that too.

BERT WEEDON 'Guitar Boogie Shuffle' 1959
After 25 years in the business helping out on other people's records, Bert Weedon, the most influential British player of the era, finally had a hit of his own with this cover version of a US single by the Virtues. It entered the charts in May 1959, rose to Number 10 and was the biggest of his eight chart entries.

JOE BROWN 'People Gotta Talk' 1959
It would be the following decade before Brown would become a UK hit-parade regular, cashing in on his 'cheeky chappie' persona, but his first releases were more rock-orientated as befitted the leader of the backing band on TV's 'Boy Meets Girls'. "I'd like to have made it with a rock number," he admitted after eventually finding success with 1962's singalong 'Picture Of You', "but if this new style is all right with the fans then it's all right with me." Nevertheless, it's 'People Gotta Talk' that kicks off the Joe Brown CD anthologies.

LONNIE DONEGAN'S 'Rock Island Line' was a hit in the US and UK. He came from skiffle in the early fifties, but endured as a fine road and recording star for many decades.

LINK WRAY & HIS RAYMEN 'Rumble' 1958
It's arguable that Link Wray invented heavy metal with this 1958 million-seller, an intense, moody guitar instrumental that successfully captured the feel of a gang fight. Wray understood the virtues of simplicity and the track has influenced everyone from the Kinks to PJ Harvey. Interestingly, the demo did not impress Cadence label boss Archie Bleyer, whose teenage daughter insisted he release it, and the result was a Number 16 'Billboard' chart hit. 'Rumble' also made history as the only instrumental ever to be banned by radio for being too suggestive!

CARL PERKINS 'Blue Suede Shoes' 1956
Though many remember it as a Presley hit, fellow Sun records singer and songwriter Perkins enjoyed his only UK Top 10 success with a track that summed up his sharp guitar-playing and equally incisive lyrics. A bad car crash in 1956 stalled his career Stateside, and Elvis' version in 'GI Blues' would become the standard for many, but his performance at an all-star concert in 1985, alongside Beatles Starr and Harrison as well as Eric Clapton, attested to the impact this song made in its writer's hands.

SANTO & JOHNNY 'Sleep Walk' 1959
The duo of Santo Farina (steel guitar) and brother Johnny (rhythm guitar) penned this Hawaiian-flavoured ditty with help from sister Ann. Yet the family hailed from un-sunny Brooklyn! The recording was the third release (and first hit) for the Canadian-American label and the last US Number 1 instrumental of the 1950s. It also helped inspire Fleetwood Mac's 1968 chart-topper, 'Albatross': "I thought that was so unique," said an impressed Peter Green.

asked by Decca to build a new studio on 16th Avenue, away from the built-up downtown area. This took the form of an extension to an existing house on a residential street – and set the trend to such an extent that the street is now known as Music Row, the Columbia office block having been built around the (now museum-piece) studio.

Chet Atkins, a virtuoso guitarist, also had a major effect on country's fast-evolving sound. He had been working part time as an A&R assistant for RCA since 1952 and was appointed to run its new Nashville studio in 1957. Along with Bradley, he softened and sweetened the raw hillbilly edge of country music, facilitating its wider public acceptance. Mellow strings and vocal choruses were added, and the result was eventually dubbed the Nashville Sound.

The industry standard microphone of the 1950s was the Neumann U47. This was the first switchable-pattern condenser microphone able to switch between cardioid and omnidirectional patterns and was so distinctive that Mercury Records touted it as its 'Living Presence' microphone, even putting pictures of it on record covers.

Many notable producers cut their studio teeth in the 1950s, including Sir George Martin. His speciality before The Beatles, however, was comedy recordings! Joe Meek also came to fame in the 1960s; he had worked as a recording engineer at IBC studios since 1953. There he engineered hits for the likes of Acker Bilk, Lonnie Donegan and Petula Clark. Meek was soon recognised as

an expert in the field of sound balance, an essential skill in these days of one and two-track tape recording.

In 1956 when recording jazz trumpeter Humphrey Lyttleton, Meek put the microphones closer to the drums to give them more impact and, in so doing, distorted the sound of the piano. Lyttleton, hearing 'Bad Penny Blues' for the first time, disliked it, but later admitted that the gimmick helped it become a Top 20 hit. The innovative Meek would use many such techniques with the Tornados (of 'Telstar' fame) and other acts in the next decade.

The end of the 1950s saw the dawn of the stereo age, after which things would never be the same again. The concept was to record sound sources separately with the intention of creating a separation of the instruments that mimicked how the listener experienced a live performance. Atlantic were first to bite the bullet, others following suit during 1958 and 1959. While both mono and stereo recordings would be issued for some years yet, mono singles often considered to sound better on radio, the new innovation would be the choice for LPs by the mid 1960s.

The end of the decade saw Atlantic in possession of the world's first eight-track recording gear – and while this would take time to become industry standard (The Beatles famously using two four-tracks synced together), it spelled the end of the small, cheap and ultimately creative recording studio. Things would never be the same – or arguably as exciting – again.

60s

Britain was the base for the guitar-fuelled beat group boom of the 1960s. Here, XTC guitarist Dave Gregory offers an insider's view of the decade.

By the dawn of the 1960s the guitar had become the must-have accessory for all British teenage boys with fire in their bellies and rhythm in their bones. Few would be capable of mastering more than a handful of basic chords, but back then little more was necessary. The pop songs of the day were undemanding in content, unsophisticated in composition. The guitar not only provided the perfect accompaniment to the singing voice, but lent the player a certain romantic intrigue into the bargain.

At the same time, America's rock'n'roll boom was a far more serious affair. Its effect was slowly but surely filtering through to the UK with hit records by Elvis Presley, Buddy Holly, Ricky Nelson, The Everly Brothers and Duane Eddy, to name but a few. At the heart of these songs, to a greater or lesser degree, was an electric guitar. As a result, guitar students soon began seeking ways to 'electrify' their acoustic archtops and Spanish guitars, sometimes attaching crude magnetic pickups to their instruments, often wired optimistically through father's radio set. British youth was finding its voice too, even if it was a little croaky.

HANK MARVIN sports specs and Strat in Shads, '63-style.

Not until 1958 had a British company produced an amplifier equal to the task of flattering the sound of these primitive electric guitars and broadcasting it at a level compatible for use among drum kits and brass instruments. The Vox AC-15, all 15 watts of it, had become the first purpose-built guitar amplifier in the UK.

By 1960 Cliff Richard and The Shadows were the nation's pop darlings. While the girls screamed, the boys were spellbound by The Shadows' leader, guitarist Hank B. Marvin. He'd borrowed Buddy Holly's image wholesale, recently completing the ensemble with a brand new Fender Stratocaster guitar... just like Buddy's, but in a glamorous red finish. Specially imported from the US by his boss Cliff, Hank's Strat was the first of its type in the country, and bore little resemblance visually or sonically to anything currently available in England. It would play a large part in transforming its handler into the first British Guitar Hero before the year was out.

Hank was special because he could actually play the guitar properly, at a time when few English rock'n'rollers could. He used his Stratocaster, a Meazzi echo unit, and a newly-acquired Vox AC-30 Twin amplifier. This was double the power of the AC-15 and had been specially commissioned by The Shadows to cope with the larger theatres they were now playing. With this set-up Hank produced a warm, clear sound coloured further by his deft use of the Strat's 'Synchronized Tremolo' vibrato system. Together with tape echo and reverb, as well as another feature of the Vox amplifiers, valve tremolo, which added a throbbing pulse to the sound of the guitar, this was virtually the full range of effects, or gimmicks, available to electric guitarists in the early 1960s. But then the instrument itself was still a novelty. It would be some years before it was taken seriously as a credible musical force.

In June 1960 Johnny Kidd & The Pirates entered the UK charts with 'Shakin All Over', arguably the first bona fide home-grown British rock'n'roll hit of the decade. The record created quite a stir among guitar nuts, its chiming hook complemented by a simple staccato bass-and-guitar riff three octaves apart. Each chorus was launched with a solo E-minor triad, guitarist Joe Moretti frantically jerking the instrument's tremolo arm. Quivers down the backbone! The record raced to number two in Britain.

Within a month The Shadows scored their first solo number one UK hit with an instrumental tune called 'Apache'. It sold a million copies and, consequently, almost as many electric guitars. Simple in construction, its tune fitted perfectly the drums/bass/rhythm-guitar/lead-guitar format that constituted the standard group line-up of the day. Youth clubs and village halls up and down Britain throbbed to the sounds of would-be Pirates and Hank-alikes negotiating their way around their heroes' tunes. Wild, cool, but most importantly easy to play, these two records did more than most to instigate a national craze among the young to form beat groups, giving birth to what would eventually become a massive industry as demand snowballed for modern musical equipment.

Despite the continuing growth of the pop business, few real advances had been made since the 1950s either in songwriting, recording or playing standards. The Beatles arrived and changed everything. Not because they were particularly gifted as instrumentalists – indeed, they were a league or two below The Shadows in that respect – but because they played and sang their own brilliantly innovative songs with a joyful, energetic exuberance never before heard in a British group. Their second single 'Please Please Me' shot into the UK charts in the freezing January of 1963 and heralded the arrival of the first significant British musical trend of the 1960s, Merseybeat. A slew of talented groups and singers, mainly from The Beatles' home town of Liverpool in the north of England, would light up the charts in the coming year with inventive new songs performed with a refreshing vigour and vitality.

THE SHADOWS' first album, 1961, with borrowed Tele and (just visible) that red Strat.

To be fair, Merseybeat did little to advance the technical standards of guitar playing, other than to instil a more dynamic and energetic attitude in the delivery. The Beatles' songs, on the other hand, introduced a whole new way of thinking in terms of chord structures. Suddenly every group wanted to write their own songs, which would involve a greater knowledge of chord shapes, inversions and progressions. Lennon and McCartney were constantly tossing in exotic-sounding chords such as sixths, major sevenths, augmenteds and diminisheds, many of which were a far cry from the standard three- and four-chord tricks around which most pop tunes had hitherto been based.

Meanwhile, something else was stirring in the south of England. With the country now firmly in the grip of Beatlemania, potential rivals had sprung from the London suburbs. An underground R&B band, The Rolling Stones, were making serious waves in the pubs and clubs of the metropolis and home counties with their gritty alternative to mop-top pop. Where The Beatles' music had its roots in everything from Carl Perkins and Gene Vincent through Little Richard to Buddy Holly and Roy Orbison, the Stones' influences included Muddy Waters, Howlin' Wolf, Jimmy Reed, Bo Diddley and Chuck Berry – American R&B acts and Chicago blues artists whose basic sound was built on raw, unpolished guitar playing.

Ironically, it would take a Beatle song to break the Stones. In October 1963 they covered a track specially written for them by Lennon and McCartney, 'I Wanna Be Your Man'. With loud, crudely-recorded, distorted guitars, incorporating a searing solo executed with a bottle-neck slide (the first on a UK single), the record gatecrashed the UK Top 20 at the end of November. British R&B had arrived. Youngsters everywhere were thrilled. Parents were suitably annoyed.

The Rolling Stones continued to gather momentum during 1964 thanks to some dynamic singles and a tremendous debut

SHEET MUSIC for She Loves You inexplicably came in the guitar-unfriendly key of E-flat.

LP that crystalised the current state of alternative British pop as hard-edged R&B with a heavy beat and an arrogant swagger. Guitars were mixed well to the fore, and the record celebrated Keith Richards' love of Chuck Berry's playing, a bluesy, rocking style characterised by much string-bending. This involved pushing the strings sideways, across the fret, to alter the pitch – no mean feat as the strings of the day were comparatively heavy-gauged, often with a wound G, sometimes wrapped with distinctly player-unfriendly plastic tape. Even so, aspiring soloists realised that, once mastered, this technique could add much excitement to a performance, particularly if the amplifier was overdriven slightly to distort the sound.

The Beatles returned to the UK from their first triumphant US visit in late February 1964 and brought with them an important new element to their sound. George Harrison had taken delivery of a new electric 12-string guitar from the Rickenbacker company. While not the first electric 12 ever

arresting arpeggiated solo guitar introduction that traced a brooding Am/C/D/F/Am/E/Am chord sequence. The intricacies of the performance were dissected by guitar students the world over. A little more difficult than the usual faux-Chuck Berry double-stops and reckless neck mangling, this called for a degree of accuracy with the picking hand. If you could hack it, you'd arrived! Even today the riff still occupies a place, somewhere around stage three, in the great 12-Step Master-The-Guitar programme.

The following month, Dave Berry released 'The Crying Game' which featured a guitar effect that many still believe to be an early example of wah-wah. In fact, the 'crying' effect was created with a footpedal dating from the late 1950s. Manufactured by Rowe Industries in the US, the DeArmond Volume & Tone pedal would rock vertically to raise or lower the volume, and from side to side to alter the tone. Neat footwork combining both effects could pay extraordinary

LIVERPOOL 1964: the sheer joy of being in a pop group.

produced, it was nonetheless only the second or third of its type made by Rickenbacker and had a unique sound – almost like a blend of harpsichord, guitar and piano. Its lower four strings were paired with a second set tuned one octave higher, while the top E and B strings were doubled in unison – standard stringing for 12-string guitars, except that the heavier of the octave pairs was on the 'top', not the 'bottom' (from the player's view). The group featured it on their new single 'Can't Buy Me Love', but it was the b-side, 'You Can't Do That', which really demonstrated what the guitar could do. The Beatles then started work on their first feature film, *A Hard Day's Night*, which showcased the Rickenbacker extensively, both visually and on the soundtrack. The opening multitracked Dm7sus4 chord of the title song effectively pronounced that a brand new voice, born of the 1960s, had arrived in the universe of the guitar.

More notable guitar hooks would drift across the ether during the British summer of 1964. The Animals, from Newcastle in north-east England, delivered the first six-minute single in June and sent it straight to number one in the UK charts, repeating that feat three months later in the US. Undoubtedly what sold 'The House Of The Rising Sun' was an

dividends – Chet Atkins had used it to great effect on his 1960 LP *Teensville* – although the casualty rate due to muscular cramps is not recorded.

Another striking sound assaulted the British charts in August 1964 (and three months later in the US). The Kinks, a teenage R&B outfit from Muswell Hill, north London, released their own song 'You Really Got Me'. Beginning with a dry, rasping guitar chopping out a two-chord riff, the song built to a cacophonous frenzy, exploding into an incendiary solo from the 17-year-old guitarist Dave Davies. Possibly inspired by Keith Richards' sound on the recent Rolling Stones UK hit 'It's All Over Now', but without the reverb, Davies had used a similar guitar to Keith's – a mid-priced Harmony Meteor – through a tiny Elpico amplifier, the loudspeaker of which he'd slashed with a blade to add more distortion to the sound. The song is often credited as being "the first heavy rock riff ever" – usually by The Kinks themselves – but it certainly set a new benchmark for guitar soloing and helped consolidate the electric guitar's increasing influence on the music scene.

ANIMALS guitarist Hilton Valentine was the man with the arpeggios to imitate in 1964.

From the same club circuit that spawned The Rolling Stones emerged The Yardbirds. Though not destined to be as successful, they nonetheless would prove integral to the continuing development of English pop in general and guitar playing in particular. The group had a gifted young guitarist, Eric Clapton, whose reputation among the hip cognoscenti was rapidly spreading. Clapton's hero was Buddy Holly, but he'd become hooked on the blues after hearing a Big Bill Broonzy record that had somehow found its way on to a BBC radio request programme. The Yardbirds' first single, 'I Wish You Would', was released in June 1964; it was backed with 'A Certain Girl', which displayed Clapton's prodigious talent as a soloist. His legato phrasing was strident, confident and eloquent, and together with some elegant note-bending created a perfectly woven solo, revealing an intelligence and musicianship that belied Clapton's 18 years. To colour the tone of the guitar he'd used a device that artificially distorted the sound: a fuzz box, or distortion pedal.

The earliest distortion units had been developed in the US by the Gibson company in 1962 as an optional built-in effect to their solidbody EB-0 bass guitar. Called, appropriately enough, Fuzztone, it would also be incorporated into their new custom-order-only EBSF-1250, a huge solid guitar with two necks, one for bass, the other a regular six-string. As few guitarists had need of such instruments, the company soon offered the Fuzztone unit in a separate battery-operated pedal and called it the Maestro. The problem with the Maestro was that, although it produced a novel crackling effect, there was insufficient gain running into it from the guitar to produce any sustain, resulting in the distorted sound cutting off after a few moments. It was the British session guitarist Vic Flick, of The John Barry Seven, who took the problem to Gary Hurst, a young electronics engineer. Hurst set about designing a unit similar to the Gibson pedal but with the required energy necessary to hold a note reasonably efficiently. His improved design, marketed as the Tone Bender, was one of the first effects pedals on the market in Britain, starting a trend for sound gadgets that would be central to the evolving sound of the electric guitar as the decade progressed.

The burgeoning British R&B scene would produce more significant guitar talent during 1965. In February, The Who made their chart debut with 'I Can't Explain', a thinly disguised rewrite of The Kinks' second hit, 'All Day And All Of The Night', but with a taut, jabbing Rickenbacker 12-string playing the irresistible three-chord riff. It was written and played by their leader Pete Townshend who, while perhaps not as accomplished a soloist as some of his contemporaries, had nonetheless forged a remarkable style based on feedback and heavy, thrashing chords. Feedback is the electronic howling and squealing that occurs when the sound from the amplifier feeds back into the pickups of the guitar.

In the past feedback, like distortion, had been a nuisance, something to be avoided at all costs. But with music now increasing in volume and energy it was yet another exciting element that could be used to great effect under the right circumstances. For The Who's next release, 'Anyway, Anyhow, Anywhere', Townshend turned in a solo that made the most of this sonic aberration. He hit hard chords through a loud amplifier while turning his guitar to face the loudspeakers. Rolling the tone control of the neck-position pickup of his Rickenbacker back to zero, and soloing on the brighter bridge pickup (the one most sensitive to feedback), he could make-and-break the piercing signal by toggling the pickup selector switch back and forth rhythmically.

Feedback and other not-entirely-musical approaches to

playing would often lead to the destruction of the volatile Who's stage equipment when they performed live, the intensity of the noise mounting to a horrendous climax from which there was no other way down. Maximum R&B indeed! But The Who's performances, both on-stage and in the studio, depended as much on sheer volume as they did on adolescent frustration. Before 1965 was over the group would deliver their epochal anthem, 'My Generation'. Louder, wilder and more exciting than anything that had preceded it, the recording packed a pounding two-chord riff, a gloriously sneering vocal, a ground-breaking bass guitar solo and a blur of thrashing drums and feedback guitar. The spectre of heavy rock was already looming.

By contrast, 1965 was also the year of folk-rock. Bob Dylan's new album *Bringing It All Back Home* had been recorded with an electric band. When he played at the Newport Folk Festival in the US that July he took to the stage with Paul Butterfield's Blues Band in tow, and strapped on a Fender Stratocaster. Opinion is divided as to whether the frosty reception afforded him by the assembled folkies that night was due to his electric guitar, or the fact that he'd only performed three songs. One thing was clear: the lonesome troubadour with the acoustic guitar was ready to rock.

PETE TOWNSHEND armed with a lethal Rickenbacker.

A month earlier The Byrds had appeared from America's west coast with an electric reworking of a recent Dylan song, 'Mr Tambourine Man'. Folk guitarists Jim (later Roger) McGuinn, Gene Clark and David Crosby had been so impressed by The Beatles' movie *A Hard Day's Night* the previous summer they'd decided to form a pop group straight away. Inspired by George Harrison's sound, McGuinn immediately purchased a Rickenbacker 12-string electric. It was, he discovered, a difficult instrument to play, but McGuinn's somewhat fumbling style nevertheless created a magical sonic foil to his group's sublime three-part vocal harmonies, a blend previously only hinted at by Britain's Searchers during the Merseybeat period. McGuinn's jangling guitar would dominate The Byrds' records for at least the next three years, and is today still considered to be the classic sound of the electric 12-string.

In England, however, the folk scene had scarcely dared venture beyond the pubs and coffee bars. Since The Springfields had broken up, only Donovan had made any commercial impact in recent years, his 'Catch The Wind' earning him a reputation as the teenage British Bob Dylan surrogate. Martin Carthy was the unofficial godfather of English folk guitar, a peerless traditional acoustic player who had championed the young Paul Simon during his first visit to the UK as an unknown in the early 1960s. When Simon returned to the US he took with him Carthy's arrangement of 'Scarborough Fair' and later, with his singing partner Art Garfunkel, turned it (uncredited) into a huge American hit, an event not lost on the hard-working Carthy. Bert Jansch and John Renbourn were two more luminaries from the same background who also remained faithful to their acoustic instruments, thus eluding mass recognition. Jansch's version of Davey Graham's tune 'Angie' had been the British fingerstyle player's entrance examination piece for several years; his 1966 album *Jack Orion* would include a tune called 'Blackwater Side' which would leave a huge impression on a young session guitarist and future legend called Jimmy Page.

Eric Clapton had quit The Yardbirds early in 1965, the call of the blues pulling him further from the group's aspirations to commercial success, and he'd joined John Mayall's Bluesbreakers. Mayall was an uncompromising blues purist who had been quick to recognise Eric's potential. He offered

McGUINN and jangly Rick.

THE KINKS put the riff in pop.

MAESTRO have a fuzzbox and everyone's going to abuse it.

Clapton a small room in his house, and the guitarist moved in. Immersing himself in Mayall's vast collection of rare American blues records, Clapton crammed his head with the music of B.B., Albert and Freddy King, Otis Rush, Buddy Guy, and their Chicago-based brethren.

On seeing the sleeve of Freddy King's 1961 LP *Let's Hide Away And Dance Away*, in which King is posed with an early 1950s Gibson Les Paul gold-top guitar, Clapton headed straight for London's music shop district in and around the Charing Cross Road, in search of a similar model. Clapton found a later version of the instrument, with a sunburst top and improved 'humbucking' pickups, manufactured in the late 1950s. These original-design Les Paul guitars had at that time been out of production for four or five years.

LONDON's West End music shops, 1964: happy hunting ground for would-be groups.

This seminal pairing of player and instrument would eventually lead to a revolution in history, and change forever the attitudes of players and audiences the world over. As the summer progressed, Clapton continued his single-minded pursuit of his style, building on the foundations laid by his Chicago heroes. The unique tone and long, natural sustain he'd discovered in the Les Paul guitar was sweetened further by an exemplary left-hand vibrato, which added an eloquent authority to the new musical language he was exploring.

String-bending was by now a firmly established technique among guitarists, many of whom had discovered it could be achieved a lot easier by 'slack-stringing' their instruments. This involved discarding the low E-string, moving the remaining five one notch upwards, and tuning the top E down to B, the B down to G, and so on. The top E would be replaced by a thin banjo A which could be purchased separately. By using this method, players could bend their now-lighter strings through as much as a tone and a half if necessary, depending on how far they scaled the fingerboard. It was also easier to add vibrato with the left hand, as some of the more adept Chicago bluesmen had done. By gently rotating the wrist, the string could be 'pushed and pulled' repeatedly across the fret, creating a more human tone and even adding to the note's sustain. This difficult technique, once perfected, was far more musical than the tremolo-arm method, enhancing the expression of notes and phrases and lending the more accomplished player a musicianly credibility. Vibrato soon became the latest trick to master.

Eric Clapton's place in The Yardbirds had been filled by another guitar genius from the Surrey area in south-east England, one Jeff Beck. On arriving at the studio to record their first single with Beck (Graham Gouldman's 'Heart Full Of Soul') the band discovered that their manager and producer, Giorgio Gomelsky, had hired two Indian musicians to play on the session – a tabla player and a sitar player. The opening riff to the song did emote a very Indian flavour, but the delicate sound of the sitar was not dynamic enough to carry the necessary impact that the track demanded. It was therefore down to the new guitarist to imitate the sound and playing style of the Indian instrument, which he did with a Fender Telecaster played through a Tone Bender fuzz pedal borrowed from his friend Jimmy Page. In so doing, Beck accidentally created the first example of another new style, one that would come to be known as psychedelia. Coined in allusion to the latest drug fashion to hit the US, the hallucinogenic LSD, the term when applied to music suggested an altered mind-state that might be realised – under its influence – by swirling, reverb-drenched, fuzz-tone guitars, often borrowing phrases and riffs from Indian scales. This novel effect would soon catch on in a big way.

By the year's end, two of the biggest-selling records in the UK would feature fuzz guitar: The Rolling Stones' 'Satisfaction', and 'Keep On Running' by The Spencer Davis Group. Even the mighty Beatles had made use of fuzz on their ground-breaking *Rubber Soul* LP, for Paul McCartney's bass part on 'Think For Yourself'. Although none of these songs could be considered remotely psychedelic, the new sound had nonetheless established itself in the minds of both musicians and the record-buying public alike. The gadgets began selling and a number of similar products soon found their way onto the market.

The inclusion of a real sitar on The Beatles' *Rubber Soul* album inspired a popular curiosity in Indian music, and all manner of Eastern instruments would pepper many a recording over the next couple of years. The Yardbirds continued a quest for exotic textures. Their ambitious 'Shapes Of Things' shot into the UK Top Five in February 1966, its abstract message borne on a marching two-chord guitar motif, breaking into double-tempo for Jeff Beck's awesome solo where his guitar assumes the guise of some psychedelically deranged gypsy violin. 'Over, Under, Sideways, Down' followed in May, taking another Indian-flavoured guitar hook into both UK and US charts. Untouchable in his field, the ever-inventive Beck had become Player Of The Moment.

The now massively successful Rolling Stones had temporarily abandoned their R&B roots with the spring release of the *Aftermath* album. Brian Jones' use of the sitar, both on the album and the single 'Paint It Black', was a brave departure from the tried and tested formula, and signalled real progress and a need to develop. The Beatles had begun experimenting with the studio's tape machines, slowing some tracks down, playing others backwards, all in a search for ever more weird sounds. One of the new psychedelic groups, The Creation, boasted an innovative guitarist called Eddie Phillips who, in addition to some fine pioneering work with feedback, had also been the first to apply a violin bow to his instrument. It was a period of great change, and of endless possibilities.

The recording of John Mayall's *Blues Breakers With Eric Clapton* album in April 1966 marked another watershed in the changing sound of the electric guitar. Having abandoned the use of the fuzz pedal after his initial Yardbirds recordings, Clapton discovered the perfect sound for the music he was playing with Mayall: the Gibson Les Paul hooked up to a 50-watt Marshall combo amplifier. By increasing the volume on the amp to a magical 'sweet spot', the guitar would overload it naturally, creating a smooth, more musical distortion. This did incur a problem in the studio, where engineer Gus Dudgeon experienced some difficulty in preventing the sound from bouncing around the room and into the drum and vocal microphones. Recording a rehearsal, Dudgeon and producer Mike Vernon invited the guitarist into the control room to demonstrate the problem to him. On hearing the playback, Clapton was ecstatic. "That's the sound I'm looking for!" he exclaimed. "Don't change a thing!"

EDDIE PHILLIPS of The Creation in 1966 deploying an avant-Page violin bow.

The finished product probably remains the greatest white blues album of all time. Through his use of overdrive distortion, controlled feedback and vibrato, Clapton had set new goals for aspiring guitarists, regardless of their chosen style. But when it was released in July, *Blues Breakers*, for all its peerless attributes, was something of an anachronism compared with what was happening on the current music scene. Certainly there were enough hardcore blues guitar fanatics around to hike the record into the UK album charts, but Clapton, having grown restless, had already left Mayall's group in search of new pastures. He'd teamed up with two new colleagues, drummer Ginger Baker and bassist Jack Bruce, to form what would become the first heavy rock group, Cream.

Fresh Cream, the group's debut album, caused much excitement on its release at the end of 1966. Baker and Bruce, though both veterans of the R&B scene, also had strong backgrounds in jazz. Both were fiery in temperament, and this reflected itself in their often ferocious playing, providing Clapton with a huge, powerful engine with which to drive his exquisite, improvised excursions. The group had upgraded their equipment to the new 100-watt Marshall amplifiers, and Baker had doubled the size of his drum kit. Listening to the album it was sometimes hard to believe that three musicians could create such an enormous sound.

Cream's single, 'I Feel Free', was issued at the same time as the album, and Clapton's solo delivered a sound more akin to a wind instrument than a guitar. Nothing like it had ever been heard. Clapton himself later described it as his 'woman tone'. "It's a sweet sound," he would tell *Beat Instrumental* magazine six months later, "more like the human voice than a guitar... it calls for the correct use of distortion." In fact, by rolling the tone control of the neck pickup of his Gibson back to zero and playing at high volume through the powerful Marshall, no fuzz pedals were necessary. The extraordinary effect also demonstrated how the new amplifier designs were helping to inspire the rapidly expanding vocabulary of contemporary music.

JIMI prepares to bombard an expectant Marquee audience.

No sooner had Cream rewritten the book of rock guitar than Jimi Hendrix arrived from the US and tore it up completely. Throughout 1967 and 1968 he reinvented the sound of the instrument time and time again, expanding its horizons, presenting undreamed sonic possibilities, and bringing the blues into the nuclear age. 'Stone Free', the b-side of his first single 'Hey Joe' (released in December 1966),

JIMI HENDRIX and Pink Floyd in one week at London's Marquee Club in 1967.

provided the first evidence of the incredible prowess of Hendrix, who played left-handed yet operated on a normal Fender Stratocaster restrung and turned upside down. On 'Stone Free' he played a heavily overdriven guitar solo, spitting out a blistering scatter of notes, the Strat's tremolo arm wrenched to near breaking point. It was a staggering performance, despatched with sheer adrenalin-rush abandon. The song faded with its final chord mutating into a ludicrously distorted, wildly undulating low F as the instrument's bridge hardware was brutally abused by its master. This was light-years from 'Apache'!

The release of his debut album, *Are You Experienced*, in the spring of 1967 confirmed beyond question the genius of Hendrix. Thirty years on, few guitarists have come close to matching his sound or can approach the depth of feeling which underscored his work. That he would all but burn out within two years was, perhaps, inevitable. *Are You Experienced* and the two albums that followed – *Axis: Bold As Love* and *Electric Ladyland* – still stand as the decade's creative high points in guitar-based rock. By 1969, under intolerable pressure to tour, write, record... and tour some more, Hendrix could produce little to compare with his astonishing achievements on those early albums where he had embraced many musical styles. He ranged effortlessly from simple two-minute pop songs to grand psychedelic masterpieces, through funky soul tunes to heavy riff rock, all forged from a rich seam of the deepest, darkest blues.

Much apocrypha has come to light concerning Jimi's uncanny insight and mythical gifts, one for example claiming that he instinctively knew exactly how a solo would sound when recorded backwards. Yet one only has to hear the reverse-track solo on the title song of his first album to appreciate that miracles were indeed possible, that somewhere a god exists. Hendrix's legacy is more widely felt today than it was during his brief lifetime, and this is testament to his phenomenal gift: that of a blues musician with a universal message, delivered with a showman's swagger, the whole blessed – or cursed – with a poet's heart and a seemingly limitless imagination.

Always underrated as a rhythm guitarist, Hendrix had a style that owed much to his early apprenticeship backing the likes of Little Richard and The Isley Brothers on lengthy one-nighter tours of the States in the early 1960s. These were acts specialising in energetic dance music where the guitarist was very much the sideman, his function to provide a solid rhythmic foundation in tandem with the bass and the drums. From this tradition came the Tamla Motown organisation of Detroit, a phenomenally successful outfit during the 1960s, producing hit after dance hit by a variety of black artists, all backed by the same coterie of writers and studio musicians on whom their success depended. Strangely, few people knew – or cared – who these faceless geniuses were. After all, they were simply doing a job in providing backing tracks for stars like The Supremes or The Four Tops, and there would be no ostentatious solo flights on their records. Even so, Robert White, Joe Messina, Eddie Willis and Marv Tarplin, to name but a few, were all brilliant guitarists who knew their place in the Motown studio, unsung heroes happy to do the job for which they were paid, but with little or no recognition. Their real contribution would eventually be acknowledged in the next decade as the funk phenomenon took hold.

Another American guitarist gaining popularity with his minimal, brittle yet deeply soulful style was Steve Cropper. The studio guitarist at Stax Records in Memphis, he was also a member of Booker T & The MGs who scored a huge US hit in 1962 with 'Green Onions', a simple 12-bar instrumental with an infectious, easy-to-master guitar hook. Cropper had gone on to write and record with such soul legends as Aretha Franklin, Otis Redding, Sam & Dave, Wilson Pickett and Eddie Floyd, as well as creating many legendary tracks with the MGs. Yet his style remained the complete antithesis of much of what was currently in vogue, his Telecaster producing clean, precise, economical chords and phrases that never once upstaged the vocalist, always finding the perfect riff for the perfect moment. Never using two notes where one would do, Cropper remains the master of the less-is-more school of musical thought, his contribution to the progress of guitar playing every bit as valid as those who played twice as many notes, twice as loud and at twice the speed.

Manufacturers would continue to keep pace with the ever-changing fads of musicians as more and more experimental playing styles continued to evolve into the latter half of the 1960s. Light-gauge, wire-wound strings had been available for some time, and it was now possible for players to create their own custom-gauge set of strings to suit their individual playing style. Jimi Hendrix hit upon the idea of tuning his guitar down by approximately one semitone. This not only made string-bending easier, as the tension was decreased, but fortuitously gave his Stratocaster a more mellow midrange tone quality, which became central to his unique sound. Hendrix, like Cream, endorsed the use of the popular Marshall 'stack' – a 100-watt amplifier perched atop two

NEW HORIZONS in sound as Roger plays a solo on the wah-wah trousers.

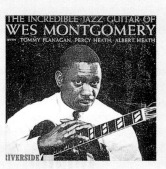

WES MONTGOMERY was the greatest jazz guitarist of the 1960s. He had an instantly distinctive sound, due in part to using his thumb rather than a pick, and often featured fluid octave runs. Montgomery had signed to Riverside in 1959 at the age of 34 when he was at the hub of the thriving local jazz scene in Indianapolis, working with many excellent musicians including his brothers Buddy (piano/vibraphone) and Monk (the first jazz bassist to play the electric bass), with whom he recorded three albums. But it was this aptly-named 1960 album (left) that really established Montgomery as a guitarist of world-class quality.

△ GIBSON L-5CESN
Produced 1960-1969 (this style); this example July 1964

Jazz guitarists entered the 1960s with their conservative view of the instrument intact. Their electric guitar of choice was a large hollow-body, either with "floating" pickups added, or with pickups built-in. Gibson was still considered the leading brand for jazz guitarists, and many players chose from the company's best electric-acoustic models, the Super 400CES and the L-5CES. Both had been launched in the early 1950s, but during 1960 a design change occurred when the earlier "rounded" cutaway style was changed to a "sharp" cutaway, providing improved high-fret access. Wes Montgomery, the most famous jazz guitarist of the 1960s, often used a custom L-5CES with one pickup.

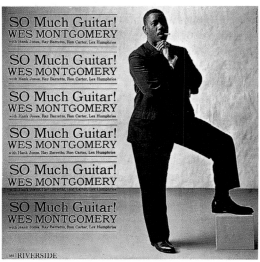

WES MONTGOMERY made 19 albums for Riverside, including this 1961 record (left), until the label closed in 1964 and the guitarist shifted to Verve. Around 1962 he told writer Ralph Gleason that he'd tried conventional plectrum picking for a few months but came back to his unusual thumb-picking style, opting for feel over precision. "I just didn't like the sound [of the plectrum]," said Montgomery, "I liked the tone better with the thumb, but the technique better with the pick. But I couldn't have them both."

△ HÖFNER VERITHIN
Produced 1960-1965; this example c1961

During the 1950s Höfner of Germany had kept many European players supplied with decent, affordable guitars when American instruments were hard to get. As US guitars became more plentiful in the early 1960s, Höfner lost some of its individuality and competed more directly with American instruments. The Verithin, based on Gibson's Thinline series, was a staple among up-and-coming pop groups. This one belongs to Bert Weedon.

BERT WEEDON was a busy British session guitarist who also helped to popularise guitars through his regular appearances on children's TV shows. Weedon used Hofner's new narrow-body Verithin model in the early 1960s (right) until Guild built him a special "signature" model (see p.37).

JAZZ GUITARS

By the close of the 1950s the sound of the electric guitar was familiar in jazz, but few guitar players had band-leading ambitions. Most were content to play in the familiar trio or quartet format rather than place the guitar as a frontline instrument in a larger ensemble. However, during the 1960s the emergence of some major new guitarists would take the instrument to the forefront of jazz.

The complex bebop lines of guitarists Tal Farlow and Jimmy Raney, inspired by the harmonic intricacy of saxophonists like Charlie Parker, had become the benchmark for a generation of jazz guitarists in the 1950s. Johnny Smith had unveiled a lush, relaxed sound, Herb Ellis with the Oscar Peterson Trio had built on the work of Charlie Christian to create a hard-swinging bluesy style of jazz guitar, and Barney Kessel was the best-known and most popular jazz guitarist of the 1950s, in constant demand as an accompanist.

But jazz music had moved on. The major innovators by the late 1950s were saxophonists, trumpeters and pianists whose line-ups seldom featured the guitar, which did not really fit into the hard-bop style of Art Blakey's Jazz Messengers or the small groups of Miles Davis.

Stylistically, guitar players were slow to respond to the possibilities of the modal approach to jazz unveiled by the ever-questioning Davis on his seminal 1959 album *Kind Of Blue*. The guitar in jazz was certainly in the front pack, but not yet among the leaders. Soon that would change dramatically.

In September 1959 the jazz saxophonist Cannonball Adderley was playing a concert in Indianapolis, Indiana. Later in the evening he dropped into the Missile Club and took a seat

near the back. On stage a trio of guitar, organ and drums was playing a selection of jazz standards and originals. Within minutes Adderley had moved to the front row and sat right in front of the guitarist, Wes Montgomery, spellbound by the sheer brilliance of his playing.

Idea after idea poured out of Montgomery's Gibson L-5CES guitar, perfectly executed with precision even at fast tempos, even though he picked the strings with his right-hand thumb instead of the customary plectrum. Like a master story-teller, Montgomery kept Adderley's attention for chorus after chorus as he unravelled his tale and drew it to a satisfying conclusion. Starting his solos with single-line improvisation, he would shift up a gear by playing entire choruses in unison octaves, thickening the sound. To bring his solo to a climax, he'd outline fast-moving melodic lines with block chords, played on the upper strings of the guitar. The effect was stunning!

Back in New York, Adderley swept into the offices of Riverside Records in a state of excitement and persuaded producer Orrin Keepnews to go to Indianapolis to hear this master musician. On the same day Keepnews read a magazine article by composer and writer Gunther Schuller praising the guitarist, and off he set. Keepnews' journey echoed that of producer John Hammond two decades earlier, who went to Oklahoma City to hear electric guitar pioneer Charlie Christian (and Montgomery's primary inspiration), a trip that launched the innovative Christian's recording career.

Within three weeks Keepnews had recorded *The Wes Montgomery Trio* in New York. Although the album caught the attention of musicians, it received mixed reviews and sales were disappointing. Montgomery played well throughout, however, and his interpretation of Thelonious Monk's 'Round Midnight' is a masterpiece. For the guitarist's second Riverside

album, 1960's *The Incredible Jazz Guitar Of Wes Montgomery*, Keepnews teamed him with a top-flight New York rhythm section, and the result more than vindicated the album's title. Many sides of Montgomery's talent were on display here: his delicate treatment of a ballad ('Polka Dots And Moonbeams'), his breathtaking up-tempo soloing ('Airegin'), his skilful development of a solo over five or six minutes ('Gone With The Wind'), his mastery of the blues form ('D Natural Blues') and his ability to write memorable tunes ('West Coast Blues', 'Four On Six', 'Mister Walker'). This album was absolute confirmation that a major new jazz guitar voice had arrived.

From 1959 to 1964 Montgomery recorded 19 albums for Riverside and its subsidiary label Fantasy and regularly topped the annual *Down Beat* readers' and critics' polls. He was partnered on record with several leading jazz artists including vibraphonist Milt Jackson, organist Jimmy Smith and pianist George Shearing. An outstanding release from this period was *Full House*, recorded live at Tsubo's Coffee Shop in San Francisco in June 1962 with the saxophonist Johnny Griffin and the rhythm section from Miles Davis' group: Wynton Kelly (piano), Paul Chambers (bass) and Jimmy Cobb (drums). It includes a beautiful solo performance of the ballad 'I've Grown Accustomed To Her Face' which Montgomery played entirely solo in chord-melody style.

For his final Riverside album, *Fusion*, Montgomery was featured with a string orchestra under the direction of Jimmy Jones. This radical shift from the familiar jazz combo setting was too much for many jazz critics, who felt that the result lacked bite, but Montgomery himself regarded it as his best recording so far. Attractively recorded and with excellent

HARMONY claimed to be the world's biggest guitar-maker of the 1960s. Models such as the H-75 shown on this 1960 catalogue (left) served to introduce the electric guitar to many a young player. One such was Keith Richards (far left) who used a Harmony Meteor in the early days of his musical career with The Rolling Stones.

△ HARMONY METEOR H-70
Produced 1960-1968; this example c1965

Harmony, based in Chicago, did a good job turning out plenty of mid-priced, average guitars for aspiring guitarists of the 1960s, providing players such as Keith Richards – seen playing his Meteor above – with a cheap instrument to get things rolling. Left-handed versions such as this are rarely encountered.

Gibson, the workingman's guitar.

Wes Montgomery & Gibson at work for MGM/Verve records.

scoring, it captures Montgomery's reflective side perfectly and showcases his ability to breathe life into a melody with sensitive single-line and chordal statements.

When Riverside ceased recording activities in 1964, the guitarist switched to the Verve label, and producer Creed Taylor pushed Montgomery more and more into a commercial direction. Some exciting jazz albums emerged from this association in its early days, but following the success of *Goin' Out Of My Head,* which won a Grammy award in 1967 for Best Instrumental Jazz Performance, Taylor increasingly restricted Montgomery's creative role on the records. Gone were the extended solos which had allowed the guitarist to unfold and develop ideas; now he rarely got more than a chorus of improvisation on each piece, while the trademark 'octaves' sound was brought to the fore and emphasised almost to the point of cliché. Montgomery was swathed in strings, struggling to extract musical value from trivial material. On the plus side, the records did get valuable radio airing and sold in quantities of which most jazz producers could only dream.

Sadly, Montgomery had only a short time to enjoy this success. He died of a heart attack on June 15th 1968 at age 43. The impact of this artist on the development of the guitar in jazz cannot be overstated. For many jazz players and listeners it was Montgomery who finally brought the guitar from the periphery to centre-stage as a jazz instrument. He was steeped in the language of jazz – a jazz musician first and a guitarist second. He'd absorbed the current innovations and could play the jazz music of the period with the authority of a star saxophonist and, like all great jazz artists, he was equally

1961

GEORGE BENSON began recording in his own right in the 1960s with records like this 1966 LP, although his greatest success came in the following decade with luxurious pop-jazz records such as Breezin'. An assured technician with a penchant for hard, driving bop and an ear for melody, Benson had started playing sessions as a teenager with organists Jimmy Smith and Brother Jack McDuff. But once he'd been spotted by Wes Montgomery a record contract was inevitable, and he signed to Columbia. In the 1960s Benson most often used the Gibson Super 400 (pictured on the album sleeve, right), as well as picking on a D'Angelico and a Guild.

strong on ballads and up-tempo numbers and could play a soulful blues. Montgomery had extended the vocabulary of the strong on ballads and up-tempo numbers and could play a soulful blues. Montgomery had extended the vocabulary of the guitar in jazz and his octaves and block-chord runs had introduced a new sound to the music.

There can be few jazz guitarists since 1960 who owe nothing to the influence of Wes Montgomery. Among the many who freely admit to Montgomery as an inspiration are Larry Coryell, Lee Ritenour, Pat Metheny, George Benson, the late Emily Remler, Terry Smith, Jim Mullen, Ronnie Jordan and, not least, Pat Martino.

During the 1960s Martino had become friendly with Montgomery and frequently jammed and worked on musical ideas with him. A professional musician from age 15, Martino had a robust, round sound, and under the influence of plectrum-guitar master Johnny Smith developed a formidable technique. The legacy of the association with Montgomery is most evident in Martino's fluent octave passages which were such a hallmark of Wes's style. But it was Martino's brilliance as an improviser – his ability to weave long, involved melodic lines through any chord progression with unerring drive and swing – that gave him his own identity. And on albums such as 1967's *El Hombre* Martino underlined his confident approach and solid jazz chops, but also applied a questing spirit to research possibilities beyond mainstream jazz, demonstrating his interest in typical late-1960s passions such as Indian music and jazz-rock fusion. A contrast to Montgomery and Martino was Joe Pass, the epitome of the all-round jazz guitarist. A superb single-line improviser with an impeccable technique, Pass was also an outstanding accompanist and chordal player. His mastery of bebop harmony and his ability to apply it to the guitar were legendary, but his technical skill was counterbalanced by an equally profound artistic sense, so that the results were always truly musical. Born in 1929 and raised in the Italian community of Philadelphia, Pass's promising career was interrupted by a 12-year period of drug dependence, and he finally entered the Synanon drug rehabilitation clinic in 1960 at the age of 31, staying for three years. A recording he made there in 1961 with fellow patients, *Sounds Of Synanon,* signalled his talent to the wider public and, after leaving the clinic, two outstanding albums, *Catch Me* and *For Django,* firmly established his reputation as a brilliant and soulful improviser whose clear, melodic lines sounded fresh and relaxed at any tempo. From the early 1970s Pass would develop an innovative unaccompanied style, epitomised by *Virtuoso*.

The 1960s were exciting years for popular music. The

△ GIBSON BARNEY KESSEL CUSTOM
Produced 1961-1971; this example March 1967

Gibson produced a number of new "signature" models in the 1960s named for jazz players such as Barney Kessel, who had been the most famous jazz guitarist of the 1950s. The body of his Gibson featured an unusual twin "sharp" cutaway.

THE BRILLIANT improviser Pat Martino made his finest album, El Hombre (far left), in 1967. Joe Pass came back from drug dependence to record the outstanding Catch Me LP (centre) in 1962, while at the very end of the decade John McLaughlin's first solo album appeared, the adventurous Extrapolation (left).

BARNEY KESSEL (below) wears a bow-tie in this Gibson promo shot to echo the "bow-tie" fingerboard markers of the Barney Kessel model.

worldwide dissemination of blues music, the explosion of talent in rock music and the emergence of the new breed of singer-songwriters changed the face of the music industry forever. But while many profited, others lost. For many established jazz musicians the release of the first Beatles, Stones and Dylan albums coincided with the end of their careers. As the public's attention shifted from jazz to rock, so the jazz clubs closed or changed their music policy, and sales of jazz records declined.

But the younger generation of jazz guitarists coming up in the 1960s could hardly ignore the blues and rock music that surrounded them. Indeed many, like John McLaughlin and Larry Coryell, had progressed to jazz from an initial interest in blues or rock. In the midst of this revolution, London's jazz scene in the mid-1960s was a hotbed of musical experimentation and development. While some musicians were rejecting the established structures of post-bebop jazz in favour of a freer approach to improvisation, others were blending elements of blues and rock with jazz.

John McLaughlin arrived in London from the north-east of England and immersed himself in this activity, working in a music store by day and playing in groups by night alongside Alexis Korner, Georgie Fame, Graham Bond, Jack Bruce and trumpeters Ian Carr and Kenny Wheeler. McLaughlin's driving guitar style had more than an echo of saxophonist John Coltrane's contemporary jazz approach, but also reflected his early interest in the blues of Muddy Waters and the jazz guitar of Django Reinhardt and Tal Farlow. By the late 1960s

McLaughlin too had begun to study Indian music, and recorded his first album as a leader, Extrapolation.

Moving to New York in 1969, McLaughlin recorded with Miles Davis, and In A Silent Way signalled the beginning of jazz-rock fusion. But it was McLaughlin's work with drummer Tony Williams' group Lifetime that finally confirmed him as an innovative guitarist of immense talent. Lifetime performed with extraordinary intensity and its complex rhythms, demanding tempos, intricate melodies and dissonant harmonies outlined a fresh musical language. No other jazz or rock guitarist could approach McLaughlin for rhythmic and harmonic sense, or inventive power. Later McLaughlin would form the Mahavishnu Orchestra which came to define guitar-led fusion in the 1970s.

The influence of outstanding players active outside jazz in the 1960s such as B.B. King and Jimi Hendrix transcended stylistic boundaries and filtered into jazz guitar in many ways. Players opted for solidbody guitars alongside the traditional archtop Gibsons and fitted lighter-gauge strings for greater string-bending facility. Improvising over a rock pulse as readily as jazz swing, they sought inspiration in the simpler chords of rock music and the cyclic harmonies of bebop.

By the end of the 1960s many jazz guitarists were no longer content simply to replicate the music of the saxophone and other jazz instruments on the guitar. They were prepared to use the unique sounds and qualities of the electric guitar to create a fresh vocabulary and assume a leading role in the jazz-rock fusion of the 1970s. ■ CHARLES ALEXANDER

YURI GAGARIN is the first man in space. The Russian orbits earth in Vostok-1 for a little under two hours. A month later Alan Shepherd is the first American in space, fired 116 miles up for a 15-minute leap. In August, Gherman Titov orbits in Vostok-2 for 25 hours.

GEORGE FORMBY, British screen star and ukulele wizard, dies. David Evans is born in Dublin, Ireland; at the end of the next decade he will become guitarist Edge in U2.

THE BERLIN WALL is built to prevent East Berliners reaching the West. Elsewhere the contraceptive pill goes on general sale, aimed to control more personal incursions.

CATCH-22, Joseph Heller's comic-surreal novel about American airmen in the wartime Mediterranean, is published. The title will pass into the language to describe deadlock.

THE TWIST is the latest dance craze to rock America. Less rhythmically bound, Bob Dylan debuts in New York folk clubs and is signed to the Columbia record company in September.

AMERICA's recently elected president John F Kennedy faces trouble abroad as an invasion of Cuba at the Bay of Pigs fails, and as the number of "military advisers" sent by the US to Vietnam steadily increases.

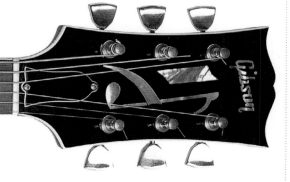

▽ GIBSON TAL FARLOW
Produced 1962-1971; this example July 1964

A year after the Barney Kessel and floating-pickup Johnny Smith models, Gibson released the Tal Farlow, complete with its ornate cutaway decoration. This example received gold-plated hardware, which was unusual.

RICKENBACKER made one of the first electric guitars back in the 1930s, and during the 1960s established themselves through the use of their stylish, modern guitars by The Beatles and The Byrds. Later in the decade, the company's 1968 catalogue cover (left) reflected the fashionable op-art style of the time, mirroring the work of artists such as Bridget Riley.

▽ RICKENBACKER 460
Produced 1961-1985; this example 1961

An idiosyncratic maker based in California, Rickenbacker introduced two of its most distinctive features on the 460: a control layout with an extra fifth "blend" knob, and triangle fingerboard markers.

▽ GRETSCH CHET ATKINS COUNTRY GENTLEMAN
Produced 1961-1981 (this style); this example 1963

Chet Atkins had helped design a number of Gretsch models since the mid 1950s. The thin-bodied Country Gentleman, for example, had first appeared in 1957, but during 1961 Gretsch launched an updated version with a twin-cutaway body for better high-fret access. It became enormously popular after George Harrison, a big Atkins fan, took up the guitar in 1963 and used it on many of The Beatles' live dates.

Ready for the Storms?

THE IN SOUND IS ENGLISH

ELECTRIC GUITARS *became so popular in the 1960s that even flat-top guitar makers such as Ovation (centre) and Martin (far left) tried to sell electrics. Guitar distributors sought out electric suppliers and invented new brands – St Louis Music created Custom Kraft (left), for example – while old hands like Kay (inset, below centre) just upped production and enjoyed the cash-flow.*

AMERICAN GUITARS

The two most revered US guitar makers of the 1960s, Gibson and Fender, are covered elsewhere in this book. But what of the other American companies whose instruments fuelled the decade's music? How did they deal with the boom in electric guitars following The Beatles' arrival on US soil in 1964, and did they survive the slump at the end of the 1960s? Here we consider ten years' output from the likes of Rickenbacker, Gretsch and Harmony, to National, Danelectro and Mosrite.

Throughout most of the 1960s an old guitar was called 'used', not 'vintage', and players didn't think about its value unless they were trading it in for something flashier. People looked ahead to a thrilling future, not back to a romanticised past. I mean, a double-cutaway must be better than a single-cut. Why? Because it's new, it's different... and Gretsch says so. What more do you need to know?

In the previous decade, departures from tradition had been the exceptions. Dealers maligned Flying Vs because they weren't, well, Gibson-like. But some of those departures became the new norms, and by the 1960s the defining philosophy dictated that innovation wasn't a bonus – it was expected. The go-go vibe was described by Andrew Edelstein in *The Pop Sixties* as "the spirit of the now" and it permeated everything from paisley pullovers to presidential politics.

For guitar buyers it was a time of unprecedented variety. Small firms like Carvin continued to build reliable solidbodies, while Micro-Frets offered wireless guitars with built-in FM transmitters and length-adjustable string nuts. Archtop master builder Jimmy D'Aquisto brought the highest standards of craftsmanship to electric designs. Even the historic Martin company dipped its toes into the electric stream with their DeArmond-pickup-equipped F-series archtops.

Of course, by the dawn of the 1960s the pillars of the electric temple were already in place: Les Pauls, Strats, Teles, classic Rickenbackers and Gretsches. In fact, most of them had preceded the rock'n'roll for which they would prove so suitable. But if in the 1950s the gear had led the music, in the 1960s it was often the other way around. The unrelenting demand for guitars left manufacturers struggling to catch up, to look cool, even to survive. In retrospect some of their 1960s 'innovations' look more like mere refinements, and some were borderline silly. Still, there were important advances among the rush.

A turning point occurred on February 8th 1964 when George Harrison encountered his first Rickenbacker electric 12-string. He was quite taken with it and debuted it on the cowbell-bonkin' intro to 'You Can't Do That'. Sitting in a Hollywood theatre, Jim (later Roger) McGuinn saw *A Hard Day's Night* and he, too, fell in love with the keening chime of the 12-string Rick; thus was born the instrumental sound of The Byrds (it's not much fun to imagine 'Mr. Tambourine Man' performed on an SG). Many of the decade's finest records – The Beatles' 'A Hard Day's Night',

The Byrds' 'Eight Miles High', The Who's 'I Can't Explain' – were energised by the jingle-jangle of the Rick 12, one of the decade's greatest contributions to guitar design.

In fact, Rickenbacker popularised a slew of advances during the 1960s, including Rick-O-Sound stereo and a brilliantly engineered headstock that allowed 12 tuners to fit on a standard sized peghead, avoiding the top-heaviness of most 12-string guitars. Other ideas never got off the ground, such as slanted frets, or the Convertible guitars that featured interesting if unwieldy comb-and-handle contraptions intended to pull six strings out of the way, converting a 12-string to a regular guitar.

At Gretsch, the seeds of innovation and whimsy planted in the 1950s came to full flower in the 1960s, with feature-laden heavy cruisers like the Viking and the White Falcon, typically with Super'Tron or 12-screw patent-number Filter'Tron pickups. The big news was the shift to double cutaways for the leading models in '61 and '62, but otherwise there was little in the line that had not been introduced or at least foreshadowed in the previous decade. Exceptions included the Monkees six-string; a vaguely 335-ish 12-string; and the seldom-seen Bikini, a double-neck with slide-in, fold-up components reminiscent of some automatic weapons.

While these guitars may not rival their single-cut forebears as top-rung collectibles, they're among the Gretschiest Gretsches ever, some sporting a mix of 1950s carryovers and 1960s ideas like angled frets, sealed hollow bodies (with fake f-holes), twin 'mufflers' (string mutes), Tone Twister vibratos, telescoping whammy handles, interior tuning forks, 'zero' frets, whoopie

GRETSCH enjoyed a huge increase in business during the 1960s, and struggled to survive the cramped New York factory they had occupied since 1916. So in 1965 Gretsch's drum operation was moved to another site and the guitar workspace expanded, as these shots (right) inside the Brooklyn HQ reveal.

CHET ATKINS (right) was country music's best known guitar-picker of the 1960s, and gave Gretsch priceless publicity for their Chet Atkins models.

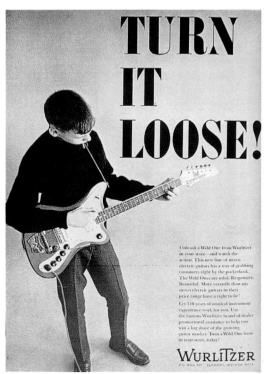

cushions (oops, I mean back pads), and even more switches and knobs than their predecessors. The Chet Atkins Hollow Body (or Nashville) was one of the decade's most lusted-after guitars; the double-cut Country Gent remains a classic by any standard; and for sheer brazenness, will any major-name guitar ever surpass or even approach the gadget-encrusted mid-1960s stereo White Falcon, the apotheosis of unabashed gizmomania?

During World War II, National-Dobro was reorganised as Valco. After the war, it bought bodies and parts from Rickenbacker, Kay, Harmony, Regal and others, part of a trend which helped lend a mix-and-match quality to so many moderately priced instruments (Valco built guitars under the Silvertone, Airline, and Oahu brands; some of its own guitars even had Gibson bodies). Although the Valco company still used the National brand in the 1960s, it generally abandoned the resonator guitars that had brought it to prominence, concentrating instead on electrics with unique shapes, colourful finishes, fragile whammies and silkscreened pickup covers. While Valco is fondly remembered for its budget models, its best guitars weren't cheap. A Glenwood 99, for example, cost as much as Gibson's gold-plated, triple-humbucker SG Custom.

Valco exec Al Frost told me, "We started using plastic more

and more... we'd take plastic, which was just like a rubber glove, and cement it to the guitars and trim it off. With the electrics you didn't need all that resonance, so we tried making the bodies out of polyester resin and fibreglass. We would take a mould, spray the finish in, then the fibreglass, pull it out of there, and the finish would already be on it. Oh, it was beautiful," Frost concluded.

This embrace of plastics technology along with an exploration of the mid-priced market niche meshed nicely with the industrial approach that had characterised National-Dobro from the beginning. By the early 1960s Valco was offering a wide selection of National and generally cheaper Supro electrics, some conventional in appearance and others like nothing players had ever seen. This latter category included Res-O-Glas models, blending fibreglass bodies with standard necks and hardware. If you wanted to step up from your bargain-basement Harmony and couldn't afford an Epiphone – or you just liked the idea of a turquoise guitar shaped like a map of the United States – then Valco was the place to go.

Valco wouldn't survive long past the mid-decade commercial tidal wave. It became involved with Kay in a complicated financial tangle and, as Al Frost put it, "When Kay sank, Valco sank." But its last-gasp guitars included nifty

EPIPHONE was established in the early 20th century, soon enjoying a reputation for top-quality archtop guitars. But by the 1950s Epi was in disarray, and Gibson bought the ailing operation in 1957. A revitalised line was introduced amid more go-ahead publicity, such as this striking 1964 catalogue (left).

TASTY GUITAR

AL CAIOLA (left) was a respected studio session guitarist who helped Epiphone design his 1963 "signature" guitar. It borrowed the five-way "Tonexpressor" tone circuit that the company had introduced a year earlier on its Professional model. Neither guitar proved very popular.

▽ EPIPHONE SHERATON E212T
Produced 1961-1970 (this style); this example November 1961

At first Epiphone prospered under its new owner, Gibson, which developed Epi as a separate but related line. Unfortunately, this led some people to view Epiphone as a kind of second-rate Gibson – although as fine guitars such as this Sheraton prove, this was far from the truth. Nonetheless, Epi sales declined, and in 1970 the brand was moved to Japanese-made guitars.

TED McCARTY (left), Gibson's president until 1966 when he left for Bigsby, controlled the Epiphone lines with production manager Ward Arbanas. Epis were built alongside Gibsons at the Kalamazoo factory.

Incomparable
MAGNATONE
THE Starstream
PROFESSIONAL GUITAR SERIES

CALIFORNIA not only hosted well known guitar makers such as Rickenbacker and Mosrite during the 1960s, but also saw the blossoming of many smaller operations. One such outfit was Magnatone, whose 1965 catalogue (left) was inhabated by clean-cut West-coasters just short of plausible grooviness.

- Harmony's Ultra-Thin Arched "Tone Chamber" construction.
- "Ultra-Slim" Necks—Steel Rod Reinforced. Uniform "feel."
- "Straight Line" Narrow Fingerboards —Short scale for easy chording "comping," or solo work.

ROCKETS' Size 15¾ x 40½ in. Rim 2 in. deep

No. H59
$139.50

models like the $99.50 Belmont; the Bermuda, with an onboard electronic tremolo and "brilliant polyester cherry" finish; and the company's highly collectable map-shape Glenwoods, Val-Pros, Newports and Westwoods.

By the time it folded in 1968, Danelectro had become dear to the hearts of players everywhere. Most Dan'os of the 1960s were updates of late-1950s models, including hollow guitars shaped like solidbodies, and pseudo-solidbodies with pine frames, Masonite (hardboard) tops and backs, pebbled-vinyl side coverings, and those inimitable lipstick-tube pickups (which sounded great, by the way). Danelectro sold truckloads of guitars to mail-order company Sears, who distributed them under the Silvertone brand along with models made by Harmony and others.

Founder Nat Daniel's biggest contribution was a production savvy that allowed him to put cool, low-priced guitars into the hands of countless players – his stack-pot double-neck retailed for $175 – but his New Jersey-based company introduced significant new ideas, too, like the amp-in-the-case set. One period piece was an electric sitar marketed under the Coral name; complete with body-mounted drone strings and a buzzy 'Sitarmatic' bridge, it added what passed for a Middle Eastern tinge to several hits. Another Coral took the unusual course of combining Danelectro's lyre-shaped 'Longhorn' silhouette with

HARMONY's Rocket model (above) was an unmistakable 1960s guitar, with its impressive curve of control knobs skirting the lower half of the body. Although they had a simple application – a volume and tone control for each of the guitar's three pickups – the multiple controls hinted that only a rocket scientist could be trusted with such a handful.

GIBSON's 1961 pricelist with the new SG-shape Les Paul models included the $157.50 Junior, the $295 Standard and the $440 Custom. By 1963 the Junior and Standard reached the UK through Gibson's agent, Selmer, who also sold Fender in Britain at the time. Their 1963 catalogue shows the Standard (right) at the equivalent of £131.25, and also listed the Junior at £78.75.

△ GIBSON SG/LES PAUL STANDARD
Produced 1961-1963; this example November 1961

This was one of Gibson's new-in-1961 guitars, known now as SG/Les Paul models because they had the new SG body shape but (at least at first) kept the "Les Paul" name on the instrument.

COLLECTORS value the limited number of Customs that have this vibrato bridge (left) with an attractive inlaid ebony block adjoining the tailpiece.

a hollow body
to produce one of the
oddest guitars of the decade. Then there were Mosrites, the brainchildren of the late Semie Moseley, an amiable gospel musician from Bakersfield, California, who had worked for Rickenbacker. The soft-spoken Oklahoma transplant built an eye-poppin' double-neck for superpicker Joe Maphis, but it was a mid-1960s association with The Ventures that put his instruments on the map. Among the most distinctive guitars of the era, they featured curvy sculpted bodies, beautiful finishes, and ultra-low actions nicely complemented by feather-touch Vibramute tailpieces. Back in 1980, Moseley told me with a laugh, "All I did was to take a Fender, flop it over and trace around it .... [the shape] was just an upside-down Fender." The mainstays of Mosrite were the successful Ventures models, but the line was rounded out with a variety of other models that included 12-strings, basses and hollowbody guitars.

Guild's Duane Eddy models were a bit odd in one respect: Eddy had recorded his twangy landmark hits on a DeArmond-equipped Gretsch 6120, not a Guild. At any rate, Guild's Duane Eddy archtops were beautiful instruments. Two of Guild's most unusual designs were associated with jazz titan

George Barnes: the AcoustiLectric, and the small-bodied Guitar In F. Neither had soundholes, and on both the pickups were suspended in holes in the top to minimise interference with top vibration. Among the most collectible of all the 1960s Guild guitars are the hollow-body versions that the company made of the BluesBird, variations on the compact, single-cutaway Aristocrat, which Guild described as a "light-weight, semisolid midget model".

Guild's thin-body Starfires were well-made guitars somewhat reminiscent of Gibson thinlines; they came in both single- and double-cutaway versions, usually in cherry red. Guild also excelled in building jazz-style archtops, such as the Epiphone-inspired Stratford; it was equipped with six tone pushbuttons that looked a little clunky but were more versatile than any stock Strat or Les Paul Custom. One of the more unusual features introduced by Guild during the 1960s that didn't catch on among other makers was the hinged guitar stand set into the backs of Thunderbirds and Polaras.

By mid-decade Kay had moved into a huge new facility near Chicago's O'Hare airport and was producing up to a reported 1,500 guitars a day, most of them budget models that allowed countless aspiring rockers to get started on electric guitar.

Kay's Jazz II, for example, one of many double-cutaways more or less derived from Gibson's 335, featured big pickups with grid-pattern covers and a V-crested peghead that owed more to rocket-inspired auto styling (or perhaps modernistic coffee-shop appliances) than any guitar tradition. The guitar boom tapered off rapidly, leaving Kay hopelessly over-extended. By the end of the decade it had changed hands several times, but none of the new owners could save it, and in 1969 the Kay brandname was ignominiously sold at auction.

Kay's history was paralleled by Harmony's. Both were old Midwestern companies that moved into enlarged facilities just in time for the mid-1960s surge and then faltered as the boom subsided and imports increased. Harmony president Chuck Rubovits told me that in the 1964-65 production cycle Harmony employed 600 workers, produced more than 1000 guitars a day, and grossed $11 million. By 1968, he estimated, Harmony was making most of the guitars produced in America, certainly more than anyone else. Before the company fell to the same market forces that had toppled Kay, it produced a vast amount of reasonably good-quality budget electrics (some of them sold through the Sears mail-order operation). A typical example of a 1960s Harmony was the

SOLID HIT
the Les Paul guitars —
by GIBSON

Gibson
KALAMAZOO, MICHIGAN

LES PAUL & MARY FORD

LES PAUL and Mary Ford
(left), the husband-and-wife
duo who had enjoyed big hits in
the 1950s, fell from favour in
the 1960s, and divorced in
1963. Paul did not renew his
contract with Gibson, fearful of
new earnings being sucked into
divorce settlements, and so the
SG guitars stopped appearing
with "Les Paul" on them.

△ GIBSON SG SPECIAL
Produced 1961-1971 (this style); this example
January 1966

*The SG-body version of the Special never appeared
with the Les Paul name on the instrument. This SG
Special was originally finished in Pelham Blue, but the top coat
of clear lacquer has yellowed with age to make it look green.*

LES PAUL (below right) first
shot to fame in the early 1950s
with hit records such as 'How
High The Moon' which bristled
with plentiful layered-up
guitars in brilliant homemade
productions. Les Paul & Mary
Ford continued to record into
the early 1960s, but by 1963 the
duo was personally as well as
professionally finished.
However, Paul emerged from
his "retirement" in 1968
with the Les Paul Now! LP,
re-recordings of his best
material, and the same year
Gibson bowed to popular
demand and reissued the
original-design Les Paul
models (see also p.70).

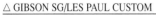

△ GIBSON SG/LES PAUL CUSTOM
Produced 1961-1963; this example October 1962

*Because of declining sales and a feeling that their solidbody
guitars were beginning to look old fashioned, Gibson completely
redesigned the Les Paul Junior, Standard and Custom models in
1961 with this modern twin-cutaway body. The "Les Paul" name
was dropped during 1963, and Gibson began to call the new
models the SG Junior, SG Standard and SG Custom.*

KAY
INSTRUMENTS
1967-68 EDITION

three-pickup Rocket III, with a hard-to-miss crescent of six big
white knobs along the lower bout.

While the joint was jumpin' at established companies, some
of the boldest ideas were coming from newcomers like Dan
Armstrong, a New York repairman/designer who at the end of
the decade came up with one of the era's most intriguing
guitars. For the body he chose a hard, clear plastic, but not for
the easy-production reasons behind Valco's Res-O-Glas models.
Armstrong said, "My intention was to make a guitar that
sustained extremely well," thus invoking a consideration that
dominated design discussions for years.

Although best remembered for their see-through bodies,
Armstrong's Ampeg-made guitars also featured inter-
changeable, slide-in pickups co-designed by Bill Lawrence. The
idea that a player could readily change pickups for different
applications helped spawn a near-obsession with versatility
that would characterise scads of multi-switch/coil-tap designs
in the coming decade. But the biggest contribution of Dan
Armstrong and other like-minded builders of the 1960s was
more subtle than any single feature. It was, simply, the notion
that the industry giants hadn't taken the electric guitar as far
as it could go after all. ■ TOM WHEELER

Musical Instruments of Quality
by KAY

ELECTRIC GUITARS
AMPLIFIERS
GUITARS
BANJOS
MANDOLINS

*KAY had by 1961 become one
of the biggest guitar producers
in America, as this expansive
view (above) of its new Chicago
factory in 1964 conspicuously
demonstrates. The company
dates back to 1890, although
the brandname itself was not
used until the 1930s. A group
of investors bought Kay in 1955*

*and ex-Harmony man Sidney
Katz became president. He
turned Kay into another
Harmony by aiming primarily
at mass sales of budget guitars.
By 1964 Kay had made its
2,000,000th guitar. During the
flurry of corporate buy-outs of
guitar makers in 1965,
Seeburg, a vending machine*

*company, bought Kay. In 1966
Katz resigned amid losses and
"mutual disappointment".
Meanwhile Valco, owner of the
National brand, bought Kay
from Seeburg in 1967, but
Kay took Valco with it when it
folded in 1969. Both the Kay
and National brandnames were
sold at auction that year.*

THE SHADOWS *became the biggest endorsers of Burns guitars when Hank Marvin spurned his famous Strat and helped to design the 1964 Burns Marvin model (seen, right, with Marvin, centre, and Bruce Welch, far right). Other Burns guitars included the Split Sonic and Vista Sonic models, as displayed in this shot from the 1963 catalogue (left).*

△ BURNS BISON
Produced 1961-1962 (this style); this example 1961

Britain's supreme moment of 1960s guitar engineering, the Bison was a handbuilt four-pickup wonder that was the aim of every flagwaving beat-group musician. But at £157 it was pure unattainable luxury for most, on the same level as an imported Strat (£148), and at a time when the average knockabout electric could be had for around £20. According to one insider, only 49 four-pickup Bisons were made before a "simplified" three-pickup version replaced it during 1962. The four-pickup Bison is one of the finest (and rarest) British guitars ever made.

EUROPEAN GUITARS

An embargo on US musical instrument imports to the UK was lifted during the summer of 1959, and the following year American-made guitars at last began to hit British shores. Players thought they'd never had it so good. Long-desired but hitherto unobtainable transatlantic electrics came over in quantity, and at first it seemed as if guitars made closer to home were in danger of being forgotten in the rush. Sales of un-American instruments did suffer, of course, but soon a new picture emerged.

In 1960s Britain, as now, the leading players exerted a great influence on those striving to emulate their styles and successes. Guitars fingered by the famous were important. While local hero Bert Weedon stolidly stuck with his Höfners, rising guitar star Hank B. Marvin had other ideas. He was assuming an increasingly high profile as lead guitarist in Cliff Richard's backing band, The Shadows, and inspiring a multitude of imitators. Marvin's Buddy Holly-like horn-rimmed glasses may have made a big impression, but it was his red Fender Stratocaster that became the main focus of attention for a multitude of aspiring axe-wielders.

That Fiesta Red Strat had come direct from America in the

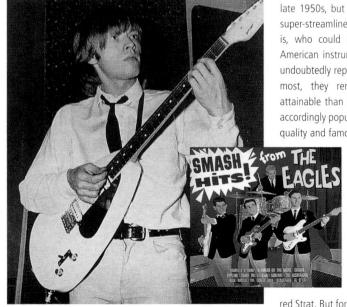

VOX guitars, originally made by Jennings in Dartford, Kent, were seen with the famous (Brian Jones with distinctive two-pickup teardrop Mk VI, above) and the not-so-famous (the "other" Eagles, right, with a handful of Vox Fendalikes).

late 1950s, but now anyone could go and buy one of these super-streamlined solids in their local music shop. Anyone, that is, who could afford it. To many hopeful British players, American instruments were over here and overpriced. While undoubtedly representing the epitome of design and sound to most, they remained mere dream machines, no more attainable than before. The more affordable US guitars were accordingly popular, but usually lacked the degree of charisma, quality and famous-artist associations of Fender.

The fact that this brand was already the clear leader in the UK was directly attributable to the success of Cliff and The Shadows. The influence they exerted during the early 1960s, both in their homeland and in many other countries outside America, should not be under-estimated, although it tends to be overshadowed by the Beatles-led beat group boom which followed. For a while it seemed that every player wanted a red Strat. But for many it cost well over six months' wages, and so they had to settle for something more finance-friendly. It was this economically-induced void that guitar makers in Britain and elsewhere tried to fill with a succession of cost-conscious alternatives to Fender's favourite creation.

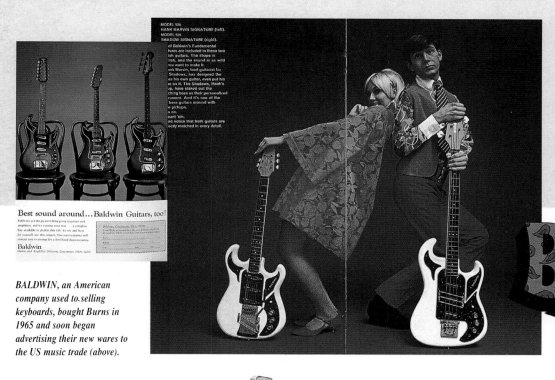

MODEL 524.
HANK MARVIN SIGNATURE (left).
MODEL 526.
SHADOW SIGNATURE (right).
...of Baldwin's fundamental features are included in these two ...ish guitars. The shape is ...lish, and the sound is as wild ...row want to make it. ...nk Marvin, lead guitarist for ...Shadows, has designed the ...as his own guitar, even put his ... so on it. The Shadows, Hank's ...up, have staked out the ...ching bass as their personalized ...roment. And it's one of the ...e bass guitars around with ...o pickups. ...o ah. ...ount 'em. ...nd notice that both guitars are ...ectly matched in every detail.

Best sound around...Baldwin Guitars, too!

BALDWIN, an American company used to selling keyboards, bought Burns in 1965 and soon began advertising their new wares to the US music trade (above).

BALDWIN joined the rush of large American corporations to buy up smaller guitar makers in the mid 1960s. Observing the boom in demand, they sensed irresistible profit potential. What they did not know, of course, was that the boom would become a slump in a few short years, and that losses and closures would replace the general euphoria. Having bid unsuccessfully for Fender, Baldwin bought the vastly cheaper Burns set-up in 1965. Burns had already toyed with US collaborators, badging some models with the Ampeg brand, and enjoying low-key distribution by Lipsky. But the Baldwin deal quickly soured – despite glorious spirit-of-the-times publicity (left) – and the operation ceased in 1970.

BALDWIN

▽ WATKINS RAPIER 33
Produced c1961-1965 (this style); this example c1964

The average British guitarist of the decade was more likely to be saddled with something like the cheap Rapier, a stalwart of the early 1960s beat-group scene. Charlie Watkins' London-based company was also well known for decent, low-priced amplifiers, and any British group member of the time will remember the stylish WEM logo (inset here), the initials standing for Watkins Electric Music. Toward the end of the decade Watkins used the Wilson brandname.

WATKINS did venture a little more up-market, leaning on amp expertise for models such as the Circuit 4 (left).

PRESENTING THE LATEST CONCEPT IN MODERN SOUND • PERFORMANCE AND LASTING QUALITY, COMBINED WITH A CIRCUITRY SYSTEM UNIQUE IN ITS COMBINATION OF TONE & OUTPUT

CIRCUIT 4
BY WATKINS
47 GNS
WATKINS
CRAFTSMANSHIP IN SOUND

German maker Höfner had long since capitalised on Gibson's popular concept of thinline semi-acoustic guitars, but the twin-cutaway Verithin, launched in 1960, targeted this market in a more obvious manner. Höfner's small-bodied Club semis remained popular during the early part of the decade, and the company managed to stay in the solid fray by replacing earlier Gibson-derived influences with distinctly Fender-ish features and styling. The Strat was an initial inspiration, and a variation on this theme provided the basis for the popular Galaxie, bedecked with switches and roller controls. The Jazzmaster outline later found favour too, and the shape also proved popular with the other significant German maker, Framus, who used it on a succession of solids, again adorned with complex control layouts. Fellow rivals Hopf and Klira followed a similar course, and the use of multiple slide switches, rollers and rotary selectors typified the German approach to the electric guitar of the 1960s.

In Britain, the Futurama brand had originally appeared on Czech-made guitars, but these were now succeeded by instruments of Swedish origin which more faithfully followed in Fender's footsteps. These second-wave Futuramas were produced by Hagström, a company hitherto best known for accordions and similarly sparkle-finished electric guitars, but

whose successful switch from squeeze-box to Strat styling was yet another sign of Fender's ever-spreading dominance.

In Italy, too, numerous accordion makers such as Eko, Crucianelli and Galanti saw that the electric guitar was the coming thing and got in on the act. Like Hagström, they opted not to abandon their heritage, and early efforts were outfitted with an abundance of sparkle and pearl plastic. Many based their creations on the Jazzmaster rather than the Strat, while others, such as Wandre, had very original ideas regarding guitar design, some quite bizarre and works of art rather than tools of the electric revolution.

Watkins, Vox and Burns were the most prominent and prolific makers in Britain. All three enjoyed quite a healthy export record to back up national sales of instruments which represented the best that the UK could offer. At the start of the

1960s Watkins began producing guitars to partner their popular budget-price small amps. The instruments trod similar territory, the Rapier model becoming a successful mainstay for many Marvin maybes.

Vox too already enjoyed amp success but the 1960s saw them add electric guitars, from entry-level planks up to ostensible alternatives to America's best. The top models initially came in Fender-inspired form, but later Vox explored less obvious avenues, resulting in the angular Phantom and the equally distinctive teardrop-shaped Mark (or 'Mk') models, perfectly capturing 1960s adventurousness.

By the start of the decade maverick maker Jim Burns had set up his own company, and typically chose to tread a decidedly different path, although Fender influences became increasingly apparent through commercial necessity. Regardless of their sometimes over-complex design quirks, Burns instruments tended to be superior in construction and components to most British-made competition. Some were aimed at first-time buyers; others at discerning players, promoted as ultimate instruments – or at least as high quality stepping stones.

In 1964 The Shadows surprisingly switched to Burns instruments, strapping on a smart set of matching models which combined Fender-derived features with original ideas. It was quite a coup for the company, although by now both band

1962

FOR EVERY top European 1960s band there were thousands of also-rans. At least some of them made it as far as the studio, as the Fender-armed Hunters prove on this obscure 1961 document (right) of pre-Beatles British beat. A year later and a step up the ladder were the deranged Swedish Spotnicks (far right), carrying a Levin guitar from home among the more familiar shapes.

and brand were beginning to feel the impact of change – in the music, those who made it, and the tools the players chose for their ever-evolving trade. The days of matching suits and stage movements were numbered, and the time when a group deliberately sported an identical array of instruments was certainly at an end, principally thanks to The Beatles.

By the mid 1960s pop music and the electric guitar had become a virtually global partnership, and this ever-growing appeal had encouraged makers everywhere to jump on an already burgeoning bandwagon. The fruits of their labours sometimes filtered through to the UK courtesy of an enthusiastic importer or two. This meant the appearance of Matons from Australia, Musimas from East Germany and Egmonds from Holland, to name just a few. Japanese-made imports actually dwindled in the face of the increasing numbers coming from elsewhere, and this position wouldn't change until much later in the decade.

Whatever the source, the underlying motive was to satisfy a seemingly undiminished demand, and to meet it with anything even remotely resembling the real thing. Many players were far from discerning

Maton

or knowledgeable, so indifferent quality and gimmicky ideas were fostered and allowed to flourish, often ably assisted by adroit marketing. As the 1960s progressed there was a growing emphasis on playing ability and an accompanying awareness of what constituted a good guitar in terms of design and performance.

Most of the new guitar heroes of this era were from blues-based rather than pure pop backgrounds – high-powered players such as Eric Clapton and Jeff Beck. Their misuse of a Gibson Les Paul through a hard-pressed valve (tube) amp gave birth to a new sound that soon became de rigueur for many followers desperate to emulate the whining sustain that such a combination produced. The Strat's popularity faltered, until given a boost by the fiery fingers of Jimi Hendrix. Whether favouring Gibson or Fender, British players now focused squarely on American instruments, and so those from UK makers and elsewhere were increasingly left out in the cold and out of touch with guitarists' evolving demands.

Of the original British 'big three', Watkins seemed least affected by such market vagaries, content to stay within and supply a small but established niche. While the brandname varied (Watkins, Wilson,

WEM) the company's commitment to the lower end of the market remained constant, despite a few excursions into slightly higher-priced realms. Burns had been bought in 1965 by the US Baldwin Piano & Organ company. Apart from the change of name and a rationalised line, it was business as usual in Britain, which meant a diminishing share of both home and export markets. Baldwin showed little real interest or incentive to stop the rot, preferring to concentrate on consolidating their keyboards, and they called a halt to all guitar production just five years later.

Like Burns, Vox had enjoyed success in the first half of the 1960s, enough to cause problems regarding supply and demand. So they enlisted the aid of a major Italian maker, Eko, to help with manufacturing. Initially this was on a shared basis, but by the latter part of the decade all production had been switched to sunny Italy. While the American Vox guitar catalogue contained numerous novelty items, the line in Britain was more compact and conservative, although it did include the Guitar Organ and a spin-off active electronics package offered as an option on certain high-end models. But by now the company was also feeling the cold wind of change, and even Vox amplification was struggling to maintain its once-prominent position. The future of the guitars looked

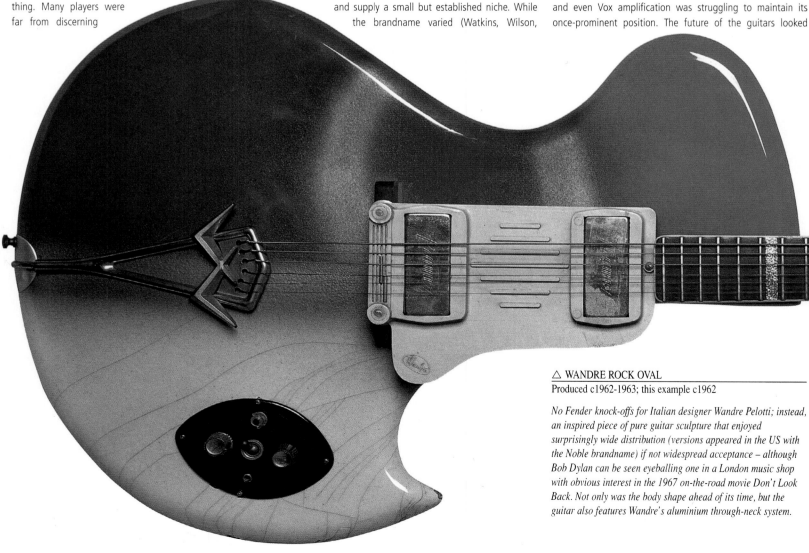

△ WANDRE ROCK OVAL
Produced c1962-1963; this example c1962

No Fender knock-offs for Italian designer Wandre Pelotti; instead, an inspired piece of pure guitar sculpture that enjoyed surprisingly wide distribution (versions appeared in the US with the Noble brandname) if not widespread acceptance – although Bob Dylan can be seen eyeballing one in a London music shop with obvious interest in the 1967 on-the-road movie Don't Look Back. Not only was the body shape ahead of its time, but the guitar also features Wandre's aluminium through-neck system.

FRAMUS built solidbody (see Strato below) and thinline models (such as the Fretjet) that fired the music of many a budding 1960s Euro star. But their more esoteric archtop models included the Attila Zoller (right), named for the Bosnian jazz guitarist who lived in New York in the 1960s.

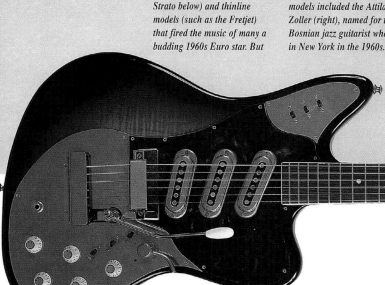

△ FRAMUS STRATO DELUXE 5/168
Produced c1962-1968; this example 1965

Fender's "offset-waist" body shape informed the designs of many European guitars, including this German Framus. The small bent handle below the bridge controls an organ-like "swell" effect.

NELSON MANDELA is jailed in South Africa. In 1964 the leader of the banned African National Congress gets a life sentence for treason resulting in his internment until 1990.

ITALIAN electric guitars of the 1960s, with brands such as Crucianelli, Bartolini and Gemelli (right), often appear gloriously free of the usual range of design influences. Instead they seem to combine elements of espresso machines, accordions and motor-scooters with wonderfully idiosyncratic results. The Gemelli model on this catalogue cover (right) is the Twins, a typically demented piece of work with baby twins crawling over the body. Clearly, this was not a Fender copy.

decidedly dim and by the end of the decade the line had dwindled to a few Italian- and Japanese-made models.

The latter constituted an early portent of things to come, as the Japanese began to perceive the commercial potential of providing very affordable copies of currently popular electrics. Previous Far-Eastern production policy had been to incorporate only the influences of classic designs and to suggest their sources in approximate rather than exact terms. Now, however, more overt mimicry made commercial sense: the era of the 'copy guitar' had begun. In Britain the Rose-Morris company provided some of the earliest examples of this new trend, under their own Shaftesbury brand. These included Gibson and Rickenbacker lookalikes, ironic in view of Rose-Morris's previous role as Rickenbacker's UK distributor.

With no new UK makers to take the place of Burns or Vox, the market for home-grown guitars had undergone a significant shift in the 1960s, having begun the decade so optimistically in terms of demand, design and sales, but finishing up as a commercial calamity. The majority of British guitarists undoubtedly preferred to play Uncle Sam's instruments. This loyalty proved to be so established and unswerving that the British guitar-building industry would never be the same again. ■ PAUL DAY

SPIDERMAN appears in Marvel comics for the first time, and becomes their most famous hero. The Beatles appear on Parlophone Records for the first time as 'Love Me Do' is released in October. They will become quite famous too.

TELSTAR, a communications satellite, is launched. It enables the first live TV transmissions between Europe and the US.

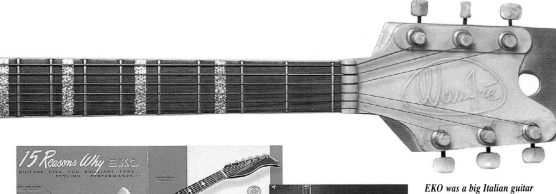

EKO was a big Italian guitar manufacturer of the 1960s, available throughout Europe, and in the US via Lo Duca. Bearing clear evidence of the company's accordion-making heritage, models such as the 700 (far left) featured typical heat-moulded plastic finishes and multiple control layouts.

JAMES BOND appears on film for the first time in Doctor No. The British secret service agent is portrayed by Sean Connery; the twangy guitar of the Bond theme tune is played by Vic Flick of The John Barry Seven.

JAMES MEREDITH enrols as the first black student at the University of Mississippi, despite riots by white students.

THUMBS CARLLILE
all thumbs
PHILIPS

FENDER's Jaguar came in standard sunburst (above) at $379.50 in 1962, or in blond or custom colour at $398.49 (plus gold-plated hardware, $456.88).

RADIO & TELEVISION

If the progress of the 20th century has a crossroads, it occurred in the 1960s, for it was during that heady decade that the international electronic experience emerged. For guitar lovers, their instrument finally triumphed as the voice of contemporary music. This victory was inseparably tied to the growing importance of radio and TV, as people around the world increasingly tuned in and joined Marshall McLuhan's "global village".

In the United States, the path to the guitar's pre-eminence was not always a smooth one. Indeed, as the decade began, it seemed as though the guitar was losing ground. In the 1950s rock'n'roll had breathed new life into AM radio – and into

△ FENDER JAGUAR

Produced 1962-1975, reissued 1986; this example 1966

Fender's first new electric model of the 1960s was the top-of-the-line Jaguar, bearing the same offset-waist body shape as the earlier Jazzmaster. It was the first Fender with 22 frets, on a shorter-than-normal 24″ scale. But the general impression was that Fender piled too many of the wrong features on the Jaguar, and the guitar has always languished in the shadow of the Strat.

FENDER continued its amusing ad series in the 1960s where an unusual scenario was matched to the line, "You won't part with yours either." In this example, a precarious Jaguar is given the important gigging-by-motorcycle test.

TOMMY Tedesco (left) was the busiest session guitarist working in the TV and film studios of California during the 1960s, and could be heard on all manner of small-screen classics such as Rawhide, Bonanza, and Route 66.

guitar playing. But by 1960 a bunch of rock's rising stars were dead, including Buddy Holly and Eddie Cochran. And what's more, Little Richard had got religion, Chuck Berry was in the slammer, and Elvis was in the army.

American pop radio faced a crisis of major proportions. During 1960 AM radio was rocked with the infamous payola scandals, where DJs had accepted money and gifts to promote specific records. Among those brought down by the scandal was Alan Freed, the man most known for promoting the new guitar-driven music in the 1950s.

Instead of rock, AM airwaves in the early 1960s were filled with mostly vocal-oriented pop. Guitars weren't totally absent from the radio, of course, but most continued 1950s traditions of instrumental pop or country. Guitars on American television continued pretty much in the same vein as in the 1950s. Programming was dominated by dramas, particularly Westerns, with a growing number of situation comedies (or 'sit-coms', such as Leave It To Beaver) joining the blend of musical variety and game shows.

While Marshall Dillon, Adam, Hoss and Little Joe ruled the screen, guitar lovers continued to enjoy weekly 'rock videos' by Ricky Nelson, backed by Tele ace James Burton, on The Adventures of Ozzie and Harriet, and the smiling picking of Buddy Merrill on The Lawrence Welk Show, both holdovers from

the 1950s. Even brush-cut comedian Gary Moore frequently ended his show plunking amateurishly on a guitar singing a novelty song. Guitars also showed up on variety shows such as the evergreen Ed Sullivan Show, and the Ford Show Starring Tennessee Ernie Ford where top country players were often showcased. Perhaps more importantly, teens got to tune in a weekly dance party hosted by Dick Clark which, while not boasting too many guitars, at least featured the music that would become the guitar's main vehicle.

TV soundtracks often had plenty to interest the guitar fan. Scored and performed by top LA studio musicians, they were loaded with memorable melodies and guitar riffs. Players such as Laurindo Almeida, Bob Bain and Al Hendrickson routinely contributed guitar parts, but no one more than Tommy

Tedesco, whose chops were heard by millions on shows such as Bonanza, Gunsmoke, Rawhide, Maverick, Have Gun Will Travel, The Rifleman, Wagon Train, Route 66 and countless other classic TV shows as well as movies from the decade.

Significantly, one other place guitars did show up on American TV was the vapid The Many Loves of Dobie Gillis (1959-63), a sit-com which parodied late-1950s beatniks and in which Gillis constantly fled homely Zelda Gilroy and tried to learn how to play guitar. The guitar in the corner was a sign of what was to come: the folk revival that would indicate the first signs of the 1960s guitar boom.

The impact of folk music was felt almost immediately on both TV and radio. Catching the trend, in 1961 the prolific Columbia record producer Mitch Miller successfully translated his popular, saccharine choral singalong records of folk music onto the small screen with Sing Along With Mitch. While this had more to do with bouncing balls than guitars, it did serve to reassure parents that the folk music their kids were playing on guitar was safe and healthy. Little did they know.

Radio stations also quickly caught the wave, and chart success of the more commercial folk singers, as well as Mitch Miller, finally did bring guitar to the fore on TV with Hootenanny (1963-64), an artificial recreation of popular college events featuring acts such as The Smothers Brothers,

Fender JAGUAR

DUANE EDDY ROCK 'N ROLL GUITARS

DUANE EDDY (left) fired most of his twangy instrumentals with a Gretsch 6120, but used a Guild "signature" model on stage for a while in the 1960s.

▽ GUILD DUANE EDDY
Produced 1962-c1969; this example 1962

Based in New Jersey, the Guild company had a reputation for making fine jazz-style archtop acoustic and electric guitars, but tried to entice 1960s rockers with this Duane Eddy model. The guitar shown here belongs to Duane "Twang" Eddy himself.

△ NATIONAL NEWPORT 84
Produced 1962-1965 (also Val-Pro 84); this example c1964

Valco was never short of impressive names for its guitar innovations, marketed mainly with National or Supro brands. These new fibreglass-body guitars were no exception: "Res-O-Glas" and "Hollow-Glas" appeared in Valco catalogues and ads to describe the material used in its new line of National non-wood instruments. In fact, the bodies were made from fibreglass-reinforced polyster, which Valco thought would provide a longer-lasting guitar. But this brave and stylish plastic experiment ended with Valco itself in the late 1960s.

READY, Steady, Go! was the hippest British pop TV programme of the 1960s, beamed into millions of homes on a Friday evening ("the weekend starts here") from a Swinging London studio, at first with Manfred Mann's '5-4-3-2-1' as its theme. It featured all the right groups – seen in action here (right) are regular guests The Kinks – but incidentally showcased the right clothes, the right dances and the right atmosphere. Unusually, RSG stopped at its peak, lasting for just three years after its debut in 1963.

Josh White and The Carter Family, all sporting guitars. The idealism of the folk revival quickly yielded to a stark intrusion of a darker reality. Within minutes of President Kennedy's assassination in Dallas, Texas, in November 1963, moving pictures of the event floated over TVs. Viewers in the US and, thanks to the newly-launched communications satellite Telstar, around the world were transfixed in heart-stopping horror and grief. Never before had an entire population watched real-life tragedy – which would include the killing of Kennedy's accused assassin – unfold live on the tube. Innocence had come face-to-face with experience.

The Kennedy assassination was significant because it was a culmination of changes that had been creeping into the artificiality of TV-land, asserting reality in the form of news reportage. Slowly but surely world events were coming into American living rooms via the TV set, from Gary Powers' U-2 spy plane incident in 1960 through 1962's near-apocalyptic Cuban missile crisis. For the rest of the decade, news would become an increasingly vital function of television, the most significant being the reports of the growing military involvement in Vietnam.

Only weeks after the Kennedy assassination came the British Invasion of the US. At 8pm on Sunday, February 9th 1964, just after *My Favorite Martian*, The Beatles took the stage on *The Ed Sullivan Show* (though they'd actually been seen on American TV a month earlier in a film clip on the Jack Paar show). The Beatles' subsequent concerts caused near riots, and made newscasts across the country. Almost immediately the American airwaves bristled with British accents. The contrast between US hits of the early 1960s and 1964 is amazing: ten top hits by The Beatles, two by The Rolling Stones, plus The Animals' 'House Of The Rising Sun' and The Kinks' 'You Really Got Me', all British and all drenched in classic guitar licks.

Pop television in Britain in the 1960s didn't get any better than *Ready, Steady, Go!* which began in August 1963. The show was a mirror to the beat boom, reproducing the feel of

NATIONAL first appeared as an independent brand in the 1920s, but by the 1960s was part of the renamed Chicago-based Valco Manufacturing company. The best-known National instruments of the 1960s are the plastic- and wood-body "map shape" guitars, so-called because the body outline is supposed to resemble part of a map of the United States. The entirely un-famous Kim Sisters model a couple of map-shape Nationals in this 1966 ad (far right). As well as its more outrageous designs, Valco also produced many more conventional models, as this contemporary catalogue (right) shows. Valco bought the Kay guitar company in 1967, but unfortunately when Kay went out of business during the following year they took Valco with them.

▽ SILVERTONE 1457 GUITAR/AMP/CASE SET
Produced 1962-1967; this example c1964

A brilliant idea by the Danelectro company of New Jersey – marketed by Sears under its Silvertone brandname – was this guitar that came with a case (below) that had a built-in amplifier.

SILVERTONE's ingenious "all-in-one" outfit boasted a guitar case with built-in amplifier and speaker. "One easy-to-carry unit," said Sears' publicity, which offered the two-pickup guitar and tremolo-amp cased set for just $99.95.

ED SULLIVAN (right) presented all the top bands of the 1960s on his TV show.

a club gig in a London TV studio and featuring all the best new pop acts as well as a hip American visitor or two. It was required viewing for fledgling guitarists who could ogle a procession of rare delights from Gretsch, Vox, Rickenbacker, Höfner, Gibson, Burns, Fender and more. The show's presenters included Cathy McGowan and Keith Fordyce. With McGowan, it was as if one of the avowedly hip audience had been given a microphone seconds before the show went on air. But the avuncular Fordyce remembers that during its brief three-year run *Ready, Steady, Go!* had its finger firmly on the musical pulse: "It perfectly reflected the rising British pop scene of the time, and as an utterly contemporary news magazine it was compelling to watch. It told you exactly

what was happening in terms of dress and music and people." In contrast to this commercial TV offering, the BBC had two key shows. *Juke Box Jury* boasted a panel of stars voting new records a hit (ding!) or a miss (bzzz), famously including all four Beatles in 1963 seen by an audience of 24 million viewers, not far short of half Britain's population. *Top Of The Pops* debuted in 1964 and is still going strong today with its shameless rundown of chart hits that culminates with the week's number one single.

Radio in Britain in the first few years of the 1960s meant the BBC, where the broadcast of records ('needle time') was limited by an agreement with the Musicians' Union designed to increase work for musicians. This meant that sessions by pop groups, specially recorded at BBC studios, were put out on BBC stations throughout the decade, providing many players with their first taste of 'proper' recording as well as an early and often important connection with their potential audience. Auditions were held for these sessions – The Beatles, for

example, still with Pete Best on drums, passed their BBC radio audition in February 1962 and made their first broadcast the following month, the first opportunity that most people outside Liverpool had to hear the group. Every top British group, and a whole army of lesser-known acts, recorded sessions at the BBC, and for some it was a stepping stone to success. Guitarist Dave Edmunds of Love Sculpture, for example, recalled the run-up to 'Sabre Dance' in 1968: "We did a live session for [DJ] John Peel's *Top Gear*, and suddenly we were signed up by EMI... and we had a number two single," said Edmunds.

The down side of the 'needle time' agreement was that record companies found it difficult to get their wares broadcast over the airwaves in Britain. Radio Luxembourg did play pop records, and thousands of British teenagers would tune in to the distant station when it could be received at night, just to hear the rare music amid the static. Record plugger Ronan O'Rahilly, frustrated at the lack of outlets for his clients, decided in 1964 to begin broadcasts a little closer to Britain,

ERIC CLAPTON (right) plays his Gibson ES-335 (see also below) at London's Royal Albert Hall in November 1968 during Cream's farewell tour – later portrayed in the Farewell Cream film. Three songs from an earlier show at The Forum in Los Angeles turned up on the Goodbye Cream LP.

△ GIBSON ES-335TDC
Produced 1962-1982 (this style); this example May 1964

This Gibson 335 is owned by Eric Clapton. He bought it in the 1960s and first used it toward the end of Cream's brief if illustrious career, most notably on the group's "farewell" concerts during late 1968 in Los Angeles, San Diego and London. While Clapton's SG (see p.48-49) was his favoured studio guitar at the time, this 335 may have been the guitar he used to record 'Badge' in 1968. The guitar's original case, complete with CREAM stencil, is pictured above. Gibson's 335, a 1950s design, reached new heights of popularity in the 1960s.

1963

GIBSON started the 1960s determined to take on their chief rival Fender, designing the Firebird guitar and Thunderbird bass (1964 ad, left) with clear recognition of the solidbody style of the West Coast firm. But it didn't work, and Gibson's 1960s sales had to rely on classic 1950s designs such as the semi-solid ES-335.

What's New

and Exciting in Solid Bodies?
Firebird Guitars and Thunderbird Basses by Gibson

Chances are, you show solid body models to a large percentage of your guitar customers. After all, the new sound of today's music depends upon them for its distinctive beat.

Chances are, you will sell more of these customers when you show them the new Firebird by Gibson. Revolutionary in shape, sound, and colors, the new Firebird is sure to create sales excitement through customer preference. Its fresh and daring design . . . its brilliant, solid sound match the needs of the musicians who play today's music. Models with one, two, or three pickups are available in ten custom colors.*

Equally exciting is the Thunderbird bass with single or double pickup. And, the Gibson price range—$159.50 to $470.00—clinches sales to the amateur, semi-pro, and professional performer.

Gibson
KALAMAZOO, MICHIGAN

---

and the showmanship of custom color

Choose the color you want . . . to enhance your performance

GIBSON not only aped Fender design with the Firebirds, but borrowed their custom colour idea too, applying car paints to guitars. One Gibson colour (Golden Mist) was actually identical to a Fender colour (Shoreline Gold). Gibson used its Oldsmobile name; Fender applied the Pontiac term.

△ GIBSON FIREBIRD V
Produced 1963-1965 (this style); this example August 1965

Despite the novel sculpting of the SG design that Gibson had introduced at the start of the decade, the company still found its guitar styles compared unfavourably to those of Fender. So they brought in an automobile designer, Ray Dietrich, who was asked to out-Fender Fender. The result was the Firebird series, launched in 1963. This one is finished in Gibson's Cardinal Red.

△ GIBSON FIREBIRD I
Produced 1965-1969 (this style); this example December 1965

BRIAN JONES (left) was often seen in the mid-1960s with this attractive sunburst Firebird VII, but not even an unofficial endorsement from a Rolling Stone was enough to give Gibson the sales boost it wanted from its stylish Firebird models.

Gibson's attempt to modernise its line with the Firebirds faltered: sales were poor, and Fender complained about similarities to its patented body features. So the original Firebird design – known now as the "reverse" body – was dropped in 1965. Gibson revamped the series with this new shape – the "non-reverse" body – and dropped the more expensive neck-through-body construction in favour of Gibson's usual glued neck. Still unsuccessful, the Firebirds were grounded for good during 1969.

GIBSON GUITARS

For Gibson the 1960s began as an extension of the highly creative 1950s period which had seen the coming of age of the electric guitar. There were more new models, and record sales, thanks to the success of musical styles ubiquitously supported by the guitar. Midway through the decade, however, the company seemed to lose its flair for innovation... but fortunately at a time when the Les Paul design from the 1950s was reintroduced as a result of enormous popular demand.

On the threshold of the 1960s Gibson was a leading contender in the field of professional-grade electric guitars. Unlike most other US makers the company boasted a full line of electrics, ranging from traditional archtops to solidbodies through semi-solid thinlines, as well as basses and electrified flat-tops like the J-160E. Gibson, however, was no longer the dominant player it had been. Several brands – some old like Gretsch, others more recent like Fender – were actively challenging its electric franchise. Competition is what prompted Gibson to start the 1960s by

dropping the sunburst Les Paul Standard, widely acknowledged today as the most desirable solidbody guitar ever. At the time, though, a lightweight body with more aggressive styling and full access to the neck seemed necessary to rekindle the Les Paul Standard's flagging market appeal. With guitars increasingly used as solo instruments, players wanted to be able to play easily in the higher registers to expand their tonal range, and a double cutaway body was the answer. The first samples of the revamped Les Paul Standard came out in late 1960 showcasing an innovative double cutaway with pointed horns, highly bevelled edges and an ultra-thin rim. Another sign of the times: the new model was the first Gibson marketed with a vibrato tailpiece as a regular built-in appointment.

By 1961 the novel body shape was gradually adopted by the other solidbody variants (Custom, Junior, Special, TV) in lieu of their previous slab-body designs, whether single or double cutaway. At the end of 1962 it was applied in an elongated form to the custom-made double necks, and eventually, in 1966, it would serve for the final restyling of the low-end Melody Maker series.

Meanwhile the Les Paul markings were dropped in late 1963 and the Standard, Custom and Junior were simply called 'SG', for Solid Guitar (not Sixties Guitar). The reasons behind this removal have nothing to do with the fact that Les Paul did

not like the sculptured SG design. The wizard of Waukesha chose not to renew his endorsement contract because of his ongoing divorce with Mary Ford – he did not want money coming in that might be made part of the settlement. By coincidence, 1963 is also the year when shipments of Gibson acoustics began to exceed those of electrics for the first time since 1954, a situation that would continue during the rest of the 1960s. ('Shipment' is the official term for the number of particular guitars that left the Gibson factory.)

Making playing more comfortable in the upper register was desirable not just on solidbodies. At the end of 1960 a deep 'Florentine' cutaway was introduced on the archtop electrics that had a 17"-wide body. The pointed horn became the hallmark of the Super 400CES, L-5CES and Byrdland of the decade, since the arguably more graceful round cutaway was not reinstated until 1969.

However, Gibson's major effort in its traditional area was the release of Artist models endorsed by Barney Kessel, Johnny Smith and Tal Farlow. All of them were great guitarists, but they were 1950s jazzers in a period which would eventually be dominated by folk, pop and rock music. The artist rostrum was later completed with Trini Lopez, a nightclub act who would be the farthest Gibson would ever go in recruiting a pop endorser for a model during the 1960s (except of course The Everly Brothers on the acoustic side). Later in the decade, though,

REVISED Firebirds (the "non-reverse" models) included the I with two single-coil pickups, III with three single-coils, V (far right) with two mini-humbuckers, and VII (right) with three mini-humbuckers. Relaunch prices were set at $199.50 (I), $249.50 (III), $299.50 (V) and $394.50 (VII).

Firebird

FIREBIRD VII
Here is the ultimate in a solid-body guitar by Gibson. A completely new and exciting instrument

FIREBIRD V
Another in the revolutionary new series of solid body guitars by Gibson. Exciting in concept, exist-

△ GIBSON FIREBIRD I
Produced 1963-1965 (this style); this example April 1964

There were four original Firebird models, all fitted with mini-humbucking pickups. The I had one pickup and was the only Firebird without a vibrato; its launch price was $189.50. The III ($249.50) had two pickups and a stud bridge, the V ($325) two pickups and a tune-o-matic bridge, and the top-of-the-line VII ($445) had three pickups. Standard finish was sunburst, like the I shown here, but custom colours were offered for an extra $15.

New CORVETTE STING RAY by Chevrolet

PRESIDENT KENNEDY is assassinated in Dallas, Texas, and Lyndon B Johnson becomes president the same day; 48 hours later Lee Harvey Oswald, accused of Kennedy's murder, is shot and killed by Jack Ruby, a nightclub owner.

DR TIMOTHY LEARY and a colleague are sacked from Harvard for experimenting on students with LSD. "Drugs," writes Norman Mailer, "are a spiritual form of gambling."

THE CORVETTE Stingray is the chic new US car. Designed by Bill Mitchell, the coupe has split windows on a "boat-tail" rear, and pivoting headlights.

BRITAIN is rocked by scandal and crime. Conservative politician John Profumo resigns after disclosure of his involvement with Christine Keeler, mistress of a Soviet naval attaché. A gang steals an unprecedented £2.5 million from a mail train, achieved by hiding a green signal light with an old glove and lighting the red signal with torch batteries.

MARTIN LUTHER KING delivers a speech to a gathering in Washington: "I have a dream that one day this nation will rise up, live out the true meaning of its creed: we hold these truths to be self-evident, that all men are created equal." Meanwhile, 5000 are arrested on a civil rights march in Alabama as Governor George Wallace refuses to open the University there to black students.

GIBSON reacted to the 1960s guitar boom with apparent ease, indicative of a company that had made instruments since the turn of the century. There was luck too: a factory expansion was completed in 1961 (architect's drawing, below), doubling its size and poised for the folk boom and the Beatles boom. Gibson had used the Kalamazoo brand for cheap products since the 1930s, and in 1965 revived it (right) to feed the demand for budget

Sell Kalamazoo to a beginner buying his first guitar and amplifier.
It could keep him from buying his [...] rom somebody else.

KALAMAZOO
guitars and amplifiers

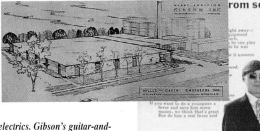

electrics. Gibson's guitar-and-amp sales grew from $10m in 1964 to peak in 1966 at $19m, falling to $14m by 1969.

there would be several certified guitar heroes using Gibsons as their workhorses, not least Eric Clapton who would play a Les Paul Standard, an SG Standard, a Firebird I and an ES-335.

The beginning of the 1960s witnessed unprecedented growth for the guitar industry, often recalled as the first guitar boom. To be sure not to miss out on market opportunities, Gibson had doubled its factory floor space up to 120,000 square feet in 1961. Two further plants were acquired, in 1962 and 1964, bringing another 80,000 square feet of space dedicated to amplifiers and electronics. These huge expansions were well inspired because by 1964, the year of the British Invasion of the US spearheaded by The Beatles, most manufacturers became unable to keep up with demand.

Given such buoyant market conditions, the sales of SG-styled electrics looked good but fell short of being spectacular. Like other Gibson guitars they were not ideal for the thunderous staccato of surf music or the twang of country styles. Besides, they were essentially monochrome (red or white) and the sideways vibrato fitted to the Standard and Custom models was inappropriate, to say the least. Something else was needed, something that could encroach upon the Fender preserve in sounds and looks while displaying typical Gibson feel and workmanship. An automobile designer named Ray Dietrich was enrolled to devise a new line of solidbodies, collectively known as the Firebird

THE VENTURES (left) had hits in the US with 'Perfidia' and 'Walk – Don't Run'. Guitarist Nokie Edwards explained to a 1964 interviewer the birth of their deal with guitar-maker Mosrite: "On the back of one of our albums we ran a credit line, 'Guitars courtesy of Mosrite Distributing Corp.' That single line in tiny type brought in over 800 letters, many from dealers."

▽ MOSRITE VENTURES
Produced c1963-1967; this example c1963

Gibson's "reverse-body" Firebird looks positively normal compared to Semie Moseley's wonderfully lop-sided concoction. A lucky marketing break came when Moseley lent a guitar to Nokie Edwards of top US instrumental group The Ventures; soon after, the Mosrite Ventures model was born. With the oriental success of both The Ventures and Mosrite that followed, the phrase "big in Japan" might have been invented for this guitar.

EARLY Ventures models, like this one, are usually indentified by a bound body and side-mounted jack socket.

series. No less than four guitars – the Firebird I, III, V and VII – and two Thunderbird basses were premiered in 1963. They were characterised by an asymmetrical body shape with a pronounced lower horn on the treble side and by a neck-through-body construction. The series was the first to be marketed by Gibson with ten optional custom colours, meant to emulate Fender's already well-established coloured finishes.

The 'reverse' body shape, as it's now known, could be viewed either as a smoothed-out variant of the Explorer or as the mirror image of an elongated Jazzmaster. Fender adhered to the second stance and claimed that the shape was infringing upon its patented 'offset-waist' design. The argument never reached the courts because disappointing sales led Gibson to modify the series in 1965. A second generation of Firebirds adopted a more conventional 'non-reverse' design (still kind of Fender-like) with a glued-on neck, but success remained elusive, despite the addition of a 12-string model.

Following on from the 1950s sunburst Les Paul Standard and 'Modernistic' Flying V and Explorer, the original Firebird series would become the third part in Gibson's revered trilogy of famous models now recognised as ahead of their time. But although their unique features are more widely praised today, the stylish Firebirds have remained less popular than other Gibson designs. This may be due to their pickups, as players tend to prefer regular humbuckers to the Firebird 'mini' variants (which were designed to be without adjustable polepieces).

Despite the Firebird hiccup, 1965 was a great year for Gibson marked by all-time record shipments. But by the following year the company was confronted with various problems, including how to replace its president, Ted McCarty, and its factory superintendent, John Huis. The two men had bought the Bigsby vibrato operation from Paul Bigsby, a long-time Gibson supplier. For Chicago Musical Instrument Co (CMI), Gibson's parent freshly quoted on the New York stock exchange, this was perceived as a potential conflict of interest, and consequently McCarty and Huis chose to resign rather than see Bigsby lose Gibson's business. Their departure is often considered as a watershed in Gibson's history, mainly because of the stalled creativity and the quality problems found in the ensuing period – not to mention the number of true classics introduced while McCarty had steered the company from March 1948 until June 1966. Quality had indeed become a serious issue. Too many models of different types were in production, and there was a much greater output compared to the 1950s. Less efficient moisture control caused plenty of wood cracking and led to a higher reject ratio, as well as to an inordinate amount of returns under warranty. Problems involving wood supplies, equipment, personnel and unions coalesced to push back-orders into tens of thousands of dollars. This was most untimely because demand was tapering off, while a bigger share of the guitar market was falling prey to oriental manufacturers.

The second half of the 1960s saw the emergence of new trends which would persist into the next decade. Production at Gibson went through a swingeing rationalisation to make the instruments stronger and less prone to warranty work. This trend gathered plenty of momentum with Stanley Rendell,

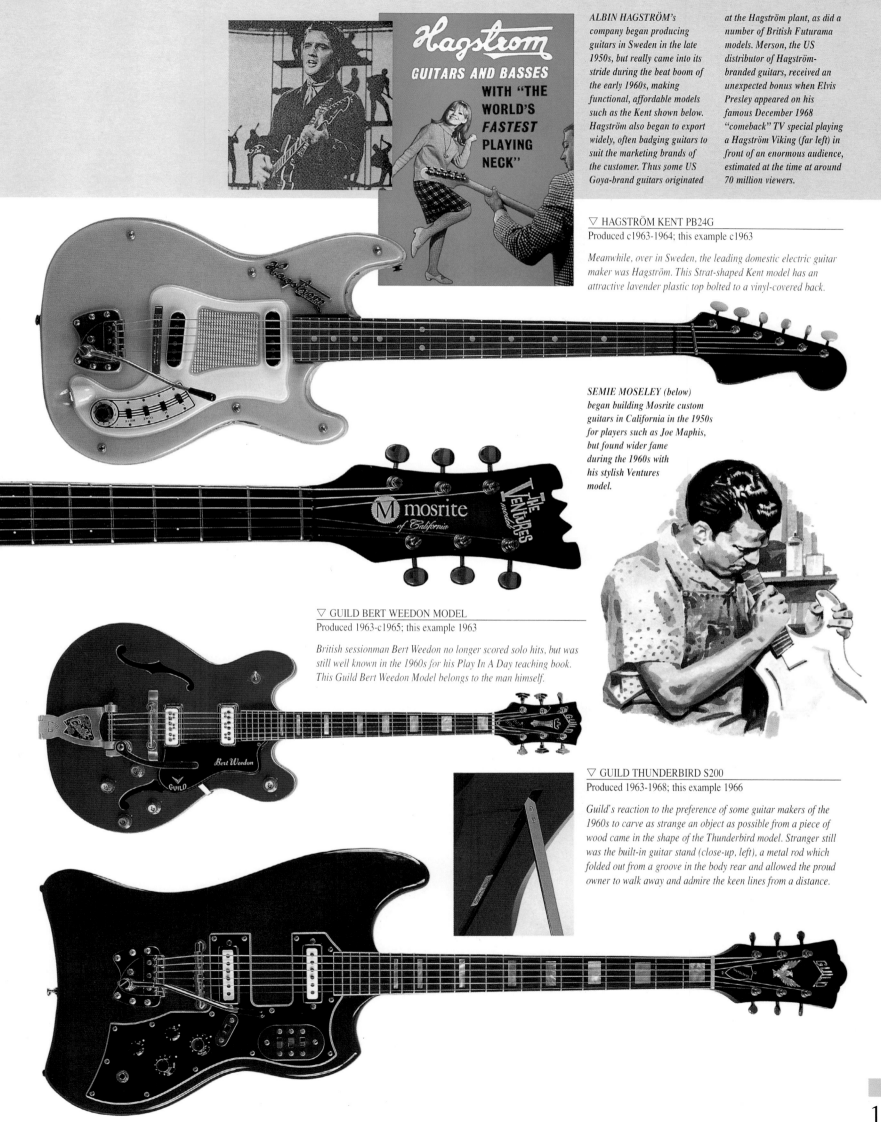

ALBIN HAGSTRÖM's company began producing guitars in Sweden in the late 1950s, but really came into its stride during the beat boom of the early 1960s, making functional, affordable models such as the Kent shown below. Hagström also began to export widely, often badging guitars to suit the marketing brands of the customer. Thus some US Goya-brand guitars originated at the Hagström plant, as did a number of British Futurama models. Merson, the US distributor of Hagström-branded guitars, received an unexpected bonus when Elvis Presley appeared on his famous December 1968 "comeback" TV special playing a Hagström Viking (far left) in front of an enormous audience, estimated at the time at around 70 million viewers.

▽ HAGSTRÖM KENT PB24G
Produced c1963-1964; this example c1963

Meanwhile, over in Sweden, the leading domestic electric guitar maker was Hagström. This Strat-shaped Kent model has an attractive lavender plastic top bolted to a vinyl-covered back.

SEMIE MOSELEY (below) began building Mosrite custom guitars in California in the 1950s for players such as Joe Maphis, but found wider fame during the 1960s with his stylish Ventures model.

▽ GUILD BERT WEEDON MODEL
Produced 1963-c1965; this example 1963

British sessionman Bert Weedon no longer scored solo hits, but was still well known in the 1960s for his Play In A Day teaching book. This Guild Bert Weedon Model belongs to the man himself.

▽ GUILD THUNDERBIRD S200
Produced 1963-1968; this example 1966

Guild's reaction to the preference of some guitar makers of the 1960s to carve as strange an object as possible from a piece of wood came in the shape of the Thunderbird model. Stranger still was the built-in guitar stand (close-up, left), a metal rod which folded out from a groove in the body rear and allowed the proud owner to walk away and admire the keen lines from a distance.

1964

▽ RICKENBACKER ASTRO AS-51
Produced 1964; this example 1964

This Rickenbacker creation was a build-it-yourself solidbody electric guitar kit aimed at the Christmas 1964 gift market, coming as an "educational and lots of fun" box of 25 parts.

ACOUSTIC 12-string guitars have been around since at least the 1930s, the idea being to make one guitar sound like at least two. Amplified – and in the right hands – the sound can be glorious, as The Byrds' 'Eight Miles High' testifies.

▷ KAWAI "AMP-IN-GUITAR"
Produced c1964-1965; this example c1964

Following the general 1960s rule that rules were there to be broken, someone wondered why the amp and speaker should be separate from the guitar. So they combined them. Although this example is brandless, the pickups suggest it was made in Japan by Kawai, and it is similar to fellow Japanese maker Teisco's more sophisticated TRG amp-in-guitar models of the period.

THE WHO established a new vitality in English pop during the 1960s. Never a great lead guitarist, Pete Townshend's skill was more to do with his ability as a rhythm player, deploying cascading chords on records such as this 1966 album A Quick One (below).

PETE TOWNSHEND (left) has explained his use of a 12-string Rickenbacker on the classic 1965 Who single 'I Can't Explain' as "a chord machine". But soon he became known just as much for the smashing time he had with his hapless guitars, and is pictured in his London flat in 1966 (left) surrounded by Ricks in various stages of dismemberment. "I sometimes feel very bad about having smashed up instruments which were particularly good ones," he said much later, "but generally I was working with production-line instruments."

▽ RICKENBACKER 330S/12 "1993"
Produced 1964-1967; this example July 1964

Although theirs was not the first electric 12-string, Rickenbacker produced the version that came to mass attention following its adoption first by George Harrison (in The Beatles) and soon afterwards by Roger McGuinn (in The Byrds). From that time on, jingle-jangle guitar nearly always meant electric Rickenbacker.

A US DESTROYER is attacked by North Vietnamese torpedo boats. President Johnson orders retaliatory air strikes, backed by Congress which in the Gulf Of Tonkin resolution authorises the president to take any steps necessary "to maintain peace".

MODS & ROCKERS go into battle at British seaside resorts. Fashionable mods take speed, drive scooters and listen to soul music. Leather-jacketed rockers drink, drive motorcycles and listen to rock'n'roll. Arbitration is not sought.

CASSIUS CLAY takes the world heavyweight boxing title. He later changes his name to Muhammad Ali.

GIBSON did not fare well in the 1960s when signing musicians to "design" guitars. Trini Lopez was an especially odd choice: he was not a guitarist's guitarist, nor was he a particularly big star ('If I Had A Hammer' was his only big hit), but Gibson still put out two Trini Lopez models, as seen in this 1965 ad (above).

appointed as Gibson's new chief in early 1968. Rendell also saw fit to restore a greater product focus by weeding out mediocre sellers, while concentrating on the more remunerative high-end models. For example, the annual shipments of the Super 400CES, the L-5CES and the Byrdland grew from, respectively, 32-44-77 in 1965 up to an unprecedented 63-200-218 by 1968. Conversely, low-end models like the one-pickup Melody Maker and SG Junior saw their totals drop from 6,753 and 3,570 in 1965 to just 338 and 561 in 1968. With plenty of cheaper imports, competition was too strong in these lower market segments.

With Gibson lacking inspiration to design new electrics, another major trend was the reintroduction of 'old' designs. The first reissue was the Flying V in 1966, but it hardly set the world on fire (despite the occasional support of Jimi Hendrix). The big coup came in 1968 with the return of the original Les Paul design. Several influential players, like Eric Clapton in the UK and Mike Bloomfield in the US, had discovered the exceptional sonic properties of 1950s Les Pauls when played at high volume. The advent of the so-called blues boom in the mid 1960s helped to create a demand that even a relatively conservative company like Gibson could not ignore. However, with the early reissues Gibson paid scant attention to details and failed to notice that the model in demand was the 1958-60 sunburst Standard. Instead the company chose to market a gold-top variant with single-coil pickups and a black Custom with two large humbuckers. Nonetheless, both models fared very well in their first year and by 1969 their combined sales topped 5000 units, enough to represent almost 20 per cent of the production of Gibson electrics. The gold-top, ineptly called the Les Paul Standard, was upgraded to Deluxe status after receiving the mini-humbuckers formerly associated with electrics from

Gibson's second brand, Epiphone (and also the Gibson Firebirds). With Epi production being relocated in Japan, the cost-conscious US factory had found themselves with a surplus inventory of pickups to use up – hence the arrival of the Deluxe.

The instant success of the reissues encouraged Gibson to expand the Les Paul line with new Personal, Professional, Jumbo and Bass models that featured the low-impedance electronics long favoured by Les Paul himself on his own instruments. Thanks to the return of Les Paul guitars, and more generally the renewed popularity of solidbodies, the sales of Gibson electrics would soon regain the upper hand over acoustics. Looking back, though, the biggest electric seller during the 1961-1969 period was the one-pickup Melody Maker, albeit with a rather paltry 23,390 shipments when compared to the 47,115 LG-0s which ruled on the acoustic side. It is also interesting to note that between 1961 and 1969 a late-1950s design like the ES-335 (20,108 units) neatly outperformed the SG Standard (14,556 units) or even the cheaper SG Junior (18,059 units).

Meanwhile, to commemorate Gibson's 75th anniversary in 1969, Stan Rendell used the finest woods he had procured for the Citation. Based on the Johnny Smith model, it was meant as a superlative flagship of Gibson craftsmanship – with a resounding price of $2,500 at a time when a Super 400CESN fetched a mere $1,360. As it turned out, the exclusive Citation helped celebrate a change of ownership as Gibson's parent, CMI, was taken over in 1969 by a concern unknown to the music industry called Ecuadorian Company Limited. ECL was subsequently renamed Norlin, and gradually took Gibson through a long and pathetic decline that would last until the mid 1980s. At Gibson, the end of the 1960s also marked the end of an era. ■ ANDRE DUCHOSSOIR

THE MUNSTERS and The Man From UNCLE debut on TV. The Transylvanian family (Lily, age 137, above left) has a simple motto: "Every cloud has a dark lining." Transcending the cold war, the United Network Command for Law and Enforcement agents Napoleon Solo (American) and Ilya Kuryakin (Russian) report to Mr Waverly (British), chiefly by talking into their pens.

PRESIDENT Johnson signs the Civil Rights Act, "ending" US racial discrimination. Three civil rights leaders who had gone missing in Mississippi are found murdered.

1965

FENDER set the pace with its colourful and stylish promotion materials, such as this 1966-67 catalogue cover (right) with artwork by Bob Perine. More unusual is the 1962 ad (far right) that, viewed today, provides an ironic premonition of the oriental domination of the industry that was to come.

ギターの名手は
フェンダーびいき
フェンダーは世界の
ギターです。

"TRANSLATION: "THE WORLD'S MOST TALENTED GUITARISTS PREFER FENDER."

THE FENDER STORY

For Fender, as for the American guitar industry as a whole, the 1960s proved the old axiom, "Be careful what you wish for; you might get it." Fender entered the new decade as one of the great American success stories, their electric solidbody guitars established as the voice of a new generation of musicians whose rock'n'roll music would dominate the 1960s and beyond.

Just as Fender's phenomenal growth through the 1950s had been impossible to imagine, so the company's continued growth through the 1960s brought problems that had been unimaginable at the beginning of the decade. By the end of the 1960s Fender would be an entirely different company. Bigger,

but not better: a victim of its own success. The 1960s started off as if they would be the Fender Decade, with the sound of Fender Telecasters, Stratocasters and Jazzmasters dominating the airwaves thanks to pop, surf and country groups such as The Ventures, The Beach Boys and Buck Owens & The Buckaroos. But in spite of Fender's success, Don Randall, a 50/50 partner with Leo Fender in Fender Sales, had never felt secure. Historically, new musical fads – rock'n'roll being a prime example – had sent once-popular instruments such as the classic (five-string) banjo, mandolin, tenor banjo, acoustic guitar and electric archtop guitar into near obscurity. Randall was understandably fearful that the electric solidbody guitar – essentially Fender's only product – was heading for the same fate in the 1960s. "You're always wondering if the public's fickleness is going to change musical taste," he says. "The electric organ came and went, and our electric piano [the mid-1960s Fender Rhodes] created quite

a stir at one time, then faded out of the picture. The funniest was when distortion came in [during the late 1960s]. We were beating our brains out trying to make a clean amplifier, and the fellas were wanting something that would distort."

The historical pattern was broken in the 1960s, however, when the guitar wave became a juggernaut, broadening into different styles of guitar music. To further break historical patterns, guitarists of the new folk music boom were not grabbing the newest, most technologically advanced guitar to create their music. Now, the next big new thing was an old thing – the acoustic flat-top guitar. For Fender's major competitors, all of whom made flat-top guitars, the folk boom was a gift

△ FENDER MARAUDER
Prototypes only 1965-1966; this example December 1966

The rarest Fender of all: the model that never made it into production. Marauder prototypes from 1965, as glimpsed in Fender's 1965-66 catalogue (opposite), show the model with an apparent lack of pickups, although they are "hidden" below the pickguard. Later test versions, such as the one shown here, have a peculiar mix of multiple controls, angled frets and (at least) conventional pickups. None ever saw the inside of a music store.

The World's Finest Acoustic and Electric Guitars
Write for Catalogues
GOYA GUITARS INC.
53 West 23rd Street, New York, N.Y. 10010
A DIVISION OF GOYA MUSIC CORPORATION

GOYA imported guitars to the US from Sweden (Hagström), Japan (Greco) and Italy (Eko).

▷ GOYA RANGEMASTER 116
Produced 1965-1969; this example c1968

Goya was a brandname used at various times by a New York importing firm, and as was so often the case with distribution companies one brandname turns up on guitars from a number of different sources. This Rangemaster model, for example, is of Italian origin, reflecting a 1960s predilection for multiple control layouts, and most likely comes from the Eko factory. The vibrato, however, was provided by another Goya supplier, the Hagström company of Sweden (see also page 37).

THE COLLECTOR who has bagged the rarest Fender, the Marauder (main guitar, below), will now require the truly ultimate collectible: the 1960s Fender delivery truck (right).

FENDER ELECTRIC XII
Produced 1965-1968; this example 1966

Fender reacted to the fashion for electric 12-strings created by Rickenbacker with this shortlived model, one of the first to appear after the takeover of Fender by CBS in early 1965.

from heaven. For Fender it was a potential death knell. But Don Randall was ready. First, he began distributing inexpensive imported acoustics made under the Regal brand, and in 1962 hired German-born designer Roger Rossmeisl (ex-Rickenbacker) to develop a line of Fender acoustic flat-tops, which debuted at the US trade show in 1963. But they never accounted for a significant portion of Fender sales.

In 1962 Fender introduced the Jaguar, its first new guitar since the Jazzmaster of 1958. The Jaguar was an extension of the earlier instrument, built on the Jazzmaster's 'offset waist' body shape, but with a shorter, 24″ scale (Fender's standard scale length was 25.5″). It had the Jazzmaster's 'floating' vibrato and the added feature of a string-mute contained in a removable bridge cover, which most players did remove. While the short scale might seem to indicate that the Jaguar was

designed for younger players, Randall says there was a movement among professionals – the jazz players for whom the Jazzmaster had been designed but who had never adopted it – toward short-scale guitars. The Jaguar's sophisticated control system, with six switches (including on-off switches for each pickup) and two control knobs, supports Randall's contention that it was aimed at pro players.

Two years later the Mustang guitar debuted, with two pickups, a new-style vibrato and a 24″ scale (with a 'three-quarter' scale length of 22″ as an option). It came in red, white or blue, making it the first Fender that did not have sunburst or the benign 'blond' as standard finish. Its target market was student or teen players, clear from its $189.50 list price, just above the other budget Fenders, the short-scale Musicmaster and Duo-Sonic models.

By the mid 1960s Don Randall was feeling comfortable for the first time. But Leo Fender was not. A chronic strep infection made him wonder how much longer he had to live. And new solid-state technology made him wonder how long his self-taught knowledge of electronics would be relevant. He decided to sell. The CBS entertainment conglomerate stepped forward with an offer of $13 million, and the deal was closed

LEO FENDER (above) set up his company in the late 1940s, and sold out to CBS in 1965.

FENDER's publicity department made a rare gaffe in this 1965-66 catalogue (below), including a couple of Marauder prototypes that never actually went into production.

US MARINES and Australian troops arrive in South Vietnam. American planes bomb North Vietnam targets in the first US retaliatory raids. President Johnson says he will continue "actions that are justified as necessary for the defence of South Vietnam". In June, US troops go on their first Vietcong offensive; by July there are 125,000 US troops in Vietnam.

THE SOUND OF MUSIC is released, achieving irritatingly widespread popularity. One reviewer thoughtfully warns moviegoers who are "allergic to singing nuns and sweetly innocent children".

RUSSIAN cosmonaut Alexei Leonov is the first man to "walk" in space, leaving his Voshod II craft for 10 minutes during its 26-hour flight.

SPIKE JONES, founder of outrageously mad City Slickers group, dies in Los Angeles. Saul Hudson is born in England. In the 1980s he will become Slash, guitarist of outrageously riotous Guns N'Roses group.

CARNABY STREET is the centre of Swinging London, selling op-art mini dresses, PVC "kinky" boots, coloured tights and soft bras, as modelled by Jean Shrimpton and Twiggy.

A SPEED LIMIT of 70mph is imposed on UK motorways. Scottish driver Jim Clark is the World Grand Prix champion for the second time.

△ GUYATONE LG-200T
Produced 1965-1969; this example c1966

The Japanese version of the multi-control/multi-pickup idea reached a zenith with this model, generally considered as the Guyatone company's finest electric guitar of the 1960s. It has 24 frets, stereo circuitry (note the twin output jacks), and a potentially large variety of sounds from its four pickups and six associated selector switches. The well-established Guyatone company, based in Tokyo, had begun to make electric guitars during the late 1950s – but for more on its 1960s activities see the Japanese section on pages 64-69.

1965

CBS bought Fender in January 1965, poured in a great deal of money, and changed many of the existing working practices. Gradually, quality suffered and reports of sloppy workmanship

filtered back to HQ from the disgruntled sales force. This alarming 1967 ad (left) was part of the PR job designed to reassure dealers that Fenders were as well-made as ever.

on January 5th 1965. A pre-sale report to CBS advised that Leo was not essential, that a competent manufacturing executive and a competent chief engineer could do a better job. So Leo was contracted, but seldom-used, as a consultant for five years. Don Randall was considered essential, and he was made vice president and general manager of Fender and later president of CBS's musical instrument division.

The future looked rosy at first. Randall didn't have Leo, but he had all the resources of CBS Labs. And popular music played right into his hands. The arrival of The Beatles in America in 1964 ensured that the guitar was here to stay. And in 1965 The Byrds, an electric guitar band, hit with 'Mr Tambourine Man', a song written by the leading folk voice, Bob Dylan. With that single blow, the acoustic/electric dividing line between folk and rock music was obliterated.

With the same line-expansion philosophy that had spawned the acoustic flat tops, Fender once again called on Roger Rossmeisl, this time to develop a line of semi-hollow archtops to compete with Gibson's highly successful ES-335. Fender unveiled Rossmeisl's thin-bodied, double-cutaway Coronado line in January 1966. With Wildwood colours available, the Coronados looked good, and with the traditional Fender neck, they felt good, but they didn't sound good. Many felt that Fender simply wasn't an archtop guitar company or, for that

△ FENDER STRATOCASTER
Produced 1965-1971 (this style)
This Lake Placid Blue Metallic example 1966

Fender's Strat changed to the slightly broader headstock style seen here during 1965, intended to ease warping problems of the earlier, narrower design (as on the 1964 example below).

△ FENDER STRATOCASTER
Produced 1959-1965 (this style)
This Sonic Blue example 1964

△ FENDER STRATOCASTER
Produced 1959-1965 (this style)
This Fiesta Red example 1960

△ FENDER STRATOCASTER
Produced 1959-1965 (this style)
This Foam Green example 1962

Fender's custom colour guitars of the 1950s and 1960s provide many a collector's prized possession today. The company used a variety of Du Pont paints, the same ones employed by the US car industry. Some were from Du Pont's Duco nitro-cellulose lines, such as this Foam Green example, others like the Lake Placid Blue Metallic at the top of the page were Lucite acrylics.

matter, an acoustic guitar company. "It was an attempt to broaden the line, but it didn't broaden," says Bill Carson, production manager at the time, of the flat-top and archtop lines. "We weren't geared for it. We didn't know how to make those things." Rossmeisl's final designs for Fender came in 1969 with a pair of full-depth archtops, the Montego and LTD, which were more respected but much less successful even than the Coronados.

In the solidbody line, Fender made no lasting advances. There was the Electric XII 12-string in 1965 and the new Bronco student model in 1968. Fender sought to bolster sales of the Telecaster by 'fixing' its weight problem in 1968 with the Thinline Telecaster – which was not thinner but hollowed out on one side to reduce weight. The hollow area was signified by the addition of an f-hole on the bass side of the body. The Thinline Telecaster would be revamped with a pair

of humbucking pickups in the early 1970s, but it never amounted to more than a footnote in Telecaster history. At the end of the 1960s two more Telecaster variations appeared – the shortlived Paisley Red and Blue Flower psychedelics, and the Rosewood model – that are more noteworthy for their collectability now than for their impact at the time.

The least noteworthy Fenders of the 1960s, but the most indicative of CBS's influence, are two obscure models from 1969 that had a total of five names: the Musiclander/ Swinger/Arrow and the Custom/Maverick. These were 'parts' guitars, put together and adapted from various leftover materials and work-in-progress of other models.

Fender's stumbling in the guitar market was symptomatic of a bureaucratic disease that was weakening the company from the inside. "CBS didn't hurt the company initially," Randall says. "It was after they had the company three or four years that they did damage to it. We had systems analysts running out of our ears, engineers running out of our ears that weren't envisioned when the sale was made and were totally unnecessary. We had to document everything we used and make where-used files for every nut, bolt and screw, and make a drawing for it."

CBS's ignorance of electric guitars began to show, and Don Randall's attention had been diverted by

corporate duties. "I was the only division president outside of New York," he says. "When they had a meeting in New York I had to jump on a red-eye special. Like most meetings they were non-productive." Increasingly frustrated, Randall resigned in 1969.

CBS had pumped plenty of money into Fender – starting with a $2.7 million, 120,000-square-foot building in 1966 – and the investment appeared to be paying off. Sales climbed "almost geometrically", Randall says. And the manufacturing staff practically doubled, from around 500 in 1964 to 950 in 1969. But the company was becoming an empty shell.

As the 1960s ended, Fender was no longer leading the guitar boom, only riding the momentum of its earlier success. When the boom ended with the recession of the early 1970s, followed by the keyboard insurrection (that Don Randall had feared), Fender would have no inner strength to pull it through. With no Leo Fender, no Don Randall, only faceless corporate management, Fender ended the 1960s, its most successful decade, set up for a long, painful decline through the 1970s. ■ WALTER CARTER

△ FENDER STRATOCASTER
Produced 1965-1971 (this style)
This Black example October 1966

Session musician Al Kooper owned this Strat, which he says was given to him by Jimi Hendrix when Kooper worked on the Electric Ladyland album in New York in 1968. Hendrix used a variety of Strats, including black models, during the 1960s.

▽ FENDER STRATOCASTER
Produced 1959-1965 (this style)
This Burgundy Mist Metallic example 1961

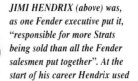

JIMI HENDRIX (above) was, as one Fender executive put it, "responsible for more Strats being sold than all the Fender salesmen put together". At the start of his career Hendrix used a tatty sunburst Strat, but soon began to acquire more, usually opting for a black or white model on-stage. He preferred maple-fingerboard models (above) from mid-1968.

131

1966

JEFF BECK was one of the most inventive and intuitive guitarists of the 1960s. As a Yardbird, Beck drew all kinds of new sounds from his Fender, even turning it into a sitar with a fuzzbox for 'Heart Full of Soul' (1965), while later he encouraged new demand for old Les Pauls. In the Jeff Beck Group he turned in some fine performances, such as the fluid instrumental 'Beck's Bolero'.

ROCK & POP GUITARS

As above, so below. Chaos theory tells us that little things reflect big ones. Or, to be more precise, that all things great and small share the same basic characteristics, and the differences are purely those of scale. If the definitive Sound Of The Sixties was the sound of rock guitar, then the reasons are simple and straightforward: the 1960s were a decade of turbulence, of change, of restlessness and hunger and boundless curiosities and a sense of infinite possibilities.

It was a decade for the creation of new ideas, and for redefining and recombining old ones – and this holds equally true for the massive shifts in the social and political spheres as it does for the comparatively smaller one of games people played with wood, wires and valves. The sound of the 1960s was the sound of barriers breaking down, of systems going into overload, distortion and – ultimately – feedback.

The guitar was the iconic signifier of the rock of the 1950s, but on record it had to jostle some heavy competition for the audio spotlight. For every totemic six-stringer like Chuck Berry, Buddy Holly or Eddie Cochran, there was an equally charismatic pianist like Little Richard, Jerry Lee Lewis or Fats Domino. It's true that in much of the classic pop of the 1960s – the cinerama-scaled epics of Phil Spector, Bacharach & David and the Tamla-Motown combine, or the funky dancefloor epiphanies of James Brown and Stax Records, where Jimmy Nolen and Steve Cropper cut through the orchestration with their six-string razors – the guitarist remained strictly part of the ensemble. Nevertheless, at the rockier end of white pop

music the guitar moved closer and closer to stage-centre until, by mid-decade, the 'guitar hero' had emerged as a fully-fledged phenomenon.

In the United States, guitar-driven instrumental singles by the likes of Dick Dale and The Ventures were an indispensable accessory to the surf music phenomenon, but The Ventures' UK counterparts, The Shadows, maintained a dual role as backing group to boy-next-door pop idol Cliff Richard, and therefore were far more closely allied to the pop mainstream.

The Beatles arrived at the tail end of 1962, revolutionising pop with their uniquely innovative blend of Motown and rockabilly and sending guitar and amplifier sales through the ceiling. They, and the first wave of 'beat group' successes following in their immediate wake, focused squarely on The Singers & The Song, their guitarists specialising in clean, tight ensemble playing with texture and rhythm prioritised over improvisation or extravagant soloing. John Lennon's rhythms were chunky and driving, Paul McCartney's bass pumping and melodic, George Harrison's leads crisp, composed and rehearsed down to the tiniest inflection. Within months The Beatles' hegemony was challenged by The Rolling Stones whose studiedly sullen bohemianism and deep roots in Chicago blues made them a very different proposition to the cheery Scousers. They did, however, share The Beatles' ensemble guitar ethic, albeit in a manner derived from the Muddy Waters combos of the 1950s. Keith Richards and Brian Jones welded their instruments together so closely and intuitively that in much of their material the distinction between 'lead' and 'rhythm' guitars

almost disappeared. Keith specialised in the Chuck Berry stuff (both signature ringin'-a-bell riffs and runka-runka rhythms) and Brian handled the slide-slinging, but almost everything else, guitar-wise, was up for grabs.

The modern guitar era – with its emphasis on cranked-up power chording, complex riffing, science-fiction sound processing and extended soloing – can trace itself back to three bands which emerged in the R&B

JIMI HENDRIX was of course best known for playing a Strat, but during the last half of 1967 this black Flying V was his favourite guitar. The extra decorations were painted by Jimi; he also converted the nut for left- or right-hand stringing.

THE MONKEES were given Gretsch gear (right) for their 1966 TV series. Session guitarists on their records included Glen Campbell, James Burton, Sonny Curtis and Jerry McGee (who probably played the driving arpeggios of 'Last Train To Clarksville').

▽ GRETSCH MONKEES
Produced 1966-1967; this example 1967

TV company Screen Gems offered Gretsch the option to sell a Monkees-related instrument. This model, emblazoned with the Monkees guitar-shaped logo, was the shortlived result.

DICK DALE (right) had a hit in 1961, 'Let's Go Trippin'', that defined the sound of the surf instrumental. Left-hander Dale poured out surging, staccato Strat lines, borrowed scales from his east-European heritage, and set it all adrift in a sea of reverb. Fans said the powerful result was the aural equivalent of catching a wave, and Dale was dubbed the "king

After surfing...

of the surf guitar". There were cash-in movies (Muscle Beach Party, far right; Dale is at the back with a youthful Stevie Wonder) and hits for other bands, including The Surfaris' 'Wipe Out', The Chantays' 'Pipeline' and The Beach Boys' 'Surfin USA'. Guitar makers (like Kent, above) exploited the upsurge in demand, but surf didn't last much beyond the British invasion of 1964.

slipstream of the Stones, though each of them swiftly distanced themselves from the blues. The Kinks and The Who distinguished themselves from R&B's huddled masses by thunderous all-action stage shows, radio-canny songcraft (provided respectively by Ray Davies and Pete Townshend) and the kind of murderously crunchy wall-of-sound guitar abuse (courtesy of Ray's kid brother Dave and, again, Townshend) which turned the Power Chord and the Killer Riff into contemporary guitar grails.

However, the real signpost to the future was provided by The Yardbirds, the first band whose key player was the guitarist rather than the singer. Their vocalist, the late Keith Relf, had the consistent misfortune to be effortlessly upstaged, first by Eric Clapton, then by Clapton's successor Jeff Beck, and finally by Jimmy Page who, in the latter part of

the decade, presided over the demise of the group and its eventual resurrection as the 1970s-dominating Led Zeppelin.

Clapton may not have been rock's first virtuoso guitarist, but he was the first to be perceived as such by fans rather than fellow musicians. 'Musicianship' had never before been an essential criterion for assessing rock groups. It had always been more important to have good songs, an exciting stage act, pretty faces and cool clothes than to include a guitarist or drummer capable of impressing jazz critics. The revelation that changed the game was Clapton's wholesale importation into rock of the 1950s and 1960s innovations of urban blues maestri like BB King, Albert King, Freddy King, Otis Rush and Buddy Guy: thick, overdriven tone, singing sustain and fleet-fingered, impassioned solo marathons, all packaged with a tight-lipped, introverted, artist-at-work persona. Clapton truly came into his own when he quit The Yardbirds on the brink of their first pop success to dive headlong into the muddy waters of straight-no-chaser blues purism with John Mayall's Bluesbreakers. In that band he once again

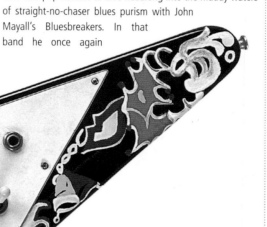

◁ GIBSON FLYING V
Produced 1966-1970 (this style); this example circa March 1967

Jimi Hendrix used this Flying V constantly in 1967. Hendrix later gave the guitar to Eire Apparent guitarist Mick Cox, since when it has been through a variety of owners, most of whom were unaware of its pedigree. The V's present owner, musician David Brewis, bought it in 1995 and restored the original black paintwork as well as Jimi's wild psychedelic additions. At first Brewis was unsure if the V belonged to Hendrix, but authenticity was confirmed when the unique patterns in its plastic fingerboard dots were found to match exactly those on a detailed period photograph of the guitar.

ONLY 44 of Gibson's reissued Flying Vs made in 1967 were not in the standard cherry finish. Hendrix's V would have been one of the few black guitars among those 44.

133

THE VOX FACTORY in England in 1965 (below). Some necks and whole guitars were also made in Italy. Vox began a reciprocal distribution deal with the American Thomas Organ Co in 1964. Soon Thomas had extra US-made Vox amps, but by 1969 the original British Vox operation would be closed.

THE HOLLIES were among the most professional British beat groups of the 1960s. They displayed good playing and fine harmony vocals amid some of the best pop songs of the time. Guitarist Tony Hicks (right) added crisp, concise solos to the singles, sometimes using a Vox

Phantom XII 12-string (right) as well as his Gibson ES-345 and Les Paul Junior. The group's albums developed from singles-plus-a-few to strong collections, with their fine Evolution LP (above) having the misfortune to appear the same month as Sgt Pepper.

ALL-VOX MAN ... that's TONY HICKS

▽ VOX GUITAR ORGAN
Produced 1966-67; this example c1966

Guitar makers have never quite managed to convince players that a guitar which can sound like a keyboard is a good idea. Vox pioneered the guitar organ, but trying effectively to put the sound generators of their Continental organ into a Phantom guitar proved highly unreliable. The fraught project was shortlived, and few fully-working models survive.

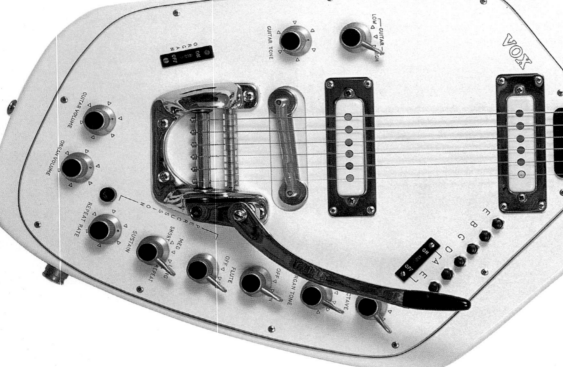

THE VOX Guitar Organ had an array of keyboard effects (left). Frets were wired to tone generators in the body; a string touching a fret completed a circuit and produced a note.

WILDWOOD was a special finish achieved by injecting coloured dyes into beech. It was available on some Coronado models, in various colour combinations (see ad, right).

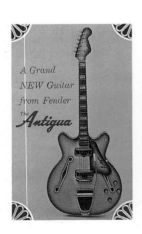

FENDER offered some Coronados in its shaded white-to-brown Antigua finish.

△ FENDER CORONADO XII WILDWOOD II
Coronado XII produced 1966-1969; this example 1968

Fender were kings when it came to solidbody electrics, but lost out to the increasing popularity of hollow-body electrics during the 1960s. So the Coronados were introduced to compete with Gretsches and Gibsons of the period, but the line proved unsuccessful and had disappeared from Fender's list by 1971.

TEISCO's Japanese-made products were available in the US by 1965 through WMI of Illinois, whose catalogues (right) stressed quality.

TEISCO were not only influenced by Fender's guitars, but as this 1966 Teisco Del Rey catalogue shows (left) the style of the Californian company's promo material also caught the eye of the Japanese. Compare this luridly illustrated piece of work to the typical Fender example shown on page 40.

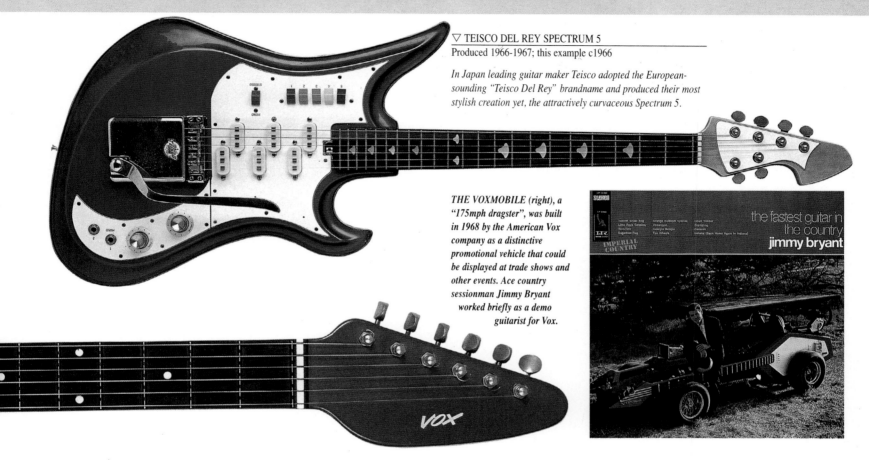

▽ TEISCO DEL REY SPECTRUM 5
Produced 1966-1967; this example c1966

In Japan leading guitar maker Teisco adopted the European-sounding "Teisco Del Rey" brandname and produced their most stylish creation yet, the attractively curvaceous Spectrum 5.

THE VOXMOBILE (right), a "175mph dragster", was built in 1968 by the American Vox company as a distinctive promotional vehicle that could be displayed at trade shows and other events. Ace country sessionman Jimmy Bryant worked briefly as a demo guitarist for Vox.

remorselessly outshone the frontman and became the primary drawing card. If Clapton was blues-rock guitar's brooding Hamlet, Jeff Beck was its cackling, demonic Joker. With little more than a slide, an echo unit and a fuzz-box as props, he delighted in peeling off ear-teasing speed-runs and aurally disguising himself as violin, sitar, train-whistle, chicken-coop or car-wreck. Enthusiastically pillaging and pastiching Indian raga, Gregorian chant and all manner of esoteric exotica, The Yardbirds eagerly embraced the omnivorous eclecticism that became a hallmark of 'progressive' guitar-based 1960s rock.

Reeling under the onslaught of the British Invasion, the empire struck back with folk-rock. Swathed in immaculately executed vocal harmonies and bristling with fingerpicked electric 12-strings, American folk-rock was essentially the creation of The Byrds. The group's leader and mastermind Jim McGuinn (later Roger – don't ask, it's a 1960s thang) wedded Beatlesque instrumentation to Dylanoid singer-songwriting via his own wavery voice and jingle-jangle Rickenbacker. Dylan's electric recordings actually placed more emphasis on layers of keyboards and The Zim's own tootling mouth-harp than it did on guitars, despite the studio presence of Mike Bloomfield whose flashy, hyperthyroid work with Chicago's defiantly unpop Paul Butterfield Blues Band had made him America's closest equivalent to Eric Clapton.

Folk-rock of a different, less shinily-packaged variety was the basis for American guitar's next major move, though LSD,

revamped 1950s beatnikism and the sudden availability of extremely powerful amplifiers were also key factors. The first wave of San Francisco 'hippie' bands essentially consisted of very loud folk groups on psychedelic drugs. The early guitar sounds of Jefferson Airplane (Jorma Kaukonen), Grateful Dead (Jerry Garcia, Bob Weir), Big Brother & The Holding Company (Sam Andrew, James Gurley) and Country Joe & The Fish (Barry Melton) seemed an uneasy meld of folk-club fingerpicking and megawatt fuzz-boxed bluesrocking performed by players who sounded like they'd only recently dumped their banjos and Martins for 335s and Marshalls.

Easily the finest and most resourceful electric guitarist to emerge from the San Francisco scene was The Grateful Dead's Jerry Garcia. Indeed, the Dead turned out to be that scene's most durable and consistent band, though they were far from a one-man show. Their high card was the synergy between the band's four core members, but Garcia's sparkling, phoenix-like guitar sparked their idiosyncratic blend of free-form improvisation and roots-music authenticity. Both Garcia as an individual and the Dead as a collective had one foot planted in folk and country, the other in blues and soul... and the head somewhere in both inner and outer space.

Brits and Yanks compared notes, famously, at the 1967 Monterey International Pop Festival. The West Coasters were a peacefully stoned bunch mostly off their faces on both Californian sunshine and California Sunshine. If they were shattered by the volume and violence of The Who they were

absolutely vaporised by Jimi Hendrix. Sounding like a Starship Enterprise co-piloted by Curtis Mayfield and John Coltrane crash landing at maximum warp on the south side of Chicago, and looking like an extremely chilled-out Brazilian buccaneer who'd just looted Carnaby Street, Hendrix rewrote the sacred texts of the electric guitar more profoundly than any other single individual, before or since.

Drawing freely on avant-garde jazz, down-home blues, grits-and-groceries funk and the brave new rock world unveiled by Bob Dylan and The Beatles, Hendrix demonstrated – more dramatically than anybody could possibly have imagined – just how broad a canvas was now at a rock guitarist's disposal, and how bright and varied a palette of colours could be applied to it.

Jimi Hendrix was to the electric guitar what Bruce Lee was to the martial arts. Famously, the Little Dragon once told a questioner who enquired what style he fought in, "My style is no style." What he meant was that he was tied to no single discipline, but drew what he needed from whatever he found, wherever he found it. Hendrix was by no means the only guitarist of his era who could play in a variety of different styles, but none of his contemporaries was capable of matching him for the sheer vision with which he melded seemingly disparate influences into a single, coherent music. He had it all covered. He could play straight, deep blues with greater emotional and idiomatic authenticity than Eric Clapton, top Jeff Beck's mastery of electronic and technique-freak special effects, and trump Pete Townshend at both on-stage showmanship and power-chord monumentalism. Hendrix's fusion of 'black' and 'white'

135

1967

MOBY GRAPE (with lead guitarist Jerry Miller), The Grateful Dead (Jerry Garcia, Bob Weir) and Jefferson Airplane (Jorma Kaukonen) were at the centre of the stoned San Francisco sound. The extended, tripped-out solos that these West Coast psychedelic bands pioneered took the guitar to its most inspired heights... and to its most tedious lengths.

and 'English' and 'American' idioms and elements also combined the advanced production techniques pioneered by The Beatles with allusive, poetic lyrics derived from Bob Dylan. In a decade obsessed with opening up and exploring hitherto uncharted areas of possibility, Hendrix was as important symbolically as musically, as iconic a figure as Dylan or The Beatles. Certainly for guitarists, he was a 100-watt revelation on legs.

Thus inspired, rock guitar was busy gobbling up every arcane influence it could find. In LA, The Doors' Robbie Krieger was enthusiastically transplanting techniques to his solidbody Gibson that he'd acquired as a student of flamenco stylings. In

Manhattan, Lou Reed super-charged his garage-band basics with avant-garde drones derived, via his Velvet Underground colleague John Cale, from contemporary minimalist composer LaMonte Young. The result was something so far ahead of its time that many had trouble recognising it as music at all until the Velvets were long disbanded. And back in England Pink Floyd's Syd Barrett was exploiting the electric guitar's potential for pure sound, while Richard Thompson and Fairport Convention laid the groundwork for a distinctively British folk-rock idiom by electrifying and psychedlicising Anglo-Celtic musical traditions.

ERIC CLAPTON's SG (below) started life with a Maestro vibrato unit, but this was not to the guitarist's taste. After a number of changes, the guitar currently has a non-original bridge and tailpiece. It has also had a new headstock fitted, part of the neck has been replaced, the knobs have been changed and the paintwork carefully retouched.

△ GIBSON SG STANDARD
Painted 1967 (SG Standard introduced 1963)

This is Eric Clapton's famous psychedelic SG. He bought the guitar probably in early 1967 to replace his stolen Les Paul Standard. Soon Clapton had a Dutch group of artists known as The Fool paint the guitar. They set a fiery-haired angel amid stars and clouds, added an idyllic landscape to the pickguard, and put an explosively 1960s version of a sunburst finish on the back (below). Clapton used the guitar widely with Cream, both on-stage and for recordings such as the Disraeli Gears and Wheels Of Fire albums. Since 1974 the guitar has been owned by musician/producer Todd Rundgren.

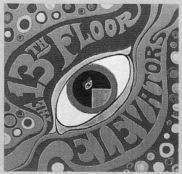

THE GRATEFUL DEAD underlined the musical superiority of the West Coast bands with the visual style of their LP sleeves (Aoxomoxoa, right). But one of the earliest psychedelic groups came from Texas. The 13th Floor Elevators used overt op-art for the cover of their 1966 album, a record which was full of Roky Erickson's blazing guitar.

JERRY GARCIA (above) defined the freewheeling improvisational spirit at the heart of The Grateful Dead, along with guitarist Bob Weir and bassist Phil Lesh.

A vogue for jazz-rock, spearheaded by Blood Sweat & Tears and Chicago, meant bolting horn sections onto rock rhythm sections, with loud, fuzzboxed, feedbacked guitar an essential ingredient. Rock-raised guitarists had little aptitude for the harmonic complexities of jazz, and younger jazz guitarists like Larry Coryell who fancied growing their hair and plugging into Marshall stacks experienced equally severe problems handling the technology that was second nature to their rocking cousins. Just about the only guys comfortable on both sides of the fence were John McLaughlin, who formed his Mahavishnu Orchestra at the tail end of the decade, and Carlos Santana, essentially a blues guitarist fronting a percussion-heavy Latin combo.

Then there were those who reacted to the preponderance of deafening, fussily over-arranged 'progressive' rock by working on their vocal harmonies and blowing the dust off their acoustics, or by crossing the cultural and ideological barriers separating long-haired, anti-war, free-loving, pot-smoking rock from patriotic, rural, God-fearing country music. The Byrds' album *Sweetheart Of The Rodeo* and the austere acousticisms of a revitalised Bob Dylan commenced a vogue for laidback, plangent, extremely white 'mellow' music which would reach its apogee in the 1970s.

Rock ended the 1960s altered beyond recognition. A once monolithic form had splintered into a series of hyphenates: folk-rock, jazz-rock, blues-rock, country-rock, and the all-encompassing 'progressive rock'. But looming above all else was the Godzilla of heavy metal: gigawatt riff-rock exemplified on the one hand by Led Zeppelin's paradoxical blend of sophisticated eclecticism and phallocentric vulgarity, and on the other by the barbiturate lumbering of Britain's Black Sabbath or America's Grand Funk Railroad. By the time their long and winding road took them to *Abbey Road*, even The Beatles were cautiously giving heavy a go. But on Planet Metal itself, singers had become almost incidental, and rock guitar had become an Olympic event wherein players were scored for strength, speed and volume. Something had to give, and in the 1970s and 1980s it did. But, for better and/or for worse, it was during the 1960s that rock guitar became, for all intents and purposes, what it still is today. ■ CHARLES SHAAR MURRAY

THE 14-HOUR Technicolor Dream takes place at London's Alexander Palace, the largest gathering of the emerging UK "underground" scene. Ten-thousand attend this all-night "happening", with bands including Pink Floyd, The Creation and Tomorrow, alongside a helter-skelter and a fibreglass igloo.

ISRAEL defeats an Arab coalition in the Six Day War.

DONALD CAMPBELL dies in his Bluebird craft on an English lake. He was attempting to break his own world water-speed record of 376mph.

THE BBC bans broadcasts of The Beatles 'A Day In The Life' because of "drug references". The Sgt Pepper track has the line "I'd love to turn you on…" Meanwhile the £ is turned down; its new value is $2.40.

THE FOOL were three Dutch artists (above, left to right): Simon Posthuma, Marijke Koger and Josje Leeger, with a Canadian, Barry Finch, added for their album. Moving to London in the 1960s, The Fool painted the exterior of the Apple boutique, as well as a car and a piano for John Lennon. They worked on Eric Clapton's SG (pictured right) in 1967.

LOTUS produce a road car with racing-team expertise, the Europa. It has a rear mounted engine in a fibreglass body.

THE MONTEREY Pop festival in June boasts a line-up including The Who, The Byrds, Jefferson Airplane, Janis Joplin, Jimi Hendrix and Otis Redding. Hendrix signs to Warner-Reprise for over $50,000. Redding dies in a plane crash in December.

GEORGE got this famous Rickenbacker in 1964, but first tried a 12-string back in April 1963. "Tom Springfield had a big 12-string," George told Melody Maker. "I sat playing it in the dressing room all afternoon. What a sound!"

THE BEATLES' first live TV appearance in the US was The Ed Sullivan Show (below) when 70 million US viewers saw Paul on Höfner bass, George playing a Gretsch Country Gent and John on his Rickenbacker "old-style" 325. Vox exploited the group's use of their amps to gain a foothold in the US market with ads such as this (right) in the trade press.

VOX! went the BEATLES USA

Thousands of would-be guitarists wrestled with a chord or three as The Beatles made the electric guitar the happening sound of the 1960s. But which guitars did the Fab Four themselves play, exactly?

It is the evening of February 9th 1964, and in CBS TV's Studio 50 in Manhattan, New York, the very first shots of The British Invasion are being fired. The Beatles have been in the United States just three days, and they're into the opening bars of 'All My Loving', the first song of their debut live American TV broadcast on *The Ed Sullivan Show*.

George harmonises with John behind Paul's lead vocal,

then adjusts the volume control on his Gretsch Chet Atkins Country Gentleman, takes centre stage, and plays a short country/rockabilly-inspired solo. As he moves over to join Paul at the other mike for the second verse, a good number of the 70 million Americans who are watching imagine themselves as the grinning lead guitarist in just such a group, with just such a Gretsch around their shoulders. Or maybe they'd prefer the moody role of John the rhythm guitarist, with his black Rickenbacker 325?

George and John are playing these particular guitars because of an American country music hero and a Belgian harmonica player. George idolises Chet Atkins, the foremost country picker in Nashville. Atkins helps everyone from Elvis to

the Everly Brothers in the studio, makes great guitarists'-guitarist records of his own, and since the mid 1950s has lent a hand to the Gretsch company of New York to design a series of Chet Atkins electric guitar models. George bought his double-cutaway Gretsch Chet Atkins Country Gent in London in summer 1963, just in time to record 'She Loves You'. Three

▽ GEORGE HARRISON'S RICKENBACKER 360/12
360/12 produced 1963-current; this example December 1963

Rickenbacker gave this 12-string to George during the group's first US visit in February 1964. It provided brand new guitar sounds, not least on the opening chord of 'A Hard Day's Night'.

△ GEORGE HARRISON'S GRETSCH DUO JET
Duo Jet produced 1953-1961 (this style); this example 1957

George's first proper US-made guitar, purchased around 1961 from a sailor who brought it back to Liverpool from an American trip. "It may have been secondhand," George said later, "but I polished that thing, I was so proud to own it." He used this Duo Jet regularly through the early years of Beatle fame until he bought his Country Gentleman in London in the summer of 1963.

△ JOHN LENNON'S RICKENBACKER 325
325 produced c1963-1975; this example February 1964

On that decisive first US trip in February 1964 Rickenbacker also had the good sense to provide John with this replacement for his old-style 325 model. He immediately took to the new gift, and used the guitar you see here on all the important Beatles live dates and recordings up to the point when he bought an Epiphone Casino (see p.53) in 1966 for the Revolver sessions.

HAMBURG provided a tough training ground for The Beatles who played five stints in the northern-German city between summer 1960 and the end of 1962. "The booze was flowing and people were having a good time," drummer Pete Best later

told Gareth Pawlowski. "The Germans really loved the Ray Charles classic 'What'd I Say' because they could participate by echoing the lyrics and banging their beer bottles on the table." This picture (above) from one of the Hamburg dives,

probably taken in 1960, shows original bassist Stuart Sutcliffe (front) playing his large-bodied Höfner bass. Behind, George plays the Neoton/Futurama guitar which provided him with workmanlike service during his first months in the group.

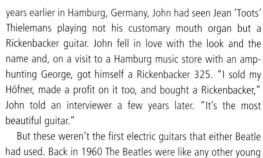

▽ THE BEATLES' GIBSON J-160E
J-160E produced 1954-1979; this example June 1962

One of the group's two "jumbo" Gibsons, which they used as normal acoustics or amplified. Owned today by George, this one was actually down originally on John's HP agreement (above).

years earlier in Hamburg, Germany, John had seen Jean 'Toots' Thielemans playing not his customary mouth organ but a Rickenbacker guitar. John fell in love with the look and the name and, on a visit to a Hamburg music store with an amp-hunting George, got himself a Rickenbacker 325. "I sold my Höfner, made a profit on it too, and bought a Rickenbacker," John told an interviewer a few years later. "It's the most beautiful guitar."

But these weren't the first electric guitars that either Beatle had used. Back in 1960 The Beatles were like any other young group starting out: they had no money to buy good instruments, and got by with anything they could scrape together – despite John's joke in a 1961 *Mersey Beat* magazine that suddenly they "all grew guitars". George moved from a Höfner President to a Höfner Club 40 hollow-body electric, and then a solidbody Neoton Grazioso (or Futurama, as it was soon renamed).

During 1960 the fledgling guitar trio – George, John and Paul – added a bass player and a drummer, and the fab five's manager rather remarkably secured them no less than 48 nights from mid-August at the Indra club in Hamburg. They took their basic guitars with them: Paul (still a guitarist) had a

JOHN and George each bought a J-160E in 1962. John is seen with his while George plays the Gretsch Country Gent on this 1963 magazine cover (above).

THE BEATLES created an enormous surge of interest in guitars and guitar playing during the 1960s. Italian guitarist and designer Mario Maccaferri (below) had moved to New York in 1939 and first made cheap plastic guitars in 1953. Sensing an opportunity with the Beatles boom, Mario's Mastro company had by summer 1964 made 500,000 plastic Beatles guitars (right) retailing at between 98¢ and $19.95. Collectors today pay rather more, especially if they have the original package.

£19 ($30) Dutch-made Rosetti Solid 7, John took his £28 ($45) German Höfner Club 40, and George the relatively luxurious £58 ($90) Czech-built Grazioso. Certainly, none of these was a great guitar. Fortunately, the Hamburg audience didn't require much more than a noise to drink to.

When the group returned to Liverpool, George managed to save some money for a new guitar, and through a small ad in the local newspaper acquired a late 1950s Gretsch Duo Jet from a sailor who'd brought it back from the States. Already enthralled with Chet Atkins' playing, George had to have a Gretsch. OK, so it wasn't a Chet Atkins Gretsch, but it was nonetheless that rare and remarkable thing, an American instrument. "Any good American guitar looked sensational to us," George said later. "We'd only had beat-up, crummy guitars at that stage." He soon gave away his dormant Grazioso as the prize in a magazine competition.

John continued to play his Rickenbacker, and on The Beatles' first single and LP recordings, made at EMI studios in

THE BACK of George's Stratocaster (left) reveals rather more of the Fender's original sonic blue custom colour, although it did not escape the artful redecoration that aligns the Beatle Fender with two other famous painted guitars of the period: Jimi Hendrix's Flying V (see p.46/46) and Eric Clapton's SG (p.48/49). The label on the rear of the headstock identifies this guitar's original sale from a music shop in Kent, England.

BEBOPALULA.

GEORGE's most famous Beatle guitars were probably his Country Gent (featured in a Gretsch promo shot, right) and his chiming Rickenbacker 12-string. But aside from these, George and his fellow Beatles inevitably acquired other electric guitars that for one reason or another turned out to be of little use. George, for example, briefly played an obscure Rickenbacker 425 in 1963, while Gretsch and Vox made him a couple of odd custom guitars. John too was given a hard-to-play 12-string version of Rickenbacker's 325, and had a fleeting dalliance with a Gretsch Nashville.

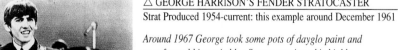

GEORGE HARRISON of the BEATLES and his GRETSCH CHET ATKINS COUNTRY GENTLEMEN-GUITAR

△ GEORGE HARRISON'S FENDER STRATOCASTER
Strat Produced 1954-current: this example around December 1961

Around 1967 George took some pots of dayglo paint and transformed his sonic blue Stratocaster into this highly personalised home-improved psychedelic appliance. The newly daubed Strat was just about visible – in glorious black and white – on the Our World global satellite broadcast of 'All You Need Is Love' that summer, but was more colourfully displayed on the 'I Am The Walrus' sequence from the group's Christmas TV film, Magical Mystery Tour. This Strat also turned up on many Beatle studio sessions of the period (see picture opposite), alongside two new 1966 acquisitions, an Epiphone Casino and a Gibson SG Standard, and is today one of George's favourite slide guitars.

George continued to use his 12-string – described by *Melody Maker* as "the beat boys' secret weapon" – all over The Beatles' studio and live performances. At the time George compared the Rick 12 sound to that of an organ or an electric piano, understandable when you hear something like 'I Should Have Known Better'. But perhaps the guitar's most famous studio moment is on the opening chord of 'A Hard Day's Night'. "That sound," George said much later, "you just associate with those early 1960s Beatles records."

'I Feel Fine', recorded in October 1964, can be seen now as a pointer toward things to come, in that the celebrated 'feedback' intro was deliberately concocted in the studio to get a weird sound, and edited on to the start of the piece. "Don't be put off by that opening noise," Paul told *Melody Maker* shortly afterwards. "It was a laugh. John was playing his jumbo guitar as we did the final run-through before recording, and when the red light came on for the actual session he played it unintentionally. The result's a sound of feedback, and after a bit of thought we decided to leave it in. It's the biggest gimmick thing we've ever used."

Not content with revolutionising the bassline by his exceptional four-string work deep down inside The Beatles' records, Paul began to take more interest in guitar playing, and bought himself an Epiphone Casino hollow-body electric in 1964. Being left-handed, Paul restrung the right-handed Casino to use it 'upside down'. Although he told one magazine that he'd got it for "composing", presumably to fend off the question of why the group's bassist should need an electric six-string, by early 1965 Paul had started to use the Casino in the studio. In February, while John was playing some new recordings to Chris Roberts from *Melody Maker*, he suddenly said: "Hey, listen! Hear that playing by Paul?" This was probably during playback of 'Ticket To Ride' or 'Another Girl'. "Paul's been doing quite a bit of lead guitar work this week," John explained to Roberts. "I reckon he's moving in."

Maybe as retaliation, John and George decided to buy a couple more guitars later in 1965 in time for the *Rubber Soul* sessions. Mal Evans, the group's trusty roadie, was sent out to get a couple of Fender Stratocasters, and apparently returned with an amazing find, a matching pair of Strats in Fender's pale Sonic Blue colour. Clear evidence of the Fenders can be heard as John and George's Strats triumphantly enter the solo of 'Nowhere Man' in unison, John giving way to George alone for the cheeky pinging harmonic at its close, the potentially twangy, toppy timbre of the Fender fully exploited.

Still the apparently ceaseless live dates continued and, despite the studio experimentation with other guitars, the stage instruments generally held to the traditional line-up of Gretsches and Rickenbacker 12-string for George, Rick 325 for John, and Höfner bass for Paul.

In December 1965 George lost his Gretsch Country Gent, smashed apart when it fell from the group's car on a drive to a gig in Scotland. Frederick James wrote soon after in *The Beatles Book*: "According to a disappointed George, at least 14 lorries must have run over the guitar before the boys located all the battered bits at the side of the motorway." Although he still had his trusty Tennessean and Rick 12-string, George soon bought a Gibson ES-345 hollow-body electric as a replacement for the Gent. Into 1966, George also got a solidbody Gibson SG Standard, and he and John acquired an Epiphone Casino each to match Paul's.

They recorded *Revolver* in 1966, an astonishing piece of work that is blatantly experimental, and as far as the guitars go is chock full of crunchy, fuzzboxed Casinos and SGs, deftly tricked into playing backwards on 'I'm Only Sleeping', or spitting blistering distortion on the glorious ensemble work of 'And Your Bird Can Sing' and fuelling Paul's superb solo on 'Taxman'. As a contrast, the group could conjure such tranquil gems as the two ghostly guitar 'statements' on 'Here, There And Everywhere' which sound like George's Rick 12-string, possibly played through a Leslie rotating speaker.

Later in the year the group played their last concerts, in Germany, Japan, The Philippines and the US. John and George mainly used the Casinos, George also taking a Rick 12, while the SG and a J-160 went along as back-ups. Paul played the familiar Höfner bass, with a Rickenbacker 4001S bass he'd acquired in 1965 as back-up. But *Revolver* had made it clear

that the studio was now the outlet for The Beatles' creativity, and at the end of 1966 they started sessions for what would become *Sgt Pepper's Lonely Hearts Club Band*.

A reporter for *The Beatles Book* magazine witnessed the studio overflowing with musical hardware. "The Beatles play far more instruments [now]," he wrote. "The total count at the moment is 14 guitars, a tambura, one sitar, a two-manual Vox organ, and Ringo's Ludwig kit, plus various pianos and organs supplied by EMI." Those 14 guitars would probably have included John's recently acquired Gretsch Nashville and certainly Paul's new Fender Esquire. Fenders dominated the few conventional guitar solos on offer during *Pepper* – the attractively frenetic contribution by McCartney and Esquire to 'Good Morning Good Morning', and George's hollow-toned, detuned, double-tracked Strat on 'Fixing A Hole'. Staccato Fenders probably power 'Getting Better', too, and the Leslie speaker is employed to colour John's ensemble guitar on 'Lucy In The Sky With Diamonds'.

In a way the guitars themselves had become less important to the group. Studio treatments and unusual colourings were now in demand from whatever source. To fill the increasingly diverse aural picture sounds and timbres were actively sought from all manner of tape sources and instruments, including orchestras and brass sections and Mellotrons.

Around the time they recorded and filmed *Magical Mystery Tour*, with its central character of a dayglo-painted coach, the group, imbued with the hippy-trippy spirit of the times,

decided to paint a few of their instruments in wildly psychedelic colour schemes. Paul decorated his Rickenbacker bass, George got out the spray-cans and attacked his Stratocaster, while John had his jumbo painted blue, red and purple, and sprayed the back of his Casino silver. "We did the cars too," Paul told me recently. "If you did the cars, you might as well do your guitars. It looked great, and it was just because we were tripping. That's what it was, man. Look at your guitar and you'd trip even more." Later – perhaps in a fit of post-trip good taste – Paul and John had the paint stripped off the coloured guitars, down to the natural wood, but George's Strat stayed steadfastly psychedelic.

By the time of the sessions in 1968 for '*The White Album*' the sound of the group's electric guitars had become heavier and more distorted, often stacked up in great riffing slabs ('Birthday') or piled on in sheets of punctuating accents ('Happiness Is A Warm Gun'). It becomes more difficult to pick out individual contributions, although the renowned solo by Eric Clapton on 'While My Guitar Gently Weeps' is unmistakable enough. Eric gave George the red Les Paul that he'd used for that wonderful piece of work, and it may well be this guitar that George uses for the distant, dejected moaning at the end of 'Sexy Sadie'.

Certainly when it came to *Let It Be* and *Abbey Road*, in 1969, George was using the Les Paul. He also got a new Fender Rosewood Telecaster around the time of *Let It Be*,

which he can be seen playing on the famous Apple rooftop concert in the film. (Fender gave some other instruments to the group at the same time, including a six-string bass and a couple of Fender-Rhodes pianos.) The Les Paul can be heard on George's rather-too-careful solo slotted into 'Something', while his heavy Tele turns up on the album version (fuzz solo) and single version (Leslie'd solo) of 'Let It Be'.

On *Abbey Road* there is some strong competition for the guitars from the fresh sounds of the group's newly discovered Moog synthesiser, but the record's parting shot is, in effect, a guitar set-piece: 'The End'. Paul, George and John, in that order, each take a two-bar solo, cycling around three times. Paul's brittle tone suggests his Esquire; George's work is pure wailing Les Paul; John makes an aggressive, distorted howl with his Casino. And that, apart from 'Her Majesty', is that.

It had been quite a journey from the late 1950s when the boys got their first guitars. George explained in 1964: "I started to learn to play when I was 13 on an old Spanish model which my dad picked up for 50 bob (£2.50, about $4). It's funny how little things can change your life. Don't ask me why he chose a guitar instead of a mouth organ or something – they certainly weren't popular at the time." As it turned out, George and The Beatles were responsible not only for creating some utterly magical and simply timeless music, but for doing much to make the electric guitar the most popular musical instrument of the 1960s. ■ TONY BACON

FENDER guitars did not become part of the Beatles' guitar line-up until 1965 when George and John acquired a sonic blue Strat each. Paul too picked up an Esquire a year or two later. Why did they wait so long? Perhaps in part it was a reaction against the Fender-toting, old-guard Shadows. But in 1967 George made 'Rocky' an even more personal friend with this psychedelic-cum-rockability paint job.

△ GEORGE HARRISON'S GIBSON LES PAUL
Les Paul produced 1952-current: this example 1957

This famous Les Paul was a gift from Eric Clapton after he'd used it to record the majestic guitar solo for The Beatles track 'While My Guitar Gently Weeps' in September 1968. When Clapton acquired the guitar it had already been refinished red; the instrument's re-stamped serial number corresponds to an entry in Gibson's log for a shipment of a Les Paul, implicitly a gold-top, to one Gartner Sweet on 19th December 1957.

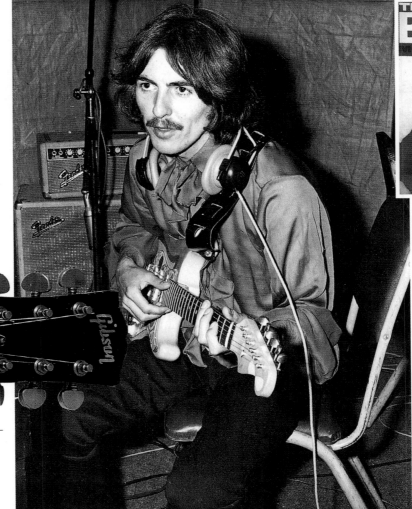

GEORGE is pictured in the EMI studios at Abbey Road (left) with his painted Strat during the recording of 'Revolution' on 4th June 1968. On the back of a 1969 edition of The Beatles Book (above) George is seen with the Rosewood Telecaster that he played on the famous Apple rooftop concert in the group's 1970 film Let It Be.

△ DOMINO CALIFORNIA REBEL
Produced 1967-1968; this example 1967

Maurice Lipsky, a distributor based in New York, imported guitars from various Japanese makers for his Domino line. This original and relatively high-quality example was probably made by Kawai. Oddities abound: note the elegant f-hole (it surmounts a sound cavity cut into the solid body), the Spanish-style slotted headstock, and edge "binding" which is painted on.

HANK GARLAND (left) was a country session player based in Nashville who put his distinctive stamp on 45s such as Elvis Presley's 'Little Sister' and Don Gibson's 'Sea Of *Heartbreak' (with Chet Atkins). In 1960 Garland recorded this jazz-flavoured LP (left), but the following year the 31-year-old was injured in a car crash that effectively ended his career.*

COUNTRY GUITARS

It was the 1960s and change was the big thing, both in and outside music. And those ten years saw country guitars and guitarists not only receiving musical currents from outside the hillbilly universe, but also serving as prime influences on the fast-developing pop music scene.

As the 1960s began, mega-stars like Jim Reeves were making mellow, pop-influenced tunes, including 'He'll Have To Go' with the brilliant Hank Garland offering only the most understated of backings on his Gibson hollow-body. Within a year Garland would release the riveting *Jazz Winds From A New Direction*, a whirlwind of high-level improvisation. The album cover shows him with an actual convertible full of Gibsons. Then, in mid-decade, the most popular group in the world featured Ringo Starr wailing Buck Owens' 'Act Naturally' – with Beatle George Harrison's hollow-body Gretsch doing its best to mimic one of country's hottest sounds, the trebly twang of Buck Owens & The Buckaroos' Telecasters. And by the end of the 1960s country-rockers such as the newly-energised Byrds were assembling Dylan-inspired songwriting, crisp California picking and Everlys-style harmonies for an enduring new sound.

But back to the beginning. Country music had survived the body blow dealt to it by Elvis and rock'n'roll by developing the

smooth, widely palatable Nashville Sound. In the studios of Nashville, this meant that a small cast of musical movers and shakers were kept wildly busy, sometimes recording for as long as 15 hours a day. "We could do four sessions a day: 10am, 2pm, 6pm and 10pm," recalls the great session guitarist Harold Bradley, referring to the standardised times for three-hour studio sessions. "If you were booked solid for four sessions, they'd say, 'We'll start at 1.30 in the morning.' They demanded it!" Bradley laughs. "The artists would say: 'We're not gonna cut it without you guys.'"

The pressure was intense to come up with great performances every time. The need for new and distinctive sounds meant players and producers were constantly on the lookout for new tools and techniques. In one famous incident the recording crew at Music Row's renowned Quonset Hut studio got creative when a malfunctioning pre-amp in the

recording console produced a wild, evenly distorted sound. Making use of the sound was session great Grady Martin, who produced the famed distortion-powered solo on six-string bass for Marty Robbins' 1961 hit 'Don't Worry'. As that record puzzled and then captivated listeners in the pop and country fields, the fuzztone era was under way. "Later when I found out what it was, I set about trying to develop that sound using transistors," recalls veteran engineer Glenn Snoddy. "We fooled around with it and got the sound like we wanted. I drove up to Chicago and presented it to Mr Berlin, the boss at the Gibson company, and he heard that it was something different. So they agreed to take it and put it out as a commercial product." The result was the first off-the-shelf fuzzbox, the Gibson Maestro.

Early echo effects like the tape-derived Ecco-Fonic and Gibson's Echoplex began to see wide use in the early 1960s, with Hank Garland making it part of his identifiable sound on records by Patsy Cline and others. Mr Guitar, Chet Atkins, continued to unleash a variety of sounds, even as he became more and more involved as a producer. Sales of his Gretsch models soared with their use by Harrison, who featured Chet-style licks on Fabs hits like 'All My Loving'. Guitars from other makers, such as the Gibson ES series and Fender's Jazzmaster that had been developed at the end of the 1950s, enjoyed increasing use in the Nashville studios by the early 1960s.

"When I started with Jim Reeves, I had a big Gibson ES-5,"

SALESMEN look glum on the
La Baye stand at a 1967 trade
show (right): not one of the
new 2-By-4 models was sold.
The same year at a British
show, Vox designer Dick
Denney (far right) demos their
Winchester small-body guitar.
Below him, Dave Roberts tries
a multi-control Vox Marauder.

△ LA BAYE 2-BY-4
Produced 1967; this example 1967

Dan Helland had a great idea. Why bother to have a body on a solid electric guitar? In theory it could be anything, so why not make it a piece of two-by-four? In typical 1960s fashion, odd theory became strange practice. Helland met guitar manufacturer Holman-Woodell (who had already made instruments for Wurlitzer as well as their own Holman brand), and La Baye was set up in Green Bay, Wisconsin. The plan got no further than prototypes at a trade show, and while some later 2-By-4s turned up branded 21st Century, no more than 90 in total are thought to have been produced, making this a rare sample of 1960s frivolity.

MESSENGER's guitar (right) used a one-piece magnesium alloy chassis that combined headstock, neck and body extension. This use of the structural strength of metal was new for guitars. Messenger explained that it permitted a neck that was thin "from first to 21st fret", as well as a fingerboard completely free of the body, allowing superb top-fret access. The guitar was also stereo-wired. However, this plethora of attributes failed to attract players, and not many Messengers were delivered.

△ MESSENGER ME-11
Produced 1967; this example 1967

Another 1960s maker destined for obscurity, Messenger made guitars with a structural "backbone" of magnesium alloy. This example has been refinished from its original sunburst to green.

JIM REEVES (above, centre) was the most successful 1960s example of how the Nashville Sound crossed over into easy-listening pop-hit territory. Leo

Jackson, guitarist in Reeves' backing group The Blue Boys, smiles (second from left) as they take delivery of a truckload of suitably blue-finished

Rickenbacker gear in 1961. However, Jackson was more often to be seen with his Jazzmaster (right), also with a special blue-boy paint job.

says long-time Reeves sideman and session musician Leo Jackson. "But I saw this guy play a Fender one time and it just knocked me out, the guy got so much out of the guitar. I said, 'I'm going to get me one of them.'" Jackson bought a Strat in 1957, but switched to a Jazzmaster by the time he accompanied Reeves on hits like 'Distant Drums' and 'I Love You Because'. There was one drawback to playing with Reeves. The singer took the name of his Blue Boys band seriously, and had Jackson spray his Fender Jazzmaster light blue with automobile paint.

A leading light of the sessions scene, Grady Martin worked zillions of dates on his famous ES-355 named Big Red, which had palm pedals to create steel-guitar-like pitch shifts. "I had an ES-335 that I bought down at Hewgley's store in 1961. That was the guitar of choice with those [session] guys," recalls guitarist-producer Jerry Kennedy, whose melodic playing appeared on countless hits such as Tammy Wynette's 'Stand By Your Man' and Roy Orbison's 'Pretty Woman'. Kennedy recalled: "A guy named Dean Porter put those string-benders on my 335 – one lever that lowered the E-string down a tone and one that raised the second [B-] string a whole tone. Now, I wish I'd had them put on some other guitar." Session player/executive Kelso Herston recalls getting an ES-345 "because Hank Garland had one".

Though Gibsons and Fenders remained the key country instruments for much of the 1960s, other makes popped up all

GEORGE HARRISON's *use of a sitar on 'Norwegian Wood' in 1965 led everybody to want one on their record. "The trouble is they are difficult to tune and obtain," sessionman Jimmy Page told a reporter. An electric sitar was needed: the Rajah from 1967 (right) was a false start; the winner proved to be the Coral Sitar (below).*

Vincent Bell SIGNATURE DESIGN ELECTRIC SITAR

△ CORAL SITAR
Produced 1967-1970; this example c1968

This electric sitar brought the exotic sounds of the complicated Indian instrument to guitar players. The key to the Sitar's imitation of the Indian sound was its "flat" plastic bridge, designed by session guitarist Vinnie Bell to give just the right buzzy edge... but it also meant the Sitar was virtually impossible to keep in tune. Coral was another brandname used by the New Jersey-based guitar manufacturer, Danelectro, after it was bought by MCA in 1967.

the time. Thumbs Carllile played a Mosrite electric dobro, session regular Chip Young had a Rickenbacker electric with palm pedals, and Harold Bradley was one of the first to try the Coral electric sitar. Baldwin, eager to get in on the Nashville scene, gave several key players some electric models, which were rarely used. Kelso Herston played the rampaging solo on George Jones' 'The Race Is On' on a Danelectro six-string bass, getting a startling sound by using lots of echo and an early in-studio phasing effect – more than three years before The Small Faces' celebrated phase-laden 'Itchycoo Park'. Herston's playing on the Jones record was pure twang. "I guess probably it was a steal from the West Coast. Don Rich and all those guys out there were doing it, so we just did it an octave lower," he recalls.

Bradley kept an enormous assortment of guitars in a room known as the 'closet' of the Quonset Hut. Included was his Jazzmaster that was passed around by many of the studio masters of the day. "Hank Garland was playing a Gibson and he called me," Bradley says. "He said, 'My guitar doesn't twang like yours. I've got this Elvis session coming up:

CHET ATKINS worked hard to establish the Nashville Sound in the 1960s, both as a record producer and guitarist. As a well-respected professional, Atkins' continued use of Gretsch guitars (Country Gentleman, above) did much for that company's image.

BUCK OWENS (above right) and his guitarist Don Rich (left) spearheaded the Tele's popularity in 1960s country music after Fender gave them each a silver-sparkle model.

ELECTRIC SITAR proved to be an irresistible flavour for many late-1960s record producers. Inventor Vinnie Bell played his Coral Sitar on many East-coast records, such as Joe South's 'Games People Play', and 'Green Tambourine' by The Lemon Pipers (left). Al Nichol of The Turtles (centre) was another enthusiastic Sitar player, using it here for one of the group's many live shows.

VINNIE BELL was a session guitarist who spotted a demand for trendy sitar sounds in New York studios in the mid 1960s. Bell had already worked with Danelectro in 1961 to design their early electric 12-string, the Bellzouki model, and his Coral Sitar was launched by the company *in 1967. Bell shamelessly appeared in a turban (left) that year to publicise the new instrument. As well as a special "buzzy" bridge the Sitar had 13 extra drone strings with a separate pickup and controls to assist the sitar impersonation.*

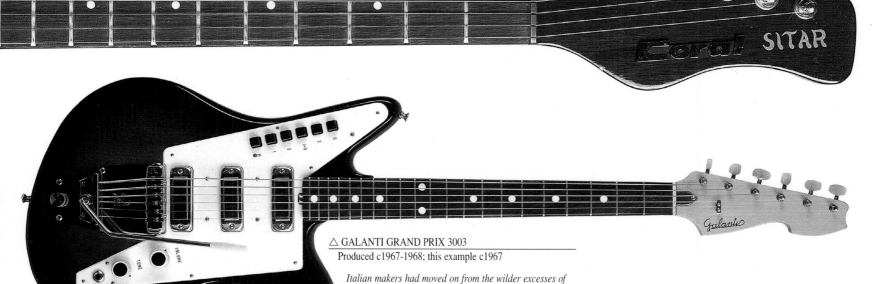

△ GALANTI GRAND PRIX 3003
Produced c1967-1968; this example c1967

Italian makers had moved on from the wilder excesses of the early 1960s (see Wandre, page 24) to produce more sober and approachable models such as this decent instrument, imported into the US by Galanti. Nonetheless, accordion influence remains in the pushbutton selector strip.

---

can I borrow your Fender?'" The session was on June 26th 1961, the tune was Presley's 'Little Sister', and the guitar part's trebly, bluesy tone prompted many imitators. Presley, recording for RCA in Nashville at the time, was only one of a slew of pop artists who hit town to make use of the casual but highly creative session scene on Music Row.

Meanwhile, pop of a different kind had worked its way into country through the innovations of a young Buck Owens. His country roots and his wide-ranging interests in other styles married and gave birth to The Twang. "I think that probably came from playing 'Jenny Jenny Jenny' and 'Tutti Frutti' and those things," remembers Owens, who freely mixed rock and country during his years of playing the honky-tonks in Bakersfield, California. The treble-heavy sound of the guitar's low end was a necessity because Owens had to work hard to be heard over the noisy night-life crowd. The sound also gave a nod to the kind of tone popularised by pop guitarists such as Duane Eddy and The Ventures' Nokie Edwards (the latter of whom worked with Owens for a while).

Seldom has an artist been more closely associated with a guitar than Buck Owens and the Telecaster. In 1963 the Fender company presented him and his guitarist Don Rich with

MERLE HAGGARD was an ideally named country star. His tough, real-life songs celebrated the downtrodden, drawing on his own unruly youth and prison spells.

Haggard's group The Strangers included guitarist Roy Nichols who produced an inventive Tele-driven mix of string abuse, heard to great effect on the 1967 album pictured above.

matching crushed-mirror sparkle-finish chequered-binding Teles. The act returned the favour by featuring them on a string of huge, hard-hitting records – including 'Act Naturally', later covered by The Beatles. An amazing nine of *Billboard*'s Top 50 US singles of the decade were by Buck and the Buckaroos. "When Buck came out with 'Tiger By The Tail' [in 1965] there was a big revival of Fender," Bradley says.

Out in California the honky-tonk strains begun in the 1950s by Tommy Collins, Wynn Stewart and others came to full flower as Owens and then Merle Haggard came up with hit after hit based on true-life heartache and guitaristics of a wholly new sort. West Coasters including Phil Baugh, James Burton and Roy Nichols were twisting strings, choking strings, slapping strings and chicken-picking strings in ways that arose organically out of the solidbody, highly-responsive Tele.

"I remember going down for the first session on a song that we were working on," Haggard says. "Roy Nichols and I were sitting on the steps of my little old apartment and talking about the necessity of having some kind of different guitar style – something that people like and remember and identify with," Haggard says. "And I remember Roy said, 'What would happen if a guy took the string and pushed it up and then hit

1968

THE BYRDS changed dramatically in 1968. Gram Parsons joined briefly, steering the group to a new course that resulted in one of the period's most influential country-rock LPs, Sweetheart Of The Rodeo (left). Bluegrass/country picker Clarence White (right) was also added to the line-up; his steely Tele was another vital element in The Byrds' new sound.

it and let it come down, rather than hitting it while it's going up?' I said, 'Let me see what you mean.' He showed me, and that was the beginning of the Merle Haggard style, coming down with the guitar string."

The 1966 Hag hit 'I'm A Lonesome Fugitive' finds Nichols chicken-picking, bending those notes down after they're hit, and popping the strings in a totally electric technique that was riveting and hit-making. James Burton, who had started making the Tele famous as a teenage sideman to Ricky Nelson, created mind-twisting licks on many of the early Haggard sessions on his way to becoming one of country's and pop's most revered twangmasters. Burton eventually joined Elvis Presley's touring band in 1969. Meanwhile, The Beatles

weren't the only pop acts tuning into country music, guitarists and guitars. The Lovin' Spoonful paid tribute to the innumerable pickers of Music City in the 1966 hit 'Nashville Cats', while Bob Dylan started a major wave of pop stars to Nashville studios beginning with his sessions there for the 1966 rock masterpiece *Blonde On Blonde*. More significantly, he came back to record the groundbreaking country records *John Wesley Harding* (1968) and *Nashville Skyline* (1969) with a new breed of Nashville picker that included studio session guitarists such as Wayne Moss, Joe South and Charlie Daniels.

Virtually single-handedly, Dylan focused the interest of the rock community on country studios and players. Of course, as

Daniels notes, "Any rock musician worth his salt has an awful lot of respect for country music – and it's been that way for a long time. How can you help from liking George Jones?" Wielding a stock 1966 Telecaster he bought in Maine during his years as a rock'n'roll journeyman, Daniels put his feisty, aggressive stamp on Dylan tunes like 'Country Pie' as well as playing a string of other country and folk sessions.

In the second half of the 1960s the cutting edge of country was definitely picking and singing its way out of California. Owens was king of country radio and Haggard was well on his way to becoming one of country's all-time innovators and creative models. And then came country-rock. As early as 1966 The Byrds had included the hillbilly anthem 'Satisfied Mind' on their *Turn Turn Turn* LP, with former folkies Jim (later Roger) McGuinn and David Crosby plus former bluegrasser Chris Hillman melding vocal harmonies and jangling

THE TELECASTER became almost a membership badge for the country guitarists' club in the 1960s. It was admired in Nashville, on the West Coast and beyond for a simplicity that allowed the voice and character of the individual guitarist to shine. Fender tried variations such as this wild paisley finish, but soon realised that a central part of the Tele's appeal is its strong resistance to change.

BOB DYLAN highlighted the move of many pop musicians toward country by making two LPs in Nashville in the late 1960s: John Wesley Harding, and Nashville Skyline (sleeve, far left). Before that, in an enforced retreat, Dylan had hidden away with The Band to record a series of demos. The Band's debut album Music From Big Pink (left) appeared in 1968, and it too drew on country as well as folk and rock, creating an atmospheric slice of Americana.

JAMES BURTON was one of the best-known session guitarists of the 1960s. He had come to fame in the 1950s and early 1960s working with Ricky Nelson (right), but in the mid 1960s began to play more country-oriented sessions for the likes of Merle Haggard and Buck Owens. For his 1969 solo album (below) he teamed up with pedal-steel man Ralph Mooney. A big Tele fan, Burton

later swapped this red one for a Paisley Red example which he used as a member of Elvis Presley's band in the 1970s.

Rickenbackers in the beginnings of a new sound. Even The Rolling Stones recorded Hank Snow's 'I'm Moving On', and The Beatles continued to release countrified tunes like 'I've Just Seen a Face' and 'What Goes On'. Then in 1968 came two

landmark records: The Byrds' all-country *Sweetheart Of The Rodeo* and The Band's country-tinged debut album, *Music From Big Pink*. Psychedelia had serious competition. The Byrds continued in a country vein throughout the rest of the 1960s, losing Hillman and Parsons to The Flying Burrito Brothers, but gaining the great guitarist Clarence White. Beginning his career as a groundbreaking bluegrasser, White became a Telecaster blaster under the tutelage of James Burton, appearing in early country-rock bands as well as developing a strap-activated string bender, still available today, along with Byrd-mate Gene Parsons.

From those country-rock roots came a host of bands. It began with Poco and culminated in the 1970s with the Eagles, who in a turnabout went on to influence mainstream country music well into the 1990s. "We definitely ruffled some feathers down there, but nothing collapsed, nothing went away," Byrds bassist Chris Hillman recalled years later of the group's 1968 appearance at the Grand Ole Opry. "We didn't destroy any tradition. People just weren't exactly ready to have a West Coast rock band on that stage."

Far from destroying tradition, the 1960s marriage of country and rock produced a vital form that, in its best incarnations, still enriches both styles. And as the century ends, the twangin' guitar sound that powered the 1960s airwaves remains as stylish as the ever-popular Telecaster. ■ **TOMMY GOLDSMITH**

MARTIN LUTHER KING is shot dead in Memphis, and Senator Robert Kennedy is assassinated in Los Angeles.

2001: A SPACE ODYSSEY has Sixties audiences enthralled by its sweeping tale from ape-man to space station, its trip-like visuals and its enigmatic message. One review describes the 140-minute movie as "somewhere between hypnotic and immensely boring".

FRENCH STUDENTS riot and heavy street fighting ensues. Workers call a general strike in support and the country comes to a halt. Elections are called amid new riots, but the Gaullists hold power, defeating the Communists in a landslide.

BLACK ATHLETES give controversial black-power salutes at a Mexico Olympics awards ceremony.

THE VIETCONG mount the "Tet Offensive", a series of continued attacks on the South Vietnamese capital, Saigon. This calls into question the ability of South Vietnamese and US forces to win the war.

SOVIET and Warsaw Pact forces invade increasingly liberal Czechoslovakia, re-imposing totalitarianism. A treaty is signed providing for Soviet troops to be stationed in Czechoslovakia, which becomes a two-state federation.

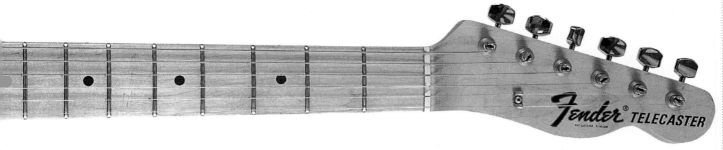

△ **FENDER PAISLEY RED TELECASTER**
Produced 1968-1969; this example 1968

This guitar shouts "Sixties!" louder than almost any other in the book, thanks to Fender's bold attempt to turn an ordinary Telecaster into a far-out psychedelic art object. Collectors would have you believe that after Fender were taken over by CBS in 1965 they became boring; clearly they do not have a paisley Tele in their collection. Fender simply went to the local wallpaper store and picked this Paisley Red design (as well as a Blue Flower pattern, left) from the self-adhesive line. Back at the factory, instead of painting Teles they stuck on the wallpaper.

FENDER's Telecaster was the least likely target for Paisley Red (opposite) and Blue Flower finishes (flyer, left). Since its launch in 1951 the Tele was rarely seen without its standard blond finish, even though custom colours were offered.

ARIA is one of many Japanese guitar brands of the 1960s that lasted for decades beyond. Aria guitars first appeared in Japan in 1956, with electrics launched around 1960. This 1968 catalogue (left) reflects the popularity of hollow-body electrics at the time, inspired by The Beatles who went on stage with Epiphones, Rickenbackers and Höfners in Tokyo in 1966.

△ ARIA DIAMOND ADSG-12T
Produced c1968-1969; this example c1968

By the late 1960s Japanese makers had absorbed many Western influences. This guitar has the Fender-inspired "offset waist" body shape that so many manufacturers found appealing. It also shows that the craze for electric 12-string guitars lasted longer in Japan – by 1968 in America and Europe the jingle-jangle sound was in decline from its first peak of popularity. The Arai company used two brands: Aria, and (as here) Aria Diamond.

SHIRO ARAI (above) was a keen classical guitarist and the president of Arai, the company which made Aria guitars.

JAPANESE GUITARS

In Japan there was no escaping the guitar in the 1960s. First there was The Ventures-inspired electric guitar boom, and then the Group Sounds fad triggered by The Beatles. Guitars became so popular that one education committee even banned them, fearful of their effect on the nation's youth. But Japan's factories poured out thousands upon thousands of guitars for a hungry domestic market – as well as for equally demanding importers in Europe, the US and elsewhere – and brandnames such as Aria, Ibanez and Yamaha made their first impressions on young guitarists around the world.

As the 1960s got underway the popularity of the guitar in America and Europe continued to grow. With an increasing number of teenage guitar players, these countries couldn't keep up with the demand on their own, and began to buy increasing numbers of instruments from exporting countries such as Japan.

During the late 1950s and into the early 1960s only Teisco and Guyatone exported electric guitars from Japan to the US and Europe. These two companies had begun producing electric musical instruments soon after World War II, gaining experience through exports. Into the early 1960s, with the instrumental surf music trend in America, this trade grew, and by 1962 Teisco and Guyatone were overwhelmed by orders.

American musical instrument importers in particular flocked to Japan, looking for new manufacturers. They visited guitar factories and offered manufacturers the chance to develop and export electric guitars. These Japanese makers didn't really have the expertise to make electric guitars, but the importers brought with them brochures and American-made guitars to demonstrate what an electric guitar should be like. Some manufacturers showed an interest and took on development, somehow managing to make guitar-like products and export solid electric instruments, as dictated by the importers.

Despite their relative lack of knowledge, these companies passionately devoted themselves to develop and learn the production techniques and very quickly were setting up mass-production systems. The Japanese manufacturers who started to produce electric guitars in this way in the early 1960s included Fujigen Gakki which made guitars with Goya, Kent and other importer brands, and Kawai Gakki, whose brands included Kawai, Domino, Kingston, Heit and Winston. Also in operation were the Arai Trading Company (Aria and Aria Diamond brands), Zen-on Gakki (Zenon, Morales), Hoshino Gakki (Ibanez, Star) and Kasuga Gakki (Mellowtone).

In 1964 surf music finally reached the shores of Japan. Songs by The Astronauts and similar groups arrived and instrumental surf music gradually grew in popularity. But the one group which caught the hearts and minds of the young Japanese was The Ventures. That year the group released two singles in Japan, 'Walk – Don't Run, 64' and 'Diamond Head', which launched their oriental success. The Ventures' Japanese tour in January 1965 triggered an unprecedented electric

guitar boom. The kids who heard The Ventures' music lost their hearts to the wild sound of electric guitars, rushed to the music stores to buy the records – and many decided to start groups of their own. One of the most successful was The Blue Jeans, led by Takeshi Terauchi, who had one electric instrumental hit after another. Young fans of the electric guitar were transfixed by Terauchi, who because of his stunning technique was nicknamed God's Hands.

Another popular guitarist was Yuzo Kayama. He made TV and concert appearances with a white Mosrite as his main instrument, and his records sold very well. Kayama, who had originally been an actor, also starred in a crucially important movie called *Eleki No Wakadaisho* (which means something like "Japanese Electric Guitar Explosion"). The film had a storyline based on the electric guitar boom, and itself helped to expand the market still further. During 1965 demand in Japan for electric guitars rose rapidly and manufacturers finally started to focus on domestic sales.

The two established companies, Teisco and Guyatone, were leading the industry in 1960s Japan, competing as friendly rivals and constantly unveiling new models. In 1962 Teisco's line consisted primarily of cheap plywood solidbody guitars, including the MJ, SD, SS and WG series. Designs were full of originality, and from 1964 Teisco began to sell better quality models. These included the TG-64 (featured in *Eleki No Wakadaisho*) which had a 'grip hole' in the body, and the TRG-1 with a built-in speaker.

Guyatone had the solidbody LG series at the start of the 1960s, and in 1963 marketed the popular LG-65T model and the hollow-body electric Musician. Two years later they announced what is arguably their best-ever model, the LG-200T.

KENT's 742 was a top-of-the-line Japanese stunner, with a figured maple body and enough pickups and controls to satisfy the most knob-crazy gadget freak. Each pickup has an on/off switch, plus a volume and tone control below.

Guyatone's LG-200T was an epoch-making instrument: it had 24 frets, stereo circuitry, and enabled various sound combinations from four pickups and six selector switches.

As the electric guitar boom took off in 1965 still more brandnames appeared on the scene, including Columbia, Elk, Mory, Pleasant, Splender, Suzuki, Tombo, Victor, Voice, and Zen-on. Among these, Pleasant and Zen-on were already exporters, but now they unveiled many new products with the accent on domestic sales.

Elk started off as an amplifier manufacturer in 1963. Because its founder, Yukiho Yamada, was an active steel guitar player, the company enjoyed a strong connection with professional musicians in Japan, and offered a top-notch, high-quality product line. In 1965 they began producing electric guitars, and from the beginning aimed at making accurate, good-quality Fender copies. One of Elk's first models was the Deluxe, a Fender Jaguar-style solidbody that was highly acclaimed by Japanese professionals.

Voice, on the other hand, manufactured small-volume, high-quality handbuilt guitars. Its founder, Yukichi Iwase, had worked for Teisco as an engineer. In 1964 his new company started to develop electric guitars and the following year released the Frontier Custom 1000. Thanks to the engineering skills and elaborate handmaking techniques he'd nurtured at

Teisco, Iwase built a guitar that was accepted by a number of professional musicians, and later by a wider public.

In many cases what was intended for export was also sold domestically, retaining the overseas customer's brand. This makes it difficult to calculate how many brands were available in Japan in the 1960s, but it was probably over 30. Some manufacturers expanded their business for export, and 1965 saw the whole industry devoting itself to the production of electric guitars.

Makers at this time enthusiastically introduced new models. Structurally, these instruments were strongly influenced by Fender, and in design and mechanical operation by Burns, Harmony, Framus, Eko and others, with each maker trying to project originality. As we've seen, at first in the 1960s Japanese-made guitars were intended for export, and destined to copy popular products – at least partly due to requests from the overseas distributors themselves. But from 1965 many makers instead of manufacturing faithful copies attempted to absorb only the best points of foreign products while pursuing their own original designs.

TV broadcasts in 1965 included electric guitar programmes with audience participation, such as *Kachinuki Eleki Gassen* ("Electric Guitar Tournament"), and guitar competitions were held throughout the country. The Ventures came to Japan for

ELECTRIC GUITARS were considered harmful influences on 1960s Japanese youth, and precautions were taken. This newspaper cutting (below) from 1965 reports a banning of electric guitars by the Ashikaga city education committee.

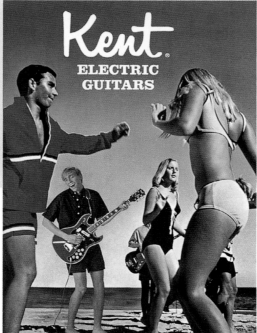

▽ KENT 742
Produced c1968-1969; this example c1968

Kent was a brandname applied by leading New York-based instrument wholesaler Buegeleisen & Jacobson to its imported line of Japanese-made guitars. At first Kents were manufactured by Guyatone, but in 1967 B&J changed supplier, probably to Kawai. This magnificent multi-control four-pickup Kent is from the new source. (The vibrato and bridge here are not original.)

▽ KAWAI CONCERT
Produced c1968-1970; this example c1968

By the end of the decade Kawai was one of the biggest guitar makers in Japan, producing instruments for the domestic market with its own brandname as well as supplying many export customers in the US and Europe. The Concert, looking more like some kind of oriental weapon than a guitar, was one of Kawai's most distinctive models.

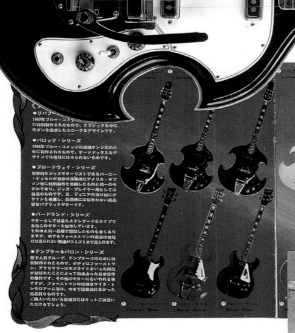

FIRSTMAN *was one of the companies set up by ex-Teisco employees who left when Kawai bought Teisco. Firstman relied on the new popularity of The Beatles in Japan by using a striking version of Höfner's "violin" body shape for the Liverpool 67 model. Its best-known player, Tunaki Mihara (right) of The Blue Comets, gave it valuable exposure.*

a second time and toured nationally for a month, ensuring the continued popularity of electric guitars. For many Japanese boys, every day started and ended with guitars, an unparalleled trend seen in every corner of Japan.

However, in any age, there are adults who feel uncomfortable about the fashions of the young. The authorities decided that playing the electric guitar turned boys into delinquents. In October 1965, Ashikaga City Education Committee in Tochigi Prefecture issued a ban on electric guitars, instantly throwing cold water on the guitar boom. Schools followed suit, with rules banning electric guitars. Many public facilities became unavailable for hire if electric guitar playing was involved. Newspapers, which up until then had supported electric guitar competitions and reported them favourably, suddenly changed their attitude. They accused electric guitars of being a hotbed of evil. The electric guitar boom imploded. Of course, there is no knowing exactly how much pressure was imposed by the authorities, and we can't presume that this was the only reason the boom declined. But the fact is that the electric guitar boom waned and sales of each maker plummeted soon afterwards.

Another reason for this decline was that people had simply got bored with instrumental music. But in the background the Liverpool Sound, personified by The Beatles, was gaining

CATALOGUE#200

Tele Star

MUSICAL
INSTRUMENT
CORPORATION

651 BROADWAY, NEW YORK, N.Y.
(212) 674-4900
SUBSIDIARY – MUSIC·CRAFT·ELECTRONIC·CORP·

YAMAHA are one of the oldest Japanese music companies, with roots that go back to organ making in the 1880s. Observing the guitar boom of the 1960s, they decided to launch a solidbody line of electrics in 1966 (with this catalogue, left) bearing clear Fender and Mosrite influences.

ELECTRIC GUITARS **YAMAHA**

JAPANESE guitar makers increasingly built instruments for export during the 1960s. Products of the bigger factories are seen with many different brands, often reflecting the marketing plans of the importer rather than the manufacturer's name. Telestar guitars (right) were made by Kawai in Japan, and the US importer has left us a document replete with such 1960s essentials as beehives, neckerchiefs and mini-skirts.

ground, and in June 1966 when The Beatles came to Japan their popularity got into full swing. Up until then the group's fans had mainly been girls, but now boys finally started to recognise The Beatles. Kids who had copied The Ventures by making instrumental music with solidbody guitars changed to vocal songs and hollow-body electric guitars, inspired by the Epiphones and Rickenbackers and Höfners they saw The Beatles playing. In 1966 many vocal groups – amateur and professional – made their debuts. The fashion was called Group Sounds, or 'GS' for short. The electric guitar boom had developed into the GS boom.

In 1967 and 1968 the GS boom swept Japan and with it sales of electric guitars increased again. Teisco had released the Framus-style V series hollow-body electric guitars. Solidbody guitars were unpopular, and so Teisco issued new models with a totally fresh design. These were the Spectrum 5 – which many consider the finest model produced by Teisco – and the tulip-shaped SM and K guitars (later taken up by

Humming Bird

OFFSET cutaways and a slanting pickup were taken straight from Mosrite for Tokai's Humming Bird, but translated into oriental style.

POP GROUPS blossomed in Japan, especially after The Beatles played at the Nippon Budokan Hall in Tokyo in summer 1966. The craze for making music that followed was called "Group Sounds", and everyone wanted to take part. Here are two examples: from the more obscure end, The Fingers (right), and the successful Sharp Five.

TOKYO SOUND CO was set up by Mitsuo Matsuki in the late 1940s to make Guyatone guitars (logo, below). With Teisco, Guyatone was the main Japanese electric guitar brand to have continued successfully into the 1960s from these early roots. The two benefitted from the initial rush of Ventures-inspired pop in Japan in 1965. Despite stronger competition during the Beatles-inspired "Group Sounds" fad of 1966, Guyatone scored by co-designing a guitar with Sharp Five's popular guitarist Nobuhiro Mine (left).

GUYATONE
TOKYO SOUND CO., LTD.

Jackson Browne/Ry Cooder collaborator David Lindley). The quality of these was far better than anything Teisco had produced before.

However, Teisco got into difficulties due to overstocking and a huge capital investment. In January 1967 they were taken over by Kawai Gakki, who began to produce Teisco guitars in their own factories. Under the umbrella of Kawai Gakki, Teisco released in 1968 a number of striking hollow-body electric models such as the May Queen, Vamper, Fire Bird and Phantom. In the uncertain period during the takeover of Teisco by Kawai, some disgruntled young engineers left Teisco to set up their own new companies, including Honey and Firstman.

Honey released a Rickenbacker copy, the SG-5, and this became a hit and made Honey almost instantly successful. Firstman released the unusual violin-shape Liverpool 67 model, as used by Tunaki Mihara, guitarist with The Blue Comets, who were at the peak of their popularity. It sold well and Firstman too became a well-known brand. Both companies began to unveil a stream of new hollow-body electric guitars (but, significantly, almost no solidbody models). If the stars of the 1965 boom were Teisco and Guyatone, it is no exaggeration to say that the heroes of the second boom were Honey and Firstman.

Another company born when Teisco was taken over by Kawai was Idol, established by a founder of Teisco, Doryu Matsuda, in September 1967. Matsuda had stayed on as a director of Kawai after the takeover, but left soon after to form Idol, which released only hollow-body electric guitars.

Guyatone too marketed a Rickenbacker-style hollow-body electric guitar, the SG-42T, as well as the solidbody LG-350T Sharp Five, jointly developed with Nobuhiro Mine who played guitar with the popular band Sharp Five.

In 1966 Yamaha entered the electric guitar market, with several solidbody models in the SG series and the hollow-body electric SA series. The latter were conspicuously high-quality models compared to other Japanese-made hollow-body electrics guitars of the period, and were taken up by a number of professionals. Arai was one of the companies which swiftly changed production from solid guitars to hollow-body electrics. In 1966 Aria's Gibson-style hollow-body electrics appeared. (Note that the company is called Arai but the brandname is Aria.)

Greco, who had until this time made instruments mainly for export, appeared on the domestic market in 1968 with Harmony-style hollow-body electric guitars. Around the same time Tokai – who would later take the world by storm with

▽ TOKAI HUMMING BIRD 200S
Produced 1968-1969; this example c1968

The Ventures instrumental group from the US enjoyed enormous popularity in Japan during the 1960s, mostly using Mosrite guitars in the process, and causing a near obsession among Japanese guitar makers with the look of the Mosrite Ventures model. This wonderful example shows how the American original was adapted to suit oriental tastes. In later decades Tokai would move to blatant copies of US designs, with notorious accuracy.

vintage replicas – entered the electric guitar market. They released Mosrite-influenced guitars under the Humming Bird brandname, the solidbody construction going against the contemporary trend. Manufacturing companies were springing up to take advantage of the demand and make money, and produced electric guitars with beautiful names but dubious identity, including brands such as Excetro, Jaguar, Liberty and Minister. One company even branded their guitars 'Burns', but with no connection at all to the UK operation.

As is so often the case, the boom didn't last long. In late 1968, GS started to decline and in '69 completely died out. The makers with excessive stocks went bankrupt – first Honey, then Firstman, followed by Idol and Guyatone (although Guyatone was later revived). By 1969 the domestic guitar industry in Japan was almost completely wiped out. It was the end of an era. Of course, some manufacturers such as Aria, Greco, Voice and Yamaha survived the crisis through sound management, and Teisco continued under the umbrella of Kawai Gakki. For these makers 1969 was a year of renewal. Greco turned its eyes to acoustic guitars and Gibson copies, and Aria tried to escape from the difficulties by joining the trend toward producing copies of classic US models. It would be these copy guitars that would dominate the Japanese guitar industry through much of the 1970s. ■ HIROYUKI NOGUCHI

◁ KUSTOM K200C
Produced 1968-1969; this example c1968

Meanwhile in Kansas, Kustom exemplified the small-scale American guitar maker trying to attract players away from big-name products. Despite designer Doyle Reading's experience gained at other modest operations such as Holman and Alray, Kustom had nothing special enough to commend its guitars, and would enter the 1970s as solely an amplifier manufacturer.

MICRO-FRETS was set up by Ralph Jones (right, with The Orbiter – and his wife Hazel – at a trade show in 1968). As well as the first wireless guitar, Micro-Frets offered a number of other models, some with the complex Calibrato vibrato system and the 'Micro-Nut', intended to stabilise tuning and improve intonation. The inventive, stylish Micro-Frets guitars did not, however, last long into the next decade.

THE ORBITER had an FM radio transmitter built into the body: the antenna can be seen on its upper horn (above). A remote receiver then picked up the signals and directed them to the player's stage amplifier.

BLUES & SOUL GUITARS

The electric guitar had become the key instrument in black American music, with the lead guitarist vying for the dominant role. Yet over the decade a fundamental change took place. In black music the electric guitar was absorbed back into a more anonymous role in the band, while during the same period a new generation of English interpreters performed the converse move, making the lead guitarist arguably the most significant force in mainstream popular music.

By 1960 the electric guitar had irrevocably changed the format of R&B. At the beginning of the 1950s, the saxophone and brass section had formed the mainstay of black music, but in a single decade they had been almost completely supplanted by small combos based around the electric guitar.

Blues music had reached an impressive state of technical sophistication. In Chicago, the capital city of electric blues, the Vee Jay and Chess record companies had enjoyed a cosy duopoly, with a definitive roster of acts including Muddy Waters, Howlin' Wolf and Jimmy Reed. However, by the late

1950s, a new generation of guitarists had appeared in the city. Buddy Guy, Otis Rush and Magic Sam – all of whom made their initial impact via the shortlived Cobra label based on Chicago's West Side – were heavily influenced by B.B. King, and along with fellow newcomer Freddy King helped establish the lead guitarist as the central figure in electric bands. Their guitar-dominated music was termed West Side blues, although as Buddy Guy points out "that word is just a label, 'cause we all played the same clubs, West Side, South Side, whatever".

Although the flowering of West Side blues was brief, it left a legacy of influential records which demonstrated how the music had developed to a form that anticipated the blues-rock of the end of the decade. Guy, Rush and 'Magic' Sam Maghett all used Fender Stratocasters amplified through Fender's beefy 4x10 Bassman combo – an amplifier designed, as its name suggests, for bass, but which was perfectly suited for powerful overdriven lead guitar sounds. Freddy King used a Gibson Les Paul gold-top or an ES-335, reportedly through a Dual Showman stack. In every case the trademark sound of these players hinged on the sustain and responsiveness of their solidbody (or semi-solid) electric guitars.

It's often remarked that the key solidbody electrics were

OTIS RUSH exemplified the West Side cocktail of blues and soul, but his career was dogged by ill-fortune. This 1969 LP, Mourning In The Morning, *produced by Mike Bloomfield, occupied similar ground to Albert King's Born Under A Bad Sign, but was released too late to enjoy similar success.*

PLAYERS *such as Eric Clapton and Peter Green had spearheaded a British blues-rock movement that relied heavily on the 1950s-style version of Gibson's Les Paul guitars, particularly the* Sunburst. *Gibson reissued a couple of models (but not the Sunburst) in 1968. As their launch ad from that year (right) admitted: "The pressure to make more has never let up. Okay... you win."*

Daddy of 'em all.

△ GIBSON LES PAUL CUSTOM
Produced 1968-current (this style); this example c1969

Even Gibson noticed the enormous interest in old-design Les Pauls during the second half of the 1960s, but in 1968 reissued the Custom and the gold-top rather than the revered Sunburst.

The Orbiter

△ MICRO-FRETS THE ORBITER
Produced 1968-1969; this example c1968

Today it's commonplace to see guitars and microphones linked from the live stage by wireless transmitters, but this innovative instrument – made by the Micro-Frets company of Maryland – was the first wireless guitar, well ahead of its time.

Micro-Frets
CORPORATION OF   FREDERICK, MARYLAND

invented by Fender or Gibson, and then reinvented by Hendrix and Clapton. But the recorded legacy of West Side blues, as well as earlier records by B.B. King, Guitar Slim and others, demonstrated that these players had developed an equally profound understanding of the electric guitar's potential. Their influence on some of the city's elder bluesmen was substantial, too. Muddy Waters drew on the services of Buddy Guy, while Howlin' Wolf, in conjunction with Chess writing mainstay Willie Dixon, recruited both Guy and Freddy King for studio duties, alongside Wolf's favoured lead guitarist Hubert Sumlin. This ensured that Howlin' Wolf enjoyed hits well into the 1960s, and according to many local commentators helped him retain a far bigger fan-base than his long-term rival, Muddy Waters.

Although the West Side bluesmen were responsible for a final flowering of the blues single, prompted in part by a realisation that the heyday of American blues was ending, artists such as Clyde McPhatter, Ray Charles and Sam Cooke had started incorporating gospel elements into their music back in the 1950s. By 1961 the commercial success of soul music was overshadowing the blues.

In many cases the difference between blues and soul was simply a question of marketing – most of the West Side bluesmen incorporated soul songs into their set, while Sam Cooke covered Willie Dixon's 'Little Red Rooster'. But the market for traditional bluesmen such as Muddy Waters and Jimmy Reed soon dried up outside their heartland in Chicago and the South.

In turn, blues labels such as Chess and Duke turned to a new generation of soul-blues performers, including Little

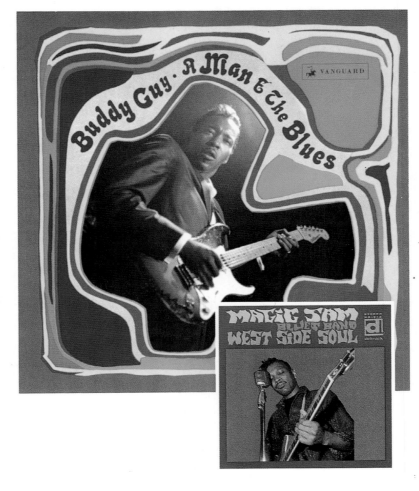

BUDDY GUY (left) was one of the key guitarists in the blossoming of 1960s Chicago blues, nicknamed West Side for the area of the city in which it developed. The tough, stinging Strat was the guitar of choice for many of the West Siders, as Guy, who began using Fenders in 1958, recently explained to Dan Erlewine. "I was always a wild man with the guitar, and a lot of times when you play like that the guitar has to be rough," he said. "So I went for the Strat, and I've had it fly off the top of a car going 80 miles an hour in Africa. The case bust open, it fell out, and there wasn't but one key out of tune." Magic Sam was another West Side bluesman, and this impressive 1968 album (left) has become a classic. Only a year later he was dead at 32.

159

1969

ROSEWOOD Telecasters were rarely seen, but an important sighting of the guitar did occur when George Harrison played one on The Beatles' famous Apple rooftop 'concert' in 1969.

▷ FENDER ROSEWOOD TELECASTER
Produced 1969-1972; this example c1969

Here was an unusual variant on Fender's enduring Telecaster design: this model had a body made entirely from heavy rosewood. Guitarists would of course be familiar with the wood from guitar fingerboards, but rosewood had rarely been used for a relatively large solid body – and apparently, when one picked up a Rosewood Telecaster, with good reason. Fender became aware of the obvious criticism quite quickly, and later versions of the rosewood Tele employed a modified body that had two separate pieces for front and back, and hollowed chambers within, all designed to ease the load on the player's shoulder.

GIBSON's Personal has a mike socket (right) on the body edge, another odd idea of Les Paul's.

▽ GIBSON LES PAUL PERSONAL
Produced 1969-1972; this example c1969

With guitarist Les Paul back in an advisory role at Gibson following the re-introduction of the original 1950s designs, the company indulged the great man's passion for low-impedance pickups with the Professional model and this Personal which, as the name implies, was based on Les Paul's own instrument.

MUDDY WATERS was a star in the 1960s. "I do the same thing for white audiences that I do for black," he said. "I get down and do real blues."

Milton Campbell and fellow Memphis singer Bobby Bland (whose outfit included the inspired lead guitarist Wayne Bennett). But their modest success on the R&B charts was eclipsed by the output of hit-oriented labels such as Motown. The Detroit company's records were masterful mini pop symphonies, but their tight musical choreography left little room for the electric guitar – if anything, the bass guitar took on more prominence, thanks to champions like James Jamerson whose imaginative basslines powered Motown hits such as The Supremes' 'You Keep Me Hangin' On'.

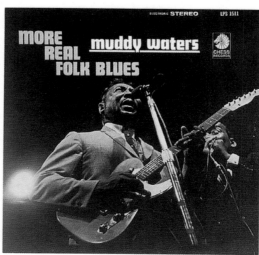

Although the role of the blues lead guitar player was becoming less prominent into the 1960s, there was no shortage of talented guitarists contributing to American R&B

hits. As well as writer/producers such as Curtis Mayfield, key soul players included Marv Tarplin, who contributed gorgeously melodic guitar to Smokey Robinson's 'You Really Got A Hold On Me' and 'The Tracks Of My Tears'. Also notable were Bobby Womack, and Robert Ward, who developed a distinctive guitar style based on subtle two-note runs and the signature vibrato sound of the Magnavox amp.

Ward played guitar on Wilson Pickett's first hit, The Falcons' 'I Found A Love', and exemplified the move to a grittier, funkier style of guitar playing. Like contemporaries such as Redding and Pickett, Ward had grown up in a musically eclectic radio-dominated environment. "I listened to Sam Cooke and the Soul Stirrers, Five Blind Boys, and the Nightingales," he says. "I listened to a lot of Jimmy Reed, Muddy Waters, and John Lee Hooker. And I played country and Western, Hank Williams and Roy Rogers. Then I tried to play all of that at once, and no

FENDER increasingly gave the impression as the 1960s drew to a close that it had lost its way. The CBS-owned operation even took to botching together a guitar called the Custom (seen at the bottom of this Fender ad from 1969) out of parts left over from obsolete models... and then had the cheek to announce that "it's new, from head to strap button".

WOODSTOCK in upstate New York hosts 400,000 music lovers cast in a sea of mud and entertained by Jimi Hendrix, Sly & The Family Stone, Richie Havens, Crosby Stills Nash & Young, Santana, Joe Cocker, The Who, Ten Years After and others.

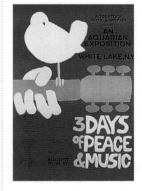

I couldn't... but I did the best I could." Blues music had always been influenced by country. Performers like Lowell Fulson or B.B. King had namechecked Western Swing bands such as Bob Wills' back in the 1950s. By the early 1960s the influence of country rhythm playing – alternating bottom-string bass notes with clipped chords, or using the two-note Memphis scale – was becoming more and more apparent in soul guitar playing. And apart from the black players who were checking out country music, a new generation of white players had been listening carefully to Jimmy Reed or Elmore James. Before long this would create an ironic situation, with black Motown musicians making hit records largely for white audiences, while a new crop of white musicians contributed to hits largely for a black clientele.

Back in the 1950s, Elvis Presley had tapped into the gloriously rich musical culture of the American South to make some of the most iconoclastic records of his era. His stint with the US army brought his influence to a premature end, but there were other musicians who, like Elvis, had been imbued with the blues music that permeated the cities. Atlantic producer Jerry Wexler was among the first to notice the significance of this development when he started licensing records from Jim Stewart and Estelle Axton of the Stax label. These Memphis partners had built a primitive studio in an old cinema, the home of the most celebrated studio band in popular music: the MGs. A racially integrated outfit led by organist Booker T, with Steve Cropper on guitar, the MGs cut the hugely successful 'Green Onions' under their own name, and contributed to countless hits by Otis Redding, Sam & Dave, Wilson Pickett and others.

Steve Cropper's distinctive style – brittle, precise rhythmic chops and vicious, stabbing solos wrenched out of a 1950s Telecaster – retained all of the emotion of classic blues guitar but packaged into short, single-friendly bursts. Cropper's style was totally distinct from that of someone like Robert Ward, for example, but was nonetheless a similarly powerful example of how classic soul guitar playing relied as much on the injection of country-type styles into blues as it did on the more generally accepted influence of gospel.

As Etta James, who would go on to record in Muscle Shoals, puts it, "A lot of that Otis Redding stuff is country to me. 'I've Been Loving You Too Long' for instance is a pure country

NEIL ARMSTRONG is the first man to step on to the moon. He is, with good reason, nervous – and fluffs his lines. He says, nonsensically: "One small step for man, one big leap for mankind." But the script remains word-perfect: "One small step for a man, one giant leap for mankind."

BRIAN JONES of The Rolling Stones drowns in his swimming pool. Meanwhile, in a British laboratory the first "test-tube baby" is produced.

BRITISH TROOPS begin patrolling Catholic areas of Belfast as unrest and violence erupt in Northern Ireland.

IN VIETNAM the first major contingent of US troops is withdrawn. The war will continue into the mid-1970s, leaving dead a million North Vietnamese troops, 200,000 South Vietnamese, 500,000 civilians, and 57,000 Americans. Journalist Michael Herr spoke for a generation of US conscripts when he wrote: "Vietnam was what we had instead of happy childhoods."

CONCORDE makes its maiden flights in France and Britain. It will enter full service in 1976.

STEVE CROPPER (above) translated the Tele's simplicity of design into musical terms as his lean, down-to-the-bone guitar lines emerged on records made at the Stax studio in Memphis. He had enough blues to entice Albert King and Pops Staples to collaborate on an album in 1969 (above right). Meanwhile, B.B. King – shown with his beloved Lucille on this 1967 LP (right) – attracted new white fans as blues-rock became the focus of attention.

AMPEG offered the Dan Armstrong See Through guitar (ad, left) with six slide-in/slide-out pickups: Rock, Country and Jazz, with a Treble and Bass variety of each. Two were supplied with the guitar; the others were available from dealers. If the "revolutionary" plastic body became scratched, Ampeg suggested buffing with a dollop of hi-tech toothpaste.

DAN ARMSTRONG · AMPEG

---

song." But Pops Staples – whose gospel guitar work with The Staple Singers would influence the sound of soul – points out, "Putting categories on those things is tricky. I called our music gospel with a blues kick, myself, but people would say to me, 'What would you call that, country?'"

The success of the MGs paved the way for several other outfits, including the Muscle Shoals studio band, with Spooner Oldham on keyboards and guitarists Eddie Hinton and Jimmy Johnson, the Hi Records house band, overseen by producer Willie Mitchell, and the American house band, established by Chips Moman. Each band featured the democratic arrangement of the Stax outfit, emphasising the new role of the electric guitar: subordinated to the song and to the rhythm. Previously there had been many blues lead guitarists – B.B. King the most prominent - who professed little interest in rhythm guitar. By the 1960s, good rhythm chops were just about the most vital qualifications on an aspiring R&B guitarist's CV.

Several performers were vying for the leadership of soul music through the mid 1960s. In 1965 James Brown achieved almost undisputed command of the title with his masterstroke,

'Papa's Got A Brand New Bag'. Brown had established a rigid format for his trademark sound, based on 'the one'. This meant hitting the first beat of a two-bar pattern in unison, then basing the rhythm on the off-beat for the rest of the phrase. On 'Bag', Brown finally found a guitarist who could inhabit this new rhythmic world. Jimmy Nolen, previously a straight blues player, had become fascinated by the complex rhythms of Bo Diddley songs. Diddley describes his own sound as deriving from his inability to play like Muddy Waters or John Lee Hooker. Instead, his distinctive style came from "playing on the guitar exactly what they play on drums".

Modifying Diddley's scratchy rhythms, and simplifying his parts to fit in with Maceo Parker's intricate horn arrangement, Nolen came up with what would soon be titled funk guitar. It was a powerful reminder that, despite being unfashionable as a lead instrument, the electric guitar would never be consigned to a completely anonymous role within the rhythm section. And of course, even as Brown recorded some of his greatest songs, white guitarists on the other side of the Atlantic were in the process of recreating the electric guitar as the ultimate lead instrument.

FREDDY KING recorded in the late 1950s and early 1960s some classic guitar-soaked

blues cuts, an influential batch of which appeared on this album (above) in 1961.

In the 1960s recording studio, guitars no longer simply strummed a backing but were thrust forward, demanding attention.

At the start of the decade recording was a simple process, but it was still considered too technical to be entrusted to musicians. A representative of the record company, the A&R man (Artistes & Repertoire), would book the studio and provide songs and arrangements. An engineer would place microphones around the instruments and in front of the vocalist, then retreat to the control room where he'd adjust the volume of the individual instruments to create a balance, sometimes adding a subtle but effective touch of artificial echo or reverberation.

A series of 'takes' would ensue, with the results recorded to a single track, or at most two tracks, of tape. When the producer was satisfied, the musicians would be told to move on to the next song, until the standard three-hour session was over. The musicians themselves were no more participants in the process than are the subjects of photography. The experience of Bruce Welch, rhythm guitarist of The Shadows, recording at EMI's Abbey Road studios in London, was typical of the period. "We were totally overawed by it all. Remember we were only 16 or 17 years old, and everything was overseen and organised for us," Welch told Brian Southall. "All we had to do was turn up and get on with it. We were overwhelmed to see an A&R man, an engineer and a tape operator on a session for us and we just did exactly what we were told."

British studios in the early 1960s tended to be rigid, bureaucratic organisations, often modelled on the BBC, with their own rules and regulations about procedures and the correct use of equipment. There were also strict controls on the length of studio sessions, and union agreements on the way recording was conducted. The overdubbing of vocals on to pre-recorded backing tracks, for instance, was technically banned by the British Musicians' Union throughout the 1960s: both band and singer were required to be in the studio at the same time, except with special permission.

Before The Beatles, British pop music was essentially a manufactured confection, with arrangers and A&R men, rather than the pop musicians, in charge. Photogenic young men and women would be allowed to sing, but the music would often be supplied by studio musicians of an older generation. This pattern was standard as late as 1963, when Ringo Starr was replaced by the experienced Andy White during the session for the Beatles 'Love Me Do' because producer George Martin didn't seem to appreciate Starr's rhythmic unsteadiness.

The role of the producer was essentially to ensure that the session was run in a cost-effective way. According to Bruce Welch: "We did three songs in each three-hour session we had. It was written into our contracts, and even if they were crap you still had to do three songs." This was not always as philistine a routine as it sounds. Engineering matters were very simple. Microphone techniques were standard, desks offered a minimum of facilities, and mixing was done live. Any time available went into honing arrangements and performances. Where the 'beat groups' of the early 1960s were concerned, these had often been

sharpened by months on the road. Muff Winwood, then bass player in The Spencer Davis Group, later told Mark Cunningham: "We'd worked on our songs so much live that as long as they sounded good when we transferred them to vinyl, that was all that counted. We only really needed a good engineer to record the performance, and it always seemed to be done without any arguments, and done well. I think the most telling thing about it all was that we cut an album in two days."

But the major British record labels didn't represent the whole story. Outside the mainstream, a few mavericks were trying to find a different way of working. Chief among these was Joe Meek, who built his own studio in a flat above a leather-goods shop in the Holloway Road, north London, and became the leading independent producer of the early 1960s. His most famous early hit was 'Telstar' by The Tornados, an instrumental in which the melody line, played on a battery-operated keyboard called the Clavioline, loomed out of a morass of weird space-age distortion and an atmospheric guitar solo by Tornados' guitarist Alan Caddy. "It earned me £30,000 ($48,000) but I haven't seen the money yet," Meek told *Melody Maker* in 1963.

At a time when most studios were wary of allowing their precious microphones too close to drums or guitar amps, Meek experimented with putting them inside pianos and bass drums, or hanging them over the front of cranked-up guitar amps and then swathing the whole lot in blankets. Meek was also among the first to experiment with 'direct injecting' bass and guitar straight into the mixing desk. "Instrumental parts mean everything, so why not bring them to the foreground more?" he said.

The records Meek was trying to make were influenced far more by the raw sounds of American R&B than by the pallid products being created in the studios of the British major labels. When Elvis Presley left the Sun label to join the giant RCA it had not meant the collapse of small record companies all over America. Instead they survived by catering for the tastes of different sections of a highly heterogenous society.

The small labels used independent studios operated by their owners, largely self-taught in the art of recording. The records they made were full of individual character, and it was these

THE FLEE-REKKERS
'Sunday Date' A-side 1960; Dave 'Tex' Cameron (lead)
"Otherwise British, the group were led by Dutch-born musician Peter Fleerackers. 'Sunday Date' was typical of many UK early-1960s guitar instrumentals to achieve fleeting fame – this one with the benefit of a Joe Meek production. For me the record's important not so much for its unsurprising guitar playing, but because it recalls the frustration of listening to interference-ridden Radio Luxembourg, the main provider of pop music in Britain at the time." PAUL DAY

JOE MEEK in his makeshift studio, and (above) with Heinz.

HOWLIN' WOLF 'Spoonful' A-side 1960; Freddy King and Hubert Sumlin (both Gibson Les Paul gold-tops)
"This Willie Dixon-penned mystery story is supercharged by the twin guitar talents of Freddy King and Hubert Sumlin, and can be classified both as primitive artefact and state-of-the-art pop song. One hundred and sixty thrilling seconds document the collision of ancient black culture and the electrified modern world. But what the hell do the lyrics mean?" PAUL TRYNKA

WES MONTGOMERY 'Gone With The Wind' from "The Incredible Jazz Guitar Of Wes Montgomery" LP 1960; Wes Montgomery (Gibson L-5CES)
"Building his ideas over several choruses, Wes unfolds a solo of sustained inventiveness and technical accomplishment. Flowing effortlessly from single-line improvisation into an extended octave passage, he draws things to a perfect conclusion with a spectacular chordal solo. Fresh melodic motifs constantly appear, to be re-shaped and sent on their way; rhythmic counterpoints pile on the pressure, before relaxing back into straight swing. A true jazz masterpiece." CHARLES ALEXANDER

sounds that the major studios would end up emulating. Interestingly, the use of independent studios and engineers did not always mean tiny, home-made productions, especially in the US. Many of the most important American records of the 1960s were independently produced but involved vast musical forces. In the vanguard was Phil Spector, who graduated from the naivety of his debut production, 'To Know Him Is To Love Him' by The Teddy Bears, to the quasi-Wagnerian efforts known as The Wall Of Sound.

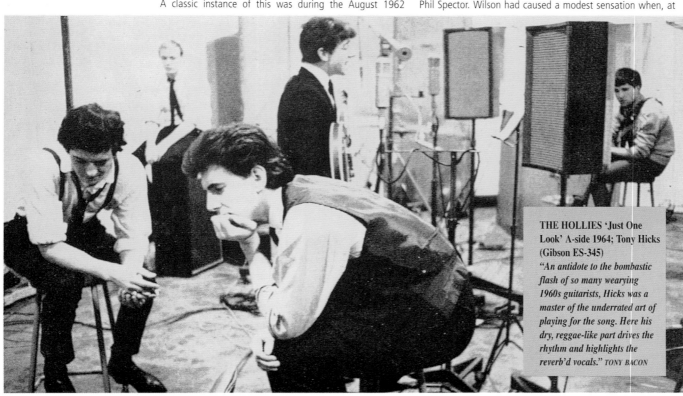

Apache—Man of Mystery—The Stranger—F.B.I. **mono**

THE SHADOWS TO THE FORE

COLUMBIA EXTENDED PLAY 45 r.p.m. RECORD

Tony

THE SHADOWS 'Apache' A-side 1960; Hank Marvin (lead, Fender Stratocaster), plus Bruce Welch
"The record that launched 10,000 bands in Britain. Hank made it all look so easy, with those stark, clever melodies wrapped in that super-clean sound. And when the man in the music store looked down his nose at you and said, "What sort of electric guitar do you want, then, sonny?" the reply was obvious: "A red one, like Hank's, please sir." Well, something like Hank's, anyway. But definitely red." TONY BACON

Spector's secret, if there was one, was simply to create massive volumes of acoustic energy in a smallish room. Then, rather than struggling to keep isolation between the players, who would invariably number at least 20, he would let sound leak in all directions and attempt to record the resultant acoustic mayhem. "The instrumental sound gets top priority when I come to think of a session," Spector told Ray Coleman in 1964. "I got the idea for this big, rolling, beaty sound from watching and hearing symphony orchestras. I decided the way to get a big sound was to mould together more than one of each instrument. So the line-up on those Crystals and Ronettes sessions, for instance, was made up of four pianos, three guitars, three basses – two electric and one upright – and one centre drummer and one additional at the side. I felt the sound had to be dynamic enough to overcome any bad material, so people would respond to the sound rather than the song."

Larry Levine, who engineered many of Spector's early-1960s hits, noted: "The lack of isolation between the musicians had a lot to do with the unique results... It was the room itself and the juxtaposition of the musicians themselves which were the leading factors in creating what would soon become known as The Wall Of Sound."

A classic instance of this was during the August 1962 recording of 'Zip-A-Dee-Doo-Dah' with Bob B. Soxx & The Blue Jeans at Gold Star studios in Los Angeles. Levine had all 12 mixer channels open attempting to make a live mix to mono tape. Despairing of getting a balance, he turned all the rotary volume controls off, before bringing them in one by one. When he got to 11, Spector told him to stop. The lead guitar microphone remained switched off, but there was enough of the sound spilling around the room for it to come through loud and clear on the other microphones.

This is a somewhat symbolic tale. The guitar was not, at first, the key instrument in the pop records of the era. It rose to prominence with the adoption of distortion, a staple of live blues and R&B since the 1950s, introduced to pop initially through the medium of the cheap transistor fuzz box. One of the first international hits to feature fuzz guitar was the Stones' '(I Can't Get No) Satisfaction', played by Keith Richards. Later, the fuzz box was to be joined by the sound of actual amplifier overdrive, coming largely from Vox and Marshall amplification, as studio engineers began to allow guitarists to make the kind of sounds they used on the road. Further 'effects pedals' followed. The bane of most engineers' lives for their tendency to introduce noise and hum, such effects as wah-wah were, in the hands of a master like Jimi Hendrix, capable of far more than the mere novelty value their makers had intended.

Jørgen Ingmann Apache ATCO 33-139

JØRGEN INGMANN 'Apache' A-side 1961; Jørgen Ingmann (probably Gibson Les Paul gold-top)
"Reworking the 'New Sound' that Les Paul invented in the late 1940s, a new breed of guitarists set the tempo of the 1960s with US hits like The Ventures' 'Walk – Don't Run' in 1960 and Swedish guitarist Jørgen Ingmann's self-produced 'Apache' in '61. The record uses multitracking, plus echo effects, bluesy bends, muted double-picking and harmonics, over a rock beat – and it all sounded great in the garage." MICHAEL WRIGHT

But the real sonic obsession of the era was with bass, which was rapidly becoming the essential underpinning of pop music, especially anything with a dance-orientated or R&B feel. Producers came under pressure to accentuate the bottom octave, even in the pop world. Brian Wilson of The Beach Boys was fundamentally a producer of pop music, but he admired R&B and was concerned to build a richer, deeper foundation for his harmonic and melodic experiments. In his great middle-period recordings he used not one bassist but a section made up of several electric and string instruments, as had his hero Phil Spector. Wilson had caused a modest sensation when, at

THE HOLLIES 'Just One Look' A-side 1964; Tony Hicks (Gibson ES-345)
"An antidote to the bombastic flash of so many wearying 1960s guitarists, Hicks was a master of the underrated art of playing for the song. Here his dry, reggae-like part drives the rhythm and highlights the reverb'd vocals." TONY BACON

THE HOLLIES at EMI's Abbey Road studio in 1964, with Tony Hicks at the mike.

BOB B. SOXX & THE BLUE JEANS 'Zip-A-Dee-Do-Dah' A-side 1962; Billy Strange
"To make a live mix, the engineer turned all 12 of the mixer's rotary volume controls off, then brought them in one by one. When he got to 11, Phil Spector said to stop. The guitar mike stayed off, but (somewhat symbolically of things to come) enough guitar sound spilled around to come through the other mikes." JOHN MORRISH

PHIL SPECTOR teaches two studio hands the chords to another little symphony.

20, he took his group out of his record company's own studios and insisted on recording them elsewhere. The Beach Boy then promptly took control of the whole artistic process, even leaving the touring band to concentrate on maintaining their punishing schedule of record releases.

Soon his favourite studios would be block-booked for weeks at a time. As he began to work with orchestral musicians and the cream of the Los Angeles session scene, laying down the tracks to which his fellow Beach Boys would later add vocals, Wilson found the studio a congenial place to write, arrange and hang out. 'Good Vibrations' was among the first recordings to be made in this way. "I tried to make a pocket symphony out of this record," Wilson told Don Traynor in 1966. In effect it is a composition for recording studio – four were used – completed over six months in 1966 at a cost of more than $50,000. The contrast with the experience of The Shadows, only a few years earlier, could not be more marked.

THE VENTURES 'Lullaby Of The Leaves' A-side 1961; Bob Bogle (lead, Fender Stratocaster) with Don Wilson
"This blasts out of the chute with a 'Walk – Don't Run' style intro and then kicks into an ascending melody that's topped off with a radical (for the time) whammy dip. One of the first hit instrumentals in which the whammy was integral to the melody, it also has a driving bass/guitar/drums unison 16th-note chorus." TOM WHEELER

But Wilson, like many artists in the coming months, discovered he liked this way of working. He told Traynor: "The stimulation I get from moulding music and from adding dynamics is like nothing else on earth. If you take the *Pet Sounds* album as a collection of art pieces, each designed to stand alone yet which belong together, you'll see what I was aiming at. I sat up in my house for five months, planning every stage of the album. I have a big Spanish table, circular, and I sit there hour after hour making the tunes inside my head. I love peaks in a song, and enhancing them on the control panel. I get such a kick out of bending electricity and recording techniques to make them work for us. They're there to be used, maximum. Top maximum." Wilson now planned a whole album made up of fragments – composed, arranged and recorded in the studio. Masses of music was recorded and dubbed on to acetate discs to allow Wilson to come up with some sort of sequence. In the event, *Smile*, as it was intended to be known, collapsed in ruins as Wilson's artistic control and self-confidence imploded.

One of the factors in Brian Wilson's decline was the imminent arrival of The Beatles' *Sgt Pepper's Lonely Hearts Club Band*, released in June 1967, a month after he had scrapped the *Smile* project. The Beatles had, if anything, been slightly behind Wilson in their artistic adventurousness up to that point. Now they took the lead. Paradoxically, it was as representatives of an unsophisticated, street-level musical consciousness far removed from anything elaborate that The Beatles had first appealed to George Martin, the unorthodox

EMI A&R man – his background was in comedy records – who was to become their producer and studio mentor.

Their first singles and their first album were done rapidly on a two-track machine, vocals on one track and instruments on the other, and the only complication was in getting an acceptable sound from the group's rather poor guitars, drums and amps. At their initial session, for instance, someone had to cobble together a monitoring amp plus a speaker from the echo chamber to make Paul McCartney a usable bass amp.

Later, though, the in-house engineering expertise of Abbey Road was to become invaluable as The Beatles began to experiment in ways that were not dependent upon mere musical expertise. Braving the wrath of EMI (written permission was required to put a microphone within 18" of a bass drum), Abbey Road engineers like Geoff Emerick began experimenting with close-miking. Later The Beatles, under the influence of either Musique Concrete, LSD or The Goons, wanted to use multiple tape loops in the recording of 'Tomorrow Never Knows'. At Abbey Road, there were always plenty of people around who knew how to do things like that.

BOOKER T & THE MGs
'Green Onions' A-side 1962;
Steve Cropper (Fender
Telecaster)
"Steve Cropper's stinging, string-torturing licks hit so hard that he only needed to launch them in the sparsest of clusters. In F, of all keys, and at the tender age of 20, Cropper wielded his stock Telecaster to devastating effect in this classic R&B instrumental."
TOMMY GOLDSMITH
"If one extreme of 1960s guitar was prolix, effects-laden and overdriven, the other was bright, tight-lipped and burnished. Memphis mofo Steve Cropper here delivered the ultimate in lean, mean and clean: elegant, understated Telecaster classicism that didn't waste a single pickstroke. Clint Eastwood was like a hysterical blabbermouth in comparison."
CHARLES SHAAR MURRAY

WES MONTGOMERY 'West Coast Blues' from "Movin' Wes" LP 1964; Wes Montgomery (Gibson L5-CES)
"Purists tend to consider Montgomery's Riverside recordings as his best, but I remember being more thrilled then by Verve LPs like Movin' Wes or Smokin' At The Half Note. The power and the swing that emanate from this shorter version of his most popular composition is incredible – and his rendition of 'Caravan' on the same LP is well worth a listen, too." ANDRÉ DUCHOSSOIR

THE VENTURES 'Slaughter On Tenth Avenue' A-side 1964; Nokie Edwards (lead, Mosrite Ventures), plus Don Wilson
"For me this is the best example of the playing of Nokie Edwards on a Ventures track, and I much prefer this to The Shadows' version. Originally bassist with the group, Edwards had swapped instrumental roles with guitarist Bob Bogle in 1963. There is a wonderful sound to Edwards' guitar on this track, where almost every guitar technique is included. This is how I was taught that lead guitar should be played." HIROYUKI NOGUCHI

THE BEATLES 'Ticket To Ride' A-side 1965; Paul McCartney (lead, Epiphone Casino), plus George Harrison, John Lennon
"The one record that occupies the cusp of beatboom and psychedelia. Behind it lies the optimistic pop of Berry and Holly. In front of it stretches a brave, frightening new world. Three guitars and a drum kit make up an almost symphonic soundstage, while the distorted guitars and drugs references are rendered even more potent by being held firmly in check." PAUL TRYNKA

THE BEATLES working on 'Paperback Writer' in EMI's No.2 studio, April 1966.

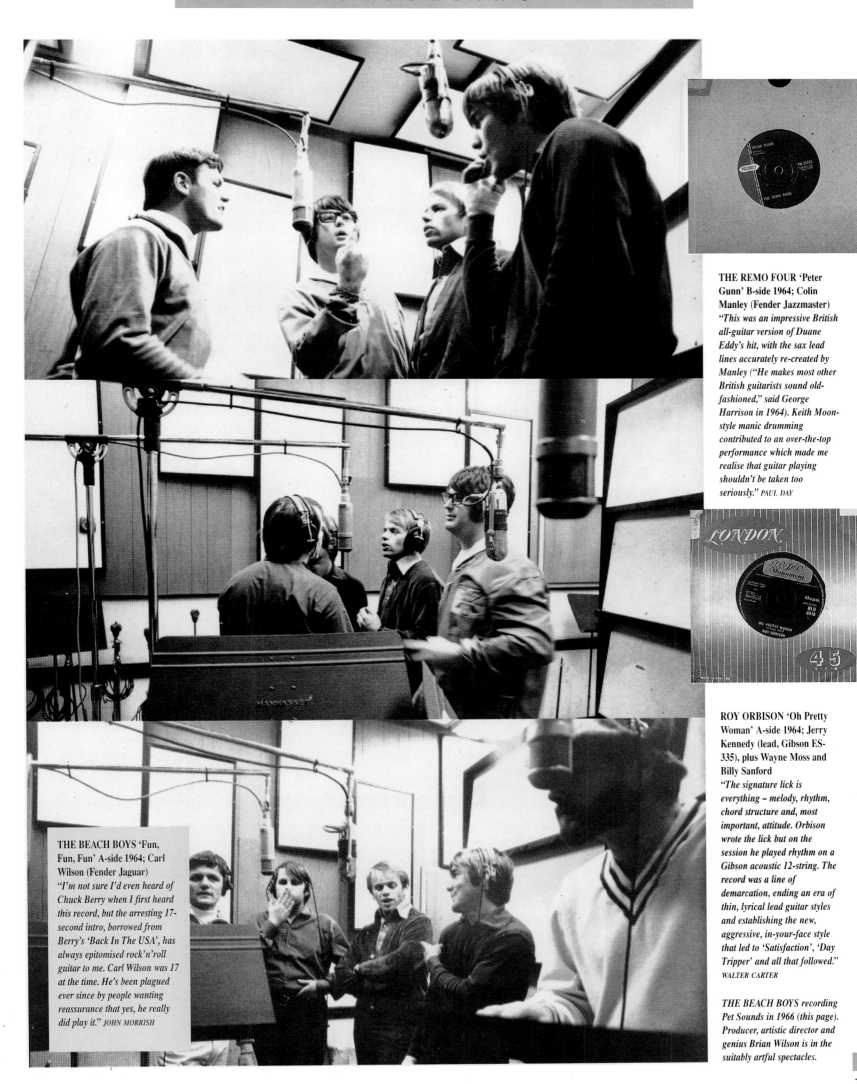

THE REMO FOUR 'Peter Gunn' B-side 1964; Colin Manley (Fender Jazzmaster) *"This was an impressive British all-guitar version of Duane Eddy's hit, with the sax lead lines accurately re-created by Manley ("He makes most other British guitarists sound old-fashioned," said George Harrison in 1964). Keith Moon-style manic drumming contributed to an over-the-top performance which made me realise that guitar playing shouldn't be taken too seriously."* PAUL DAY

ROY ORBISON 'Oh Pretty Woman' A-side 1964; Jerry Kennedy (lead, Gibson ES-335), plus Wayne Moss and Billy Sanford *"The signature lick is everything – melody, rhythm, chord structure and, most important, attitude. Orbison wrote the lick but on the session he played rhythm on a Gibson acoustic 12-string. The record was a line of demarcation, ending an era of thin, lyrical lead guitar styles and establishing the new, aggressive, in-your-face style that led to 'Satisfaction', 'Day Tripper' and all that followed."* WALTER CARTER

THE BEACH BOYS 'Fun, Fun, Fun' A-side 1964; Carl Wilson (Fender Jaguar) *"I'm not sure I'd even heard of Chuck Berry when I first heard this record, but the arresting 17-second intro, borrowed from Berry's 'Back In The USA', has always epitomised rock'n'roll guitar to me. Carl Wilson was 17 at the time. He's been plagued ever since by people wanting reassurance that yes, he really did play it."* JOHN MORRISH

THE BEACH BOYS recording Pet Sounds in 1966 (this page). Producer, artistic director and genius Brian Wilson is in the suitably artful spectacles.

Rewiring the rotating-speaker Leslie cabinet of the studio organ so that Lennon could sing through it, on the same song, was a matter of a few minutes. Invited to indulge their creativity, too, the Abbey Road engineers came up with a string of electronic inventions, most of them built around the idea of taking sound from the tape machine's 'sync' output (using the recording head to play back) and mixing it, after a suitable delay, with the normal playback output. The first was ADT (artificial double-tracking), designed to save Lennon the trouble of singing everything twice. That led directly to 'flanging' and 'STEED' (Send Tape Echo Echo Delay), a flutter-echo vocal effect showcased on 'A Day In The Life'.

Although most of *Sgt Pepper's* was recorded on four-track ('A Day In The Life' being the famous exception, using two four-track machines linked up to provide seven tracks), The Beatles were eager to exploit new resources as they became available. When they found that, inexplicably, Abbey Road was booked when they wanted to record 'Hey Jude' in 1968 they went to Trident studios and found what was then one of a very few working eight-track recorders in London.

However, returning to Abbey Road they discovered that EMI had an eight-track machine in the laboratory being

THE BEATLES 'And Your Bird Can Sing' from "Revolver" LP 1966; George Harrison (lead, Gibson SG Standard), plus John Lennon or Paul McCartney
"Someone once called this 'the best guitar playing you ever heard' and I'd be hard put to disagree. George, along with harmonies by John or Paul (memories differ), provides an ultra-bright, 16th-note rampage as intro, backing and riveting solo for the proto-hippie tune. As well as Revolver, check out the Anthology 2 version for a more Byrds-influenced take, complete with Rick 12-string." TOMMY GOLDSMITH
"In my view, the combination of George Harrison and John Lennon is one of the best in the whole of 1960s guitar playing, and on this track you can hear elaborate guitar licks and an emotional harmony at work. Listen too for the way in which the twin guitar phrasing is deployed with such a mastery of melody." HIROYUKI NOGUCHI

Clapton was to find solace at various points in his career in a different Anglo-American tradition, one of self-conscious simplicity and authenticity rather than artistic contrivance. This was not simply a matter of taking inspiration from black music – the production-line soul of Motown was as painstakingly crafted as anything by The Beatles or Phil Spector – but of black music that consciously adhered to the blues tradition. The recordings produced for Atlantic and Stax by Tom Dowd were notable for their concentration on basic musical interplay – 'feel' – rather than arrangement or tricky engineering.

Certainly Dowd used the best equipment he could get. Atlantic's New York studios were among the first anywhere to have eight-track, which had been used by producers Leiber & Stoller to create hits for The Coasters and The Drifters since the late 1950s. But Dowd insisted on the simplest of engineering: one microphone per channel, wherever possible, and no equalisation (tonal adjustment) on the desk. When Dowd went to the Stax studios, a converted 500-seat cinema in Memphis, Tennessee, things were even more basic. Recording was done straight to mono, with a minimum of microphones. A five-piece horn section might have two microphones on them, which would require them to balance themselves. But such musical skills were readily available.

In 1967, Eric Clapton's Cream came to Atlantic studios and Dowd recorded their *Disraeli Gears* album on eight-track. After initial dismay at the sheer volume produced by the three-piece, Dowd settled down and made the album in three days. This combination of musical virtuosity and engineering simplicity offered a different route to that explored by The Beatles in the latter part of the 1960s, where the sophistication was in arrangement and engineering. This was a tussle that was to be

THE BUTTERFIELD BLUES BAND 'East-West' from "East-West" LP 1966; Mike Bloomfield and Elvin Bishop (Bloomfield Gibson Les Paul gold-top; Bishop probably Gibson ES-335)
"In this sprawling 13-minute instrumental rock raga Bloomfield and Bishop intertwined modal melodies in pulsed crescendos punctuated by Butterfield's brilliant harp. It's one of the earliest flings in 1960s pop culture's emerging affair with eastern philosophy and psychedelia, creating the model for the twin-lead heavy guitar rock that was to follow." MICHAEL WRIGHT

'evaluated'. So they persuaded engineer Dave Harries to let them use it on 'While My Guitar Gently Weeps', a piece also notable for the fact that Eric Clapton's guest guitar, rather than the vocal, is put through the ADT machine. This single song took some 37 hours to record, approximately 37 times as long as the average Shadows number of a few years earlier. The Beatles were self-evidently falling apart during the making of *'The White Album'*, and subsequent efforts did nothing to slow this decline. The recording process as it had developed in the mid 1960s was often destructive of bands and their creativity. An extremely boring process for those not actually laying down tracks, it magnified minor technical failings and brought 'artistic differences' to the fore. Eric Clapton famously left The Yardbirds because a harpsichord was dropped into their 1964 single 'For Your Love'. "Where does that leave me?" he complained. "Twelve-string guitar, I suppose."

CREAM 'Sunshine Of Your Love' from "Disraeli Gears" LP 1967; Eric Clapton (Gibson SG Standard)
"The song and the riff are true classics from the late 1960s and form a timeless vehicle for improvisation. But 'Sunshine Of Your Love' also exemplifies Clapton's typical 'woman tone' which many aspiring guitarists were then keen to imitate. It looked even better when played live and loud on a painted SG Standard." ANDRÉ DUCHOSSOIR

played out again and again during the next decade. Multitrack recording – 16-track was introduced towards the end of the 1960s – had made it possible for those with no musical vision and limited instrumental expertise to produce complex-sounding music by the simple process of adding and subtracting until they found something that worked. This was entirely new. Previously, composers and arrangers had always needed a sound in their heads before they started. In the 1960s, musicians and record producers – who were increasingly enjoying 'auteur' status akin to that enjoyed by contemporary film directors – were freed from that requirement. The stage was set both for a new type of creativity and an epic era of self-indulgence.

In both respects, Jimi Hendrix showed himself to be at the forefront. He had made recordings throughout his career, right back to his days on the 'chitlin circuit', the black music clubs of America. In 1967 he took the Experience into Olympic Studios in London for the first sessions with engineer Eddie Kramer. "Basically," explained Kramer, in a 1992 article for *EQ* magazine, "he created the sound in the amp and I just took it and ran with it – expanded upon it." Hendrix's sound came from a few favourite pedals, overdriven amplifiers and his own hands. Kramer helped where he could, for instance by creating stereo phasing to give him "an underwater sound he had

heard in his dreams". For vocal recording, which Hendrix loathed, he put him behind screens and kept the lights dim. This womb-like ambience was to be central to Electric Lady, Hendrix's own studio in New York. Musicians had had their own studios before, but this was to be the real thing, with the first true 24-track mixer and tape machine.

Hendrix's dream was to be able to record day or night, for as long as he wanted. But Electric Lady also represented a sanctuary, a safe haven for a man who had always had a problem with the word "No". In particular, it allowed him to escape his touring self, a psychedelic showman for whom music came a poor second.

Electric Lady opened in the summer of 1970. Hendrix recorded some tracks for *Rainbow Bridge* there, but it was too late. He died in September of that year. But this new use for the recording studio, as a sympathetic artistic refuge in a hostile world, was to become common in the years ahead. ■ JOHN MORRISH

THE YARDBIRDS 'Shapes Of Things' single A-side 1966; Jeff Beck (lead, Fender Esquire), plus Chris Dreja
"I was 13 years old, my first guitar still a good nine months into the future. Across the fuzzy ether from Wonderful Radio London came what sounded like an alien marching tune, interrupted by the most demented, far-out musical noise my young ears had heard. Was that a guitar? It must have been – each time it came on I would leap to my feet, hands convulsing Cocker-like in ludicrous imitation of its crazy execution. It was going to be a fantastic year." DAVE GREGORY

JIMI HENDRIX EXPERIENCE 'Are You Experienced' from "Are You Experienced" LP 1967; Jimi Hendrix (Fender Stratocaster)
"As a mature 14-year-old I'd already learned to play all the songs off From Nowhere... The Troggs. So Jimi's debut album came as a bit of a shock. After 35 minutes of the music of the gods, Hendrix closed the record with this stunning track, apparently created almost entirely in reverse. It was remarkable that anything musical could be achieved from such a random process, yet here was an emotional, coherent, perfectly-executed solo that I am still unable to turn away from whenever I hear it. Who but Hendrix would have dared attempt such a feat and pull it off so perfectly?" DAVE GREGORY

JIMI HENDRIX ready to rock with Strat, Vox wah and Fuzz Face at TTG studio in 1968.

STEPPENWOLF 'Magic Carpet Ride' A-side 1968; Michael Monarch (lead, Fender Esquire), plus John Kay
"It's the rhythm. While most guitarists were concentrating on the blues, Steppenwolf followed the example of the early rockers and took the rhythm element from R&B. They kicked it into overdrive and came up with a crunching rhythm sound so strong that a conventional lead part was unnecessary." WALTER CARTER

TONY WILLIAMS LIFETIME 'Spectrum' from "Emergency" LP 1969; John McLaughlin (Gibson Les Paul Custom)
"Tipped from the mid 1960s as a guitarist to watch, McLaughlin confirmed his arrival as a major innovative force with the playing on this track. Its angular theme, crunchy chords, soaring melody and urgent rock rhythms springboard McLaughlin into a blistering solo of Hendrix-like intensity, the fresh harmonic ideas and technical fluency of which announce the agenda for the jazz-rock and fusion music that was to come in the 1970s." CHARLES ALEXANDER

Index

174